D1371517

Marble Queens and Captives:
Women in Nineteenth-Century American Sculpture

Artistic Voyagers:
Europe and the American Imagination in
the Works of Irving, Cooper, Hawthorne, Allston, and Cole

BUFFALO BILL'S WILD WEST

BUFFALO BILL'S
WILD WEST

CELEBRITY, MEMORY,
AND POPULAR HISTORY

JOY S. KASSON

🖑 HILL AND WANG

A DIVISION OF FARRAR, STRAUS AND GIROUX

NEW YORK

Hill and Wang
A division of Farrar, Straus and Giroux
19 Union Square West, New York 10003

Copyright © 2000 by Joy S. Kasson
All rights reserved
Distributed in Canada by Douglas & McIntyre Ltd.
Printed in the United States of America
Designed by Jonathan D. Lippincott
First edition, 2000

Permission has kindly been granted to reprint E. E. Cummings's poem "Buffalo Bill's," copyright 1923, 1951, © 1991 by the Trustees for the E. E. Cummings Trust. Copyright © 1976 by George James Firmage, from *Complete Poems: 1904–1962* by E. E. Cummings. Edited by George J. Firmage. Reprinted by permission of Liveright Publishing Corporation.

For

John, true partner, guide, and inspiration

Peter, brave explorer of a new West

Laura, author of adventures

ACKNOWLEDGMENTS

My interest in Buffalo Bill can undoubtedly be traced to my childhood. Growing up in the first television generation, I watched hours of Westerns — Roy Rogers and Gene Autry, Hopalong Cassidy and the Lone Ranger — and played cowboys and Indians with my brothers and friends. I recall having a cowgirl outfit and watching Gail Davis on television as Annie Oakley. In retrospect, it seems to me that my friends and I imagined the West as unselfconsciously as the audiences did at Buffalo Bill's shows: Western adventure was a thrilling but safe form of entertainment, with a relatively uncomplicated story line and a predictable happy ending. Buffalo Bill, who died the year my father was born, still rode through my grade-school curriculum on a spotless white horse surrounded by an unmistakable aura of heroism.

Western landscapes seemed less complicated, too. I played beneath the bronze buffalo in Chicago's Garfield Park and spent long hours admiring the wildlife dioramas in the Field Museum of Natural History. I went West with my family and marveled at the Badlands of South Dakota, the Rocky Mountains of Colorado, the geysers of Yellowstone, and the Great Salt Lake. Car culture and postwar prosperity attracted countless families in my generation to Western tourism as surely as the posters, fliers, and publicity campaigns drew record audiences to the Wild West's show grounds in Cody's day.

My training in American Studies led me to admire the pioneers who opened the West's academic frontier. For more than a century, historians, literary scholars, art historians, and museum curators have been placing the land and peoples of the West at the center of any discussion of American national identity. In recent years, Richard White, Richard Slotkin, Patricia Limerick, and other new Western historians have transformed the field through their wide-ranging investigations. My own involvement in the study of the West stems from my deep interest in the visual arts and their relationship to American culture. In the summer of 1991 I visited the stunning and controversial exhibition *The West as America: Reinterpreting Images of the Frontier, 1820–1920* at the National Museum of American Art in Washington; several months later I delivered a commentary on an original and thought-provoking paper given at the American Studies Association convention by a scholar who had worked on that exhibition, Alex Nemerov. While thinking about his subtle analysis of the painter Charles Russell, I began to wonder about the relationship between popular entertainment and American conceptions of history, nature, and national identity. I learned something about Buffalo Bill's Wild West then, and I have been learning more and more ever since.

I have accumulated many debts during the years I have been studying Buffalo Bill. Librarians and archivists have been exceptionally generous. Like many other scholars, I am deeply indebted to the Buffalo Bill Historical Center in Cody, Wyoming: its museum brings Cody and his era to life, and the Harold McCracken Research Library preserves books, manuscripts, programs, posters, route books, and a host of other sources for understanding the Wild West shows. Frances Clymer in the library and Elizabeth Holmes in the photography department were especially helpful. Annette Fern at the Harvard Theatre Collection helped to track down recondite materials. I want also to thank librarians at the Western History Department of the Denver Public Library; the Beinecke Rare Book Library at Yale; the New York Public Library for the Performing Arts; the Library of Congress Motion Picture, Broadcasting and Recorded Sound Division; the Library of Congress Prints and Photographs Division; the Library of Congress Books and Manuscripts Division; the Buffalo Bill Ranch State Historical Park; the Smithsonian Institution; the Chicago Historical Society; the Newberry Library; the State Historical Society of North Dakota; the Circus World Museum; Anheuser-Busch; the Theodore Roosevelt Collection at the Harvard College Library; and the Buffalo Bill Museum in Golden, Colorado. I am grateful, too, to the photography department at the University of North Carolina at Chapel Hill's Wilson Library.

My work has been aided by a number of grants. At my home institution, the University of North Carolina, the University Research Council supported research travel as well as photographic and reproduction fees, and I have benefited from a Kenan Research Leave and a Max Chapman Family Fellowship granted by the Institute for the Arts and Humanities, which also provided research services and the stimulating conversation of fellow fellows. I am deeply grateful to the National Humanities Center in Research Triangle Park, North Carolina, for a yearlong fellowship. The librarians, especially Eliza Robertson, were remarkably helpful and patient. The Center's cordial and accommodating staff made the scholar's life seem ideal, and the heady discussions among fellows challenged, inspired, and invigorated me. I thank especially Paul Berliner, Fitzhugh Brundage, George Chauncey, Jane Gaines, Don Lopez, Paul Strohm, and the redoubtable daily walking group: Trudier Harris, Nancy Langston, Susan Cole, and Pam Simpson.

This project has also benefited from the advice and criticism of two writing groups. Jane Blocker, Jacquelyn Hall, Carol Mavor, and Della Pollock helped me to formulate issues and sketch out plans. Judith Farquhar, Jane Danielewicz, Laurie Langbauer, Megan Matchinske, and Marisol de la Cadena read what must have seemed like an unending cascade of chapters and improved the manuscript greatly. My thanks also to others who read other parts of the book: Robert Cantwell, Alan Trachtenberg, Michael Green, and Laura Wexler. Barbara Michaels graciously answered a query. Jean Kempf made an enormous contribution by inviting me to a conference on memory.

At Hill and Wang, Elisabeth Sifton has been every scholar's ideal editor: gracious, wise, a keen reader, and an implacable foe of obfuscating jargon. Thanks also go to Mia Berkman for her assistance.

My greatest gratitude is due to those closest to home. John Kasson has helped me in every step of my work. His clear thinking and subtle observations have guided me in this as in every other project, and his love and support have always made an enormous difference. Our children, Peter and Laura, have patiently endured my fascination with the longhaired sharpshooter, accepting trips to libraries and archives as a natural part of family life. Both have been able to make their own contributions, talking over ideas and reading drafts of my writing. And my parents, Walter and Mary Schlesinger, have kept up the support and encouragement that began when they packed my brothers and me into the family car to explore firsthand the Western frontier. To all, my deep thanks.

CONTENTS

BUFFALO BILL'S WILD WEST

INTRODUCTION
SHOWMANSHIP AND MEMORY

*It is a sunny day in Omaha, Nebraska . . . hot and humid in Youngstown,
Ohio . . . pouring rain in Macon, Georgia . . . chilly weather in North Adams,
Massachusetts. A wind storm blows down a tent in Oswego, New York . . .
audiences flock to newly constructed grandstands in Paris . . . a stadium is lit
by the world's largest single power plant for entertainment in Staten Island . . .
a muddy field in White River Junction, Vermont, holds twenty miles of rope
securing twenty-two thousand yards of canvas.*

*For weeks before the show opens, passersby spot eight-foot posters on the
sides of barns, rows of signs along a fence, two-foot-high pictures in the shop
windows, streamers on the sides of downtown buildings. In brighter-than-life
color, a handsome rider tips a white Stetson hat; a cowboy rides a horse that
arches its back, head down and mane streaming; a gaucho swings a bola; a
pretty young woman holding a gun daintily leaps over a hurdle; a crowd of
Indians shooting arrows dashes after a stagecoach; a rider balances on the back
of a bucking steer; an Indian warrior falls from his horse, shot by an army
scout. The day before the show, special railroad cars pull into town, with the
name of the troupe written in ornamental letters and the star's portrait gleaming from the side. A band plays and the cowboys and Indians, vaqueros, cossacks, and Arabs, lead a free parade down the main street of town, followed by
boys on bicycles, men in suits and working clothes, women, children, and
grandparents.*

Before the show, spectators can stroll among the tepees of Indian perform-
ers, talk to Sioux and Pawnee men and their wives, shake hands with cowboys,
and see the big tent with the stuffed buffalo head and the carpet under the
camp chair, where, if they are lucky, the star will be spinning tales for visitors.
On the way to their seats, they can buy programs, souvenir photographs, book-
lets, food, and drink.

Finally, the show begins. Sitting in grandstands that circle or form a horse-
shoe around a dirt performance area, the audience hears the cowboy band play
"The Star-Spangled Banner" (not yet the national anthem), followed by "See,
the Conquering Hero Comes." Then the performers enter, mounted on spirited
horses, raising clouds of dust as they ride: American Indians in feathers and
war paint, whooping and waving their bows in the air; Mexicans in round hats
with fancy braid on their trousers and lariats in their hands; Arabs in white
headdresses, cossacks with fur hats, cowboys with kerchiefs around their necks,
French and German soldiers in military uniforms. When they have all dashed
around the ring to the cheers of the audience, the riders form ranks, quiet their
mounts, and look toward the entrance as one more figure appears. A large gray
horse carries a tall, handsome man wearing fringed buckskins and high boots;
his clipped goatee and long flowing hair identify him even before he gallops to
the center of the ring, sweeps off his hat, and shouts, "Ladies and gentlemen,
allow me to present the Congress of Rough Riders of the World!"

For the next two hours men, women, and children cheer a horse race
between a cowboy, a cossack, a Mexican, an Arab, and an Indian; skillful
shooting by Annie Oakley, aiming at a target behind her by looking in a hand-
held mirror; horseback marksmanship by Buffalo Bill, shooting glass balls
tossed in the air by an Indian galloping a few paces in front of him; a demon-
stration of pony-express riding techniques; an enactment of Indian dances and
ceremonies; a buffalo hunt with a live buffalo. They applaud and gasp at dra-
matic scenes of frontier life, including an Indian attack on a frontier cabin and
an assault on a wagon train of Western settlers, both of which are repulsed at
the last minute by Buffalo Bill with the cowboys and scouts. Audience members
are invited to the arena to ride in the historic Deadwood mail coach, which is
then chased around the ring by menacing Indians until Buffalo Bill swoops
down to chase away the Indians and rescue the passengers. Scenes from the
Indian wars are played out before their fascinated eyes, as Custer and his entire
company are massacred at the Little Big Horn and Buffalo Bill rescues captive
settlers at the Battle of Summit Springs. When the dust has cleared and the
sounds of gunfire die away, the entire company unites again, riding around the
ring for a final display of horsemanship from around the world while the cow-

*boy band continues to play and the audience returns to farms, small towns, or
city neighborhoods with souvenirs and memories.*

At the turn of the twentieth century, millions of people around the world
thought they remembered the American Wild West because they had seen it,
full of life and color, smoking guns and galloping horses, presided over by the
most recognizable celebrity of his day: William F. Cody, or Buffalo Bill. Buffalo Bill's Wild West brought an enormously successful performance spectacle to audiences throughout the United States and Europe between 1883
and 1916. With its demonstrations of skills such as riding, roping, and shooting and its dramatic narratives like "The Attack on the Deadwood Stagecoach" and historical re-enactments like "Custer's Last Stand," it blurred the
lines between fiction and fact, entertainment and education. Audiences
watched performers who could claim personal experience in the West—cowboys, army scouts, and, most important, American Indians who had often
participated in the very events being represented—but at the same time, they
could recognize that those interpretations of frontier life were drawn from
dime novels and sensational journalism. The performers' enacted memories
of the "real" West were always intermingled with spectators' memories of the
West as it had been portrayed for years in literature, art, and popular culture.
Buffalo Bill's Wild West created vivid personal memories that could be
understood as historical memory. In a manner that has become familiar in
the age of electronic popular culture, an entertainment spectacle was taken
for "the real thing," and showmanship became inextricably entwined with its
ostensible subject. Buffalo Bill's Wild West became America's Wild West.

Buffalo Bill was arguably the most famous American of his time. At the
end of the nineteenth century, a few military figures such as George Armstrong Custer and Robert E. Lee were widely viewed as genuine heroes, but
both were dead by the time Cody enjoyed his greatest recognition. Among
living contemporaries, Mark Twain enjoyed a substantial national and international following that rivaled his, winning acclaim for his performances on
the lecture platform as well as for his published works, charming men,
women, and children with his instantly recognizable persona: white suit,
bushy hair and mustache, and biting humor. Yet America's best-known writer
was a teller of tales, not a doer of deeds; it was his words that amused, fascinated, and provoked. By contrast, Cody, performing before the age of ampli-
fied sound, presented a living diorama that had temporal and spatial
immediacy; viewers left his performances believing that they had seen the

actual deeds for which he was famous. During his lifetime, only Theodore Roosevelt was equally charismatic as an American action hero known to millions, and Roosevelt showed that he had learned much from Buffalo Bill. The Congress of Rough Riders of the World had been a part of Buffalo Bill's Wild West for five years before Roosevelt stormed San Juan Hill; the future President rode to military and political power on the trail blazed by the consummate showman.

In a career that stretched over four decades, Buffalo Bill helped to create the modern notion of the celebrity, someone who is "known for his well-knownness," as Daniel Boorstin has put it. Like only a handful of Americans before him—but many, many others since—Cody reaped the benefits of "star-making machinery," brilliant publicity campaigns waged by his staff to shape public perceptions of his character and accomplishments. So successful were these efforts that to audiences everywhere, Buffalo Bill was an immediately legible figure. Wherever he performed, political cartoons appeared in newspapers, using the easily recognizable metaphor of the Wild West show to comment on local issues: politicians roping each other, holding up stagecoaches, shooting at targets. Audiences understood him so well that posters and advertisements could promote his show with shorthand references: the figure of a running buffalo; a sketch of a horseman with long hair, goatee, and broad-brimmed hat; or a speeding stagecoach. His performances impressed viewers as diverse as Queen Victoria and Susan B. Anthony; he was celebrated by E. E. Cummings and Ernest Hemingway. Buffalo Bill's Wild West provided the template—and the personnel—for the early film Western, and his version of frontier history cast a long shadow through the television western to the shoot-outs of George Lucas's *Star Wars*.

Of course, much has been written about Buffalo Bill, including a well-researched biography and numerous works of thoughtful analysis by present-day historians.[1] But the cultural freight he carried in his own time and ever since makes it especially challenging to evaluate anything written or said about him. So powerful was the public image of Buffalo Bill, disseminated seamlessly through publicity, dime novels, and performance, that even early accounts of Cody's life and deeds reflect an identity carefully constructed by his publicists. Much ink has been expended on the question of William Cody's "actual" accomplishments as a hunter, an army scout, an Indian expert. Friends and associates "remembered" Buffalo Bill's past in ways that harmonized with the stories he had dramatized and the public persona he had developed, and debunkers "remembered" embarrassing counter-stories.[2] My intention here is not to distinguish the "real" from the "fictional" Buffalo

Bill, but rather to examine the subtle interweaving of fact, fiction, hype, and audience desire. In Buffalo Bill's Wild West, historical events seemed to become personal memory, and personal memory was reinterpreted as national memory.

So we return to the question of what was remembered by those who saw Buffalo Bill's Wild West and how their memories were framed. Of course, a note of nostalgia rang loudest in the Wild West's later years, when a series of farewell tours enshrined Buffalo Bill as a living historical monument. The text of a 1902 program declared the days of the Wild West, like those of its performers, numbered. "Soon the dark clouds of the future will descend upon the present, and behind them will disappear the Wild West with all its glories, forever made mere memories; and as it fades behind nature's impenetrable curtain will be hallowed by a timely and dignified—FINIS."[3] A 1910 poem presented Buffalo Bill as a figure from the past but hailed him as the perpetrator of memory,

> *Graving time's footprints on history's page;*
> *The red man's grim passing, the paleface's sway*
> *. . .*
> *Re-living the scenes of a fast-fading age.*[4]

But even in the show's early days, promotional and program texts stressed a nostalgic perspective, describing the buffalo as the "fast-disappearing monarch of the plains," the coach used in the robbery scene as a "scarred and weather-beaten . . . old relic."[5] In 1884, one Denver reviewer exclaimed that Buffalo Bill portrayed "incidents that are passing away *never more to return.*"[6] While the Wild West gripped audiences with its immediacy, from the beginning it also defined itself as a preserver of memory, standing on the threshold of historical transformation, giving the Western frontier a new life to ward off oblivion. Buffalo Bill's Wild West was a representation that created, even while it claimed, its own history.

At the end of the nineteenth century, the historian Frederick Jackson Turner located the essence of the American spirit in the Western frontier, a time and place that were fading into the past. Even as Turner delivered his address on "The Significance of the Frontier in American History" at the Columbian Exposition in Chicago in 1893, Buffalo Bill's Wild West was entertaining its largest audiences ever in an arena across the street from the fairgrounds. The success of his performances underscored Turner's point: the viewing public, like the scholar, yearned to stop time and capture memory. In the shadow of the great world's fair, with its vision of a noble past and a lofty future, visitors to the Wild West could flirt with danger and uncertainty, experience vicariously the thrills and hardships that the Exposition and the historian of the West both assumed were a thing of the past, all from the security of a seat in the stands. Less than three years after the massacre at Wounded Knee, spectators at the Wild West could see the Indian wars unfolding, enacted by survivors of that very event, brought to a satisfying conclusion before the evening train departed for homes and hotels.

Buffalo Bill's Wild West represented a kind of memory showmanship. At stake were not only the invention of a great entertainment form and the creation of a worldwide celebrity, but the forging of a link that would grow stronger over the course of the next century, a link between national identity and popular culture, between Americans' understanding of their history and their consumption of spectacularized versions of it. At the end of the twentieth century, Buffalo Bill's Wild West itself was re-created at the European Disneyland, where a nightly dinner show features cowboys, Indians, and live animals who re-enact a re-enactment of American history. Understanding the complex and contradictory ways that William Cody and his collaborators invented Buffalo Bill's Wild West can shed light on the continuing relationship between performance, memory, and national desire.

PART ONE

PERFORMANCES

Buffalo Bill, c. 1878

CHAPTER ONE

INVENTING THE WILD WEST
1868–86

Wilaillim Cody was not always an icon of historical memory. He began his career on the fringes of respectability, engaged in activities that already challenged the boundaries between accomplishment and self-promotion, and he entered show business as one struggling pitchman among many. Cody tried a variety of forms of stage acting before developing the successful formula for his Wild West exhibition, and his experiments reveal the fluidity of nineteenth-century American performance culture. Leaving behind associates in the small-time arena of humbug and braggadocio and enlisting the help of experienced actors and inspired publicists and writers, William Cody became world famous; his tools for self-transformation included written texts, visual images, new performance practices, and a resonant connection with a national sense of destiny. The success of Buffalo Bill's Wild West was a triumph of good luck, good management, and good timing.

PLAINS SHOWMAN

Born in a log cabin in Iowa in 1846, Cody grew up in Kansas, where his father became embroiled in Free Soil politics and died when his son was eleven. Young Cody worked as an ox-team driver, as a messenger for the firm that later operated the pony express, and on numerous wagon trains. He prospected for gold and went on trapping expeditions, became a good hunter, and had a number of encounters with Indians and border ruffians. During the Civil War he served as an army scout and guide, and then enlisted with the Seventh Kansas regiment. At the war's end, he married Louisa Frederici, a girl he had met in St. Louis, and returned to the West, where he tried to run a hotel once owned by his mother, then joined a partnership attempting to develop a town on the Kansas Pacific Railroad line. He worked on contract for the U.S. Army and for the railroad as a buffalo hunter and a scout. By the early 1870s, he was well known among army and border men, displayed considerable frontier skills, and made a desultory living for his growing family.

Although his publicity would later present him as a solid citizen—a family man, cattle rancher, and development advocate—his early career on the plains suggests a person with itchy feet and an inability to find a permanent job. Like numerous friends and competitors, he tried his hand at various occupations in the postbellum years, looking for adventure, recognition, and cash. In the process of becoming an international celebrity, Cody both followed and diverged from familiar pathways in the search for success and respectability that led many others to debt, obscurity, and failure.

The U.S. Army was Cody's most important employer in the decade after the Civil War.[1] Although he had returned to civilian life at the end of the war, he possessed skills and knowledge that were important to American military leaders, who were pouring their talents and ambitions into the Indian wars. Like many other plainsmen, Cody worked on short-term contract as a civilian scout for the army, guiding troops through unmapped terrain, hunting for meat, carrying messages, tracking Indians, and participating in military encounters. Official reports show that Cody was liked and respected by the officers he worked for. After successfully completing a series of punishing rides as a messenger for General Philip Sheridan, he was appointed chief of scouts for the Fifth Cavalry in 1868; later that year, he reached the highest level of pay for scouting and received an extra one hundred dollars in an order approved by the Secretary of War. In 1872 he was awarded the Medal of Honor for his scouting and combat skills at the Loup River in Nebraska. Working for the army was exciting, and it gave Cody recognition and contacts that would open further opportunities for him.

Cody also detected the promise held out by the rowdy world of leisure, entertainment, and communication services that surrounded the army on the Western plains. Long before he became involved in more conventional kinds of entertainment, Cody excelled at what we might call plains show-manship. A trail of paper and archaeological evidence links him by 1868 to horse races, buffalo-shooting contests, and hunting excursions on the plains. In these activities, he displayed his prowess before spectators who might be insiders (soldiers, plainsmen, settlers) or outsiders (tourists, visitors); he was rewarded by prizes, money earned by betting, and prestige. Plains showman-ship mingled business with pleasure, compounded feats of skill with acts of self-promotion, and made frontier life inseparable from its embodiment as a spectacle.

Newspaper accounts gathered by Cody's biographers show that he raced his buffalo-hunting horse, Brigham, against Thoroughbreds, led dudes on buffalo hunts, and rounded up a band of robbers to local acclaim.[2] More dif-ficult to document, but intriguing for many reasons, was a shooting contest Cody allegedly held with a fellow scout, Billy Comstock, in 1868.[3] According to later accounts, the match was organized for the amusement of officers from two Kansas army posts, Fort Hays and Fort Wallace, who put up the prize money, and it attracted a local audience of scouts and frontiersmen as well as an audience of city folk. Louisa Cody told of seeing a poster in St. Louis promoting the event: "Grand Excursion to Fort Sheridan, Kansas Pacific Railroad. Buffalo shooting match for $500 a side and the champi-onship of the world between Billy Comstock (the famous scout) and W. F. Cody (Buffalo Bill), famous buffalo killer for the Kansas Pacific Railroad."[4] Although the advertisement has never been authenticated, the rhetoric she reported rings true. In this freewheeling world of self-promotion, anyone who could pay for an advertisement could describe himself as famous, and the winner of any contest could proclaim himself champion of the world. Though at this early date Cody was identified as an employee of the Kansas Pacific Railroad, the army officers who watched the match were also his once and future employers. Winning could lead to more work, as well as enhancing his reputation, and, of course, gaining him the prize money. Recounting this later, Cody remembered a hundred spectators, including his wife and daughter, arriving on a special train from St. Louis, and archaeological evidence—hand-blown beer and champagne bottles uncov-ered at the purported site nearly a century later—suggests a daylong event that included eating and drinking. Cody says he won the match, shooting sixty-nine buffalo to Comstock's forty-six, with the final kill taking place "close to the wagons, where the ladies were"—a dramatic conclusion to the spectacle.[5] Real buffalo were being shot, but the event itself was pure entertainment.

Plains showmanship also manifested itself in the well-documented celebrity buffalo hunts in which Cody soon participated. As a sport, hunting has always involved ritual and display, and mingled spectatorship with participation. Furthermore, as the historian John MacKenzie has pointed out, by the mid-nineteenth century, the ethics and ethos of the hunt had also come to define a leadership class for Britain's developing worldwide empire.[6] British sportsmen had mounted big-game excursions on the Western plains as early as 1853, when Sir George Gore brought two hundred men to hunt buffalo, elk, deer, and antelope. He was followed in 1869 by Sir John Watts Garland and Lord Adair, the Earl of Dunraven, for whom Cody served as a guide on several occasions. Perhaps the spectacles staged by visiting British nobility helped to awaken American public figures to the symbolic uses of the hunt. In 1871, General Sheridan organized a hunting party for a group of American business and civic leaders whose support he desperately wanted to win as the United States Army struggled to define its post–Civil War status.[7] Sheridan spared no expense and effort to give a dozen guests a thrilling but safe experience in the West, assigning to them a hundred-man escort from the Fifth Cavalry and providing army vehicles and supplies including sixteen wagons (one loaded with ice), three army ambulances, and carpeted tents for the travelers and their servants. Sheridan chose Cody to serve as guide for the group.

A privately published memoir, written as a souvenir of the hunting trip by one of its participants, gives a taste of its atmosphere. The author of *Ten Days on the Plains*, Henry Eugene Davies, was no tenderfoot, having fought with Sheridan in the Shenandoah Valley. Participants from New York, Philadelphia, and Chicago included present and former army officers (one of whom was Sheridan's future father-in-law), as well as experienced hunters and horseback riders. But Davies described his group as "tame citizen[s] of the East" who were venturing West to see "the region we had been taught by our early studies in geography to describe as the Great American Desert."[8] The group hoped for a colorful experience of the exotic, a firsthand encounter with landscape and people both known and unknown. And the trip served Sheridan's purpose, suggesting the possibilities for tourism in the land the army was rapidly making secure for Euro-Americans; it also revealed the tremendous hunger for the experience of the West that Cody would later draw upon.

While offering participants the opportunity to test their physical prowess on the plains, the hunting party also surrounded them with the amenities of urban life. When the group gathered in Chicago to embark for the West, Davies writes, "the large hall of the hotel was encumbered with a pile of gun cases, hunting boots, ammunition boxes, champagne baskets, demijohns and other necessities for a hunting campaign, that astonished and bewildered even the people of Chicago, accustomed as they are to shooting and to drinking at discretion." At Fort McPherson, Nebraska, they were met by a group of "ladies in carriages and on horseback," who joined them at a ball "until a very late hour of the night." Not surprisingly, life on the trail with this party was luxurious; as Cody later described the trip,

> There were none of the discomforts of roughing it upon that expedition. A [multi-]course dinner of the most delicious viands was served every evening by waiters in evening dress, and prepared by French cooks brought from New York. The linen, china, glass, and porcelain had been provided with equal care. . . . For years afterward travelers and settlers recognized the sites upon which these camps had been constructed by the quantities of empty bottles which remained behind to mark them.[9]

Thus the hunting party viewed the Western landscape, with its wildlife and even its threats of hostile Indians, from the safe vantage point of privilege; their adventure offered diversion and pleasure, but no hardship. Yet at the same time, this leadership elite hoped for some of the same imaginative benefits Frederick Jackson Turner would soon claim for the frontier: "rebirth . . . fluidity . . . simplicity."[10] As Davies put it at the beginning of his account,

> The man whose days were passed in the excitements of Wall street could find in the congenial society of buffalo bulls and grizzly bears an agreeable change from the ordinary associations of his life. . . . The man who had nothing to do could look forward to the prospect of abundant occupation, and he who at his home believed himself to be overworked could imagine in such a trip a period of idleness and ease.

As Americans began to prosper in the postwar years, and as prosperity brought nervous strain to the lives of successful city dwellers, the West was already identified with recreation, escapism, and renewed masculinity.

The convivial Cody found it easy to respond to his audience's hunger for a Western experience. He never seemed to lose his sense of wonder when he found himself "trotting in the first class, with the very first men of the land," as he put it in a letter to his brother-in-law in 1896, but his charm and sense of humor served him well too.[11] Members of Sheridan's hunting expedition seemed to appreciate his good-natured showmanship. As Davies expressed it, the tourists had expected to meet "the typical desperado of the West, bristling with knives and pistols, uncouth in person, and still more disagreeable in manners and address." Instead, they were pleased to find "William Cody, Esquire," to be "a mild, agreeable, well-mannered man, quiet and retiring in disposition, though well informed and always ready to talk well and earnestly upon any subject of interest. . . . Straight and erect as an arrow, and with strikingly handsome features, he at once attracted to him all with whom he became acquainted." Davies praised Buffalo Bill for his ability to shoot, manage horses, and build bridges, but it was clearly as a symbol of the frontier that Cody most impressed his Eastern audience. On the morning they left Fort McPherson, Buffalo Bill rode up with a flourish, "dressed in a suit of light buckskin, trimmed along the seams with fringes of the same leather, his costume lighted by the crimson shirt worn under his open coat, a broad sombrero on his head, and carrying his rifle lightly in his hand." Davies commented that "as his horse came toward us on an easy gallop, he realized to perfection the bold hunter and gallant sportsman of the plains."

This could be considered Buffalo Bill's first dramatic entrance; later he would open performances by galloping in on an attractive horse, sweeping off his broad-brimmed hat, and bowing to set his show in motion. When he wrote his autobiography in 1879, he described the encounter with Sheridan's hunting expedition as if it were a performance:

> As it was a nobby and high-toned outfit which I was to accompany, I determined to put on a little style myself. So I dressed in a new suit of light buckskin, trimmed along the seams with fringes of the same material; and I put on a crimson shirt handsomely ornamented on the bosom, while on my head I wore a broad *sombrero*. Then mounting a snowy white horse—a gallant stepper—I rode down from the fort to the camp, rifle in hand. I felt first-rate that morning, and looked well.[12]

Memories of performer and audience seem to mesh perfectly—until we realize that Cody had Davies's book at hand when he wrote or dictated his autobiography.

Cody's success with Sheridan's Eastern tourists made him a natural choice for Sheridan to request as a guide for an even more thoroughly publicized celebrity hunt that departed from Fort McPherson a few months later: the visit of Grand Duke Alexis, son of the Russian Czar. This event was widely reported in American newspapers and magazines, perhaps because Sheridan had done such a good job of interesting influential publishers in the romance of plains showmanship. Visits from foreign dignitaries, let alone royalty, were rare enough in nineteenth-century America, and President Grant wanted to offer a warm welcome to the Russian prince in order to cement the cordial relations that had led Russia to support the Union during the Civil War and had resulted in the purchase of Alaska in 1867. Diplomatic relations in Washington were not running smoothly, and Grant relied on Sheridan to provide the twenty-one-year-old visitor with an entertaining experience. Sheridan, for his part, had been smarting from criticism of his handling of relief efforts after the great Chicago fire in October 1871 and was eager for positive publicity and recognition.[13] The general used army resources lavishly, detailing two companies of infantry, two of cavalry, and the regimental band to accompany the hunting party, bringing its number to more than five hundred. He made special arrangements to release Cody from his commitment to follow the Fifth Cavalry to Arizona, and he brought Lieutenant Colonel George Armstrong Custer from Kentucky to take part. Cody gave the grand duke buffalo-hunting lessons and let him ride his horse, Buckskin Joe. Several hundred buffalo were killed during the five-day excursion, and the grand duke traveled on to Denver with apparent satisfaction.

With so many interests committed to making the royal hunt a success, Cody stood to reap some of its reflected glory and to learn even more about what made a frontier spectacle work. Apparently it was Sheridan who had the idea of recruiting Indians to join in the hunt and to give demonstrations of their ritual songs and dances, but it was Cody who had the task of finding appropriate participants and overseeing them. Scouting had brought Cody into contact with various hostile and friendly Indian groups, so presumably it was his scouting connections that led him to persuade the Brulé Sioux Spotted Tail, with a hundred of his band, to participate in the hunt. The presence of the Indians made the press accounts and illustrations more picturesque; when *Frank Leslie's* weekly magazine published a story about the hunt, the accompanying engraving showed the grand duke firing at a buffalo, followed by Custer and Buffalo Bill, with Indians in feathers galloping up behind.[14] Press stories detailed the Indians' feats, including an arrow shot that passed through a buffalo's body and out the other side. One journalist wrote that the visitors "were favored with a splendid view of a scene that few white men, who have lived many years upon the plains, have ever witnessed."[15] Plains showmanship acquired an air of hyper-reality, assumed to be authentic but more "splendid" than ordinary experience.

Some of the earliest photographs of Cody in scouting garb date from around the time of these two celebrity hunts, suggesting that he was beginning to attend to the production of his own image. Small, reproducible, inexpensive photographs had become popular in the United States as well as abroad during the 1860s. In sizes ranging from the carte de visite to the cabinet photograph, these visual mementos became part of the currency of business, politics, friendship, and show business. People could buy photographs of themselves to give to friends and relatives; publicists could distribute photographs of politicians or entertainers to newspapers or financial backers; and the public could collect photographs of famous people by buying prints from photographers, shops, or concessions. Evidence suggests that Cody's photographs circulated in all these ways.

Some of the photographs that marked Cody's career as a plains showman resembled the portraits that small-town photographers all over America produced to help groups record their membership: army units, volunteer fire companies, Sunday-school classes. Cody apparently had photographs taken of himself with his hunting trophies and also posed with groups of hunters who wanted to record their adventures in the West. The firearms, antlers, and animal skins arrayed in such photographs were guarantors of authenticity for frontier tourists and markers of a profession for the showman-scout.

By the time Davies published his account of the Sheridan hunting trip in 1872, Cody had ordered at least one studio portrait of himself in scouting clothing. Davies's book included pasted-in carte de visite photographs of participants, including a head-and-shoulders image of Cody that appears to be a truncated version of a small studio portrait posing the scout against a painted mountain landscape, leaning on his rifle, wearing a knee-length fringed and ornamented leather coat, engraved or embroidered high boots, and a broad-brimmed hat. His hair curls to his shoulders and he wears a thin mustache and small goatee. The inscription "To Sister Julia from W. F. Cody" on one surviving copy of the full-length photograph suggests that he gave at least some of these pictures to his relatives around this time.

The image paved the way for his public self-presentation as well. He had now found the look he would keep for the rest of his life. His wife's ghost-written autobiography, published after Cody's death, comments on the change in his appearance at about this time. When, after a long absence, she sees him dressed very much as he appeared in the photograph, she objects to his long hair but relents when he protests that if he cut it, "I'd be kind of out

Buffalo Bill in Scout Dress, c. 1870, photograph by Mathew Brady

of place with the boys." Sententiously, the narrator of Louisa's autobiography continues, "I'm afraid that even with the stories of his prowess on the plains, Buffalo Bill would not have been Buffalo Bill without that long hair, without that mustache and that little goatee—at least, he would not have been the unusual appearing character that he was, nor would he have been as handsome."[16]

DIME NOVEL AND STAGE SHOWMAN

Around the same time, Cody received some outside help in developing his frontier persona from a professional writer, Edward Zane Carroll Judson, who wrote dime novels under the pseudonym Ned Buntline. Judson, a veteran of the Union army, had an eventful career that included various kinds of posturing and imposture. A temperance lecturer and bigamist, he had been jailed for helping to incite the 1849 Astor Place riot in New York, when twenty-two people were killed in a demonstration against an English actor, and he was lynched for shooting a man in a duel in Nashville (he survived because the rope broke). Judson found a congenial profession in the emerging mass-publishing trade and earned as much as twenty thousand dollars a year producing novels for the popular publishing firm of Beadle and Adams. In 1869, Judson met Cody and used the name "Buffalo Bill" for the hero of a serial novel, *Buffalo Bill, the King of the Border Men*, published in the *New York Weekly* beginning December 23, 1869. Judson's tale featured Cody as an attractive sidekick to James Butler "Wild Bill" Hickok in a narrative culminating in the gunfight with the "M'Kandlas" gang that was already well known, thanks to an admiring article in *Harper's New Monthly Magazine*.[17]

Judson's story, the first in a series of fictional representations of Buffalo Bill, did not present him as much more than a compendium of clichés. The characterization is crude and predictable, using well-worn language to establish the fictional Buffalo Bill as a loving son ("Better son never blessed a mother, wild as he is"), a faithful comrade ("Buffalo Bill is just as good as was ever made, no matter whar you find him. . . . There isn't a bit of white in his liver, nor no black in his heart"), and an invincible ally in a fight ("On through the mass dashed Buffalo Bill, a revolver in each hand, and shot after shot, in the very face of his opponents, dropped a man at every fire. . . . Every shot had been fired from his revolver, but now his great knife-blade flashed in the air and came sweeping down here and there, as he saw foes to strike").[18]

Rescuing victims and supporting his friends, bringing villains to justice and fighting Indians and bandits without mercy, Judson's Buffalo Bill was a generic adventure hero like many others. The novel focused a spotlight on Cody as a Western personality, but it did not distinguish him from a horde of other dime-novel figures.

More effective was a play based on Buntline's serial, written by Frank Meader. Its successful run in New York in 1871 had made Buffalo Bill's name familiar to the participants in the Sheridan buffalo hunt: Davies described it as a "brilliant drama."[19] When Cody rode up to present himself as a guide at Fort MacPherson, he could draw on expectations that had already been created by his fictional and dramatic counterparts. And, in turn, his success with the Sheridan party allowed Cody to expand his own showmanship from the Great Plains to more traditional entertainment arenas.

Early in 1872, the publisher James Gordon Bennett, who had been a member of the Sheridan hunting party, invited Cody to come to New York. Sheridan, pleased with the outcome of the grand duke's hunt, smoothed the way by giving Cody a leave with pay. Bennett had just taken over the editorship of the *New York Herald* from his aging father and was eager to shed his playboy reputation, so he no doubt relished the idea of hosting this picturesque specimen of frontier masculinity. Cody transferred his plains showmanship to the big city, wearing his buckskins to a costume ball and enjoying the social life to which he was introduced.

In New York, Cody discovered the significance of his own theatricality when E.Z.C. Judson took him to a performance of the Buffalo Bill play at the Bowery Theater. When the theater manager learned that the real Buffalo Bill was present in the audience, he invited Cody to the stage to take a bow, and later tried to interest him in acting. Judson showed Cody around the city, arranged interviews for him with reporters, and began work on another Buffalo Bill dime novel. Although Cody went back to a scouting assignment with the Third Cavalry, he continued to receive letters from Judson urging him to try his luck on the stage. Finally, in December 1872, he went to Chicago to appear in *The Scouts of the Prairie*, a drama written by Judson and starring Cody, another army scout named Texas Jack Omohundro, and Judson himself, together with an Italian dancer, Giuseppina Morlacchi. December was the "off-season" for the Indian wars; although in 1868–69 a winter campaign had been waged against the Plains Indians, it was not until the mid-1870s that Sheridan began using the winter weather as his ally in the military struggle.[20] So Cody's theatrical efforts represented a low-risk venture; for the next decade he combined a winter theater season with summer scouting work.

Ned Buntline, Buffalo Bill, Giuseppina Morlacchi, Texas Jack Omohundro, c. 1870

The Scouts of the Prairie was apparently loosely based on a serialized Buffalo Bill novel that Judson had written after Cody's visit to New York, *Buffalo Bill's Last Victory; or, Dove Eye, the Lodge Queen*.[21] Like other dime novels, and like frontier stories dating back to James Fenimore Cooper (and before him to Cooper's models, Sir Walter Scott and the gothic novel), the story led its characters through captivity and danger, chases and battles. But reviews make it clear that the play was not admired for its literary qualities. "The only originality in the piece itself is the grotesque combination of absurd elements," sniffed one reviewer. "There is scarcely a vestige of plot. The characters are mainly Indians and trappers, who repeatedly amuse themselves by fierce and fatal combats. A series of these fights—always ending in tableaux—intermingled with desperately stupid monologues by a Western Pocahontas and others, and occasional temperance lectures by Ned Buntline, make up the drama, which is absolutely deficient in wit, vivacity, or sense." " 'The Scouts of the Prairie' . . . was written by Mr. 'Ned Buntline' for the purpose of affording two genuine scouts an opportunity to tread the boards and win histrionic honors and dollars," began another review. "As might have been expected, the play, considered as a literary work, is beneath contempt." The reviewer went on to lambaste the acting skills of both Cody and Omohundro. "Nothing could be worse from an artistic point of view than the performance of Buffalo Bill and his friend. . . . The lines allotted to Buffalo Bill are not arduous, and no vast amount of study and intellectual effort is required to unfold their meaning to the audience; and yet the wild and ineffectual struggles of the actor with them would make a contrary impression upon the uninformed."[22] Sample dialogue, preserved in playbills, suggests that the reviewers were not exaggerating: "We'll wipe the Red Skins out," "Then burn, ye cursed Dogs, burn," "The cage is here but the bird has flown," "Fly, fly, your enemies are too many," not to mention "Bill's Oath of Vengeance—'I'll not leave a Redskin to skim the Prairie,' " and "Buffalo Bill's red hot reception—'Give it to them, boys.' "[23] Cody himself acknowledged his awkwardness in early performances and his difficulty in learning his lines, so it is even doubtful whether these lines were actually spoken on the stage at any particular performance.

Why would anyone have wanted to see this trite and shabby play? One critic clearly pointed out the reason:

> It is undeniable that a certain interest does attach to the two white men apart from their absurd attempts to act. They are both fine-looking men, Buffalo Bill particularly, having an exceedingly handsome face and noble carriage. And then, when we see them rush in with pistols and rifles and slay a dozen Indians at a time, or watch the dexterous gentleman from Texas throw the lasso with delicate precision, or observe both of them tear the red-flannel scalps from the heads of their fallen enemies, it is comforting to know that they have done this kind of thing all their lives in deadly earnest.

Despite the ludicrous plot and ridiculous stage effects (red flannel scalps), audiences were fascinated by the scouts, their claim to authenticity, and their physical appeal: "The excitement in the gallery . . . was something wonderful to witness."[24]

Reviews of the stage plays in which Cody acted over the next few years return again and again to the solid fact of his graceful and handsome body. "As drama it is very poor stuff," wrote one reviewer. "But as an exhibition of three remarkable men it is not without interest." "Buffalo Bill and Texas Jack are fine, lusty, muscular, handsome young fellows," gushed another. "Their bodies are suppleness itself, and their bearing and glances mark their long familiarity with the free life of the prairie." "Buffalo Bill is a magnificent specimen of a man, and has a native grace of movement that is quite capti-vating. Jack has a fine physique also." "Tall beyond ordinary men, lithe and supple in form, with a finely cut head adorned by flowing black hair reaching almost to the shoulders, he is all that the pen of Buntline has ever painted him. Texas Jack is smaller in build, and would not be so marked a man in a crowd as the other."[25]

In his early stage career, then, Cody played the part of a real frontiersman playing the part of an actor playing the part of a frontiersman. Spectators responded enthusiastically to his extraordinary presence. *The Scouts of the Prairie* shared much with freak shows or the famous exhibitions of P. T Bar-num. Audiences came to see General Tom Thumb because he could sing and dance and tell funny stories, but also because he was an unusual physical being, a midget only twenty-five inches tall. Even Jenny Lind attracted audi-ences who understood little of her musical talent but simply wished to see the famous "Swedish nightingale."[26] Similarly, Cody understood that in translating plains showmanship into stage showmanship, his own physical self was the chief object of curiosity that brought in the enthusiastic, paying audiences.

A decade of stage plays traded on Buffalo Bill's recognizable character from one season to another. The dialogue seemed to matter little; other actors set up the situations in which Cody then performed actions such as shooting, fighting, tearing off disguises, and carrying dead Indians offstage. "Of course a girl is captured by the Indians," one reviewer explained, "and after much planning and following trails through the wilderness, consider-able 'Injun' fighting and dare-devil skirmishes, the maiden is rescued, falls in love with the hero who takes her from the clutches of the redskins, and then everything is lovely—until she is captured again the next night."[27] By 1876, programs reported a melodramatic dialogue between Buffalo Bill and a hos-tile Indian chief: "'Hold on, pard!' 'What! Bill Cody?' . . . 'My rifle failed me, but this will not!' . . . 'Back! back! this must not be!'"[28] No longer a bum-bling neophyte, Cody was settling into stage showmanship, mastering longer speeches and picking up the cadence of melodrama.

These early stage plays were animated dime novels, which is one reason they appealed to audiences. Critics grumbled: "The crusade against the cheap, trashy fiction which destroys the mental faculties of the youth and others who feed upon it, should extend to this alleged actor and his so-called plays." But the simplicity of the melodramatic format was clearly popular. "The Opera House was packed to suffocation, fully seven hundred boys and men paying for admission to the gallery alone . . . The vast audience was wild with delight when Bill was on the stage and manifested their delight with the most vigorous applause which broke out at times into yells of approval."[29]

The success of the plays called forth more novels, including some purportedly written by Cody himself. Judson composed a few more Buffalo Bill stories, and Colonel Prentiss Ingraham, who began writing the plays in 1876, also wrote Buffalo Bill novels during the 1870s and 1880s. By the summer of 1883, Cody was claiming authorship of thirteen novels. Some of these were later reprinted under Ingraham's name, and at least two were versions of Ingraham's scripts. It is unclear whether Cody's novels were ghostwritten, written collaboratively, or slapped together under a genuine confusion about the nature of literary originality.

Buffalo Bill's novels follow the language and plot conventions of blood-and-thunder sensationalism: "I am alone, alone, alone!" laments a beautiful young maiden lost on the prairie. "Hark! Is not that the distant howl of a wolf?" "Dare any brave of the Sioux or Cheyennes strike at the breast of the pale-face? If so, the breast of the white man is bared to the stroke."[30] This florid language resembles that of the Judson or Ingraham plays more than the earthy and rambling voice of the letters Cody wrote himself. Yet Cody's sister Helen claimed that he labored to make his writings acceptably literary. Although she acknowledged his lifelong disdain for spelling, grammar, and punctuation, she believed he worked hard to meet the expectations of the dime-novel format. In her memoir, she quotes a letter she says he sent to his publisher: "I am sorry to have to lie so outrageously in this yarn. My hero has killed more Indians on one war-trail than I have killed in all my life. But I understand this is what is expected in border tales. If you think the revolver and bowie-knife are used too freely, you may cut out a fatal shot or stab wherever you deem it wise."[31] Unlike the dime novels themselves, the letter has Cody's signature humor. Perhaps at this point Cody staked his claim to the persona that all the different texts were rapidly making famous; having mastered the delivery of dime-novel speeches, he began to reproduce them in his interviews, reminiscences, and writing. His literary identity was fast becoming his primary public role.

Over the next decade, as Cody gained more experience as an actor, his role as a frontier hero became dignified and the scripts for his plays more complex. Dialect characters appeared (Irish, German, Chinese, and Native American) and romance did, too. Cody's 1877 *May Cody; Or, Lost and Won*, written by Major Andrew Sheridan Burt, featured a character based on Cody's sister May; the opening scene takes place in a Fifth Avenue drawing room before transporting its characters to the frontier. The playbill stresses the play's claims to respectability, describing it as "the most Refined and Meritorious Sensational Drama ever written," and promising that it is "devoid of the usual trashy effects" of border dramas.[32] By 1879, *May Cody* was alternating in the repertory with *The Knight of the Plains; or, Buffalo Bill's Best Trail*, by Prentiss Ingraham. The chivalric allusion was meant to lend dignity to the adventures of the border scouts, as Cody pointed out in legal testimony in 1885. In the early 1880s, *The Prairie Waif* was praised for being more genteel than some of his earlier productions: a reviewer commented that it was "shorn of much of the blood and thunder that characterized Cody's former plays, and being thus tempered down is much more acceptable to the refined ear."[33]

As Cody's plays softened their blood-and-thunder plots, he was represented differently in the accompanying publicity, less a frontier curiosity and more a man of substance. "Receiving only a common-school education, Buffalo Bill has since educated himself for a thorough reader of human nature and close observer of men," stated one press report. "He naturally falls into the ways of polite society, and is a gentleman under any and all circumstances."[34] In interviews he stressed that he was a cattle rancher in Nebraska, and often mentioned how much money he earned in his performances. He began to speak to reporters about his views on Indians policy, and to use the title "Honorable," which he could claim because he had been elected to the Nebraska state legislature in 1872 (though a recount gave the office to his opponent, and Cody never contested it or tried to claim his seat). Buffalo Bill was evolving into a man who represented himself as spanning the worlds of campfire and parlor, West and East, battlefield and stage.

Paradoxically, Cody's attitude toward the texts that had launched Buffalo Bill became ambivalent. Although dime novels had paved the way for his career and several had been published under his name, he did not want to be associated too closely with this very popular entertainment form. In 1885, he bristled at the notion that Ned Buntline was primarily a writer of dime novels: "I have never seen a dime novel written by him and have heard him say he never wrote one."[35] Later he would protest against being considered a dime-novel scout, writing indignantly to complain about a former partner's belittling remarks. "I see you don't leave a stone unturned to give me a dig when ever you can in interviews with newspapers you say you have done more scouting in three months than I ever did, that I am a ten cent novel scout &c &c, all of which you know is false."[36] Dime novels were associated with the values and desires of their predominantly working-class readers, so

Cody's wish to minimize his connection with the genre that had propelled him into the public eye fits clearly with the other signs of his upward mobility.[37]

Similarly, as he became more famous, Cody became ambivalent about the plays. Questioned in a court case about his stage appearances, he gave humorously offhand descriptions of their plots: "I can't tell whether it was in my business to rescue that girl, or for someone else to do it, but the girl got back all the same, and you can bet on that." In interviews he gave self-deprecating accounts of his first appearance in *The Scouts of the Prairie*, claiming that Judson wrote the play in an afternoon and that when he went onstage he was so nervous he forgot all his lines, improvising with Judson's help. Much later, he would paint himself as even more of a nonprofessional: "I didn't try to act. I did what I used to do on the prairie, not what I thought some other fellow might have done if he felt that way."[38] Emphasizing the plays' artificiality allowed him to insist on his own underlying authenticity.

AUTOBIOGRAPHICAL SHOWMANSHIP

As he laid claim to the persona of Buffalo Bill outside the pages of dime novels and beyond the stage, Cody attempted a different kind of literary showmanship: the production of an autobiography. *The Life of Hon. William F. Cody, Known As Buffalo Bill, the Famous Hunter, Scout and Guide: An Autobiography* was published in Hartford, Connecticut, by Frank E. Bliss in 1879. Although the *Autobiography* had features in common with his dime novels—accounts of battles, dangers, and daring exploits—its chief purpose was very different: to establish Cody's authenticity, his "genuine" frontier credentials, and his fame as a hunter, scout, and guide. His primary identity is now that of the "Hon. William F. Cody," who is also "known as" Buffalo Bill.

The book was handsomely produced, distinguishing itself immediately from the Buffalo Bill novels. Opposite the title page, a frontispiece features a dignified steel engraving signed, in a firm and florid handwriting, "Yours Sincerely, W. F. Cody." The engraving, based on a photograph by C. D. Mosher, shows Cody dressed in a double-breasted suit, white shirt, and tie, in a bust-length image that fades gently into the ornate signature at the bottom of the page. This image could represent any substantial citizen except for Cody's trademark long hair, mustache, and goatee. The dedication establishes Cody's connection with the military establishment: "To General

Philip H. Sheridan, this book is most respectfully dedicated by the Author." Before the reader even reaches the publisher's "Introductory" remarks, the book displays a remarkable endorsement: a facsimile of a handwritten letter by Lieutenant General Philip Sheridan praising the *Autobiography* as "scrupulously correct" and "a record of actual daily life" that will be "of real service to the future historians of the country." The publisher goes on to quote from a complimentary letter about Cody from General E. A. Carr of the Fifth Cavalry.

What is the meaning of this series of prefatory endorsements? Was Cody's autobiographical project so tenuous that he needed heavy ammunition to bolster his believability? A generation earlier, publishers had presented the writings of escaped slaves wrapped in similar layers of authentication. Frederick Douglass's extraordinary autobiography, *Narrative of the Life of Frederick Douglass*, had appeared in 1845 prefaced by endorsements from two abolitionists vouching for its genuineness and declaring on its title page that the book was "written by himself." Just as a formerly enslaved person used autobiographical testimony to achieve recognition as a fully human and capable individual, Cody used his autobiography to take full possession of his own frontier persona.

Frontispiece of Cody, *Autobiography*

The publisher, too, needed to insist on the book's authenticity. Frank Bliss was trying to establish a subscription publishing business; his father, Elisha Bliss, was Mark Twain's publisher, and the younger Bliss was negotiating for A Tramp Aboard at the same time he signed Cody. Bliss hoped the *Autobiography*, profiting from Buffalo Bill's name recognition, would launch his own bid for independence and importance. In turn, Cody could only gain in stature from rubbing shoulders on the list with Mark Twain. In fact, Bliss offered Cody even closer access to the legacy of the superstar author. Several of the illustrations in the *Autobiography* were lifted directly from *Roughing It* and other Bliss books about the American West.

The note of solemn authenticity sounded in the book's introductory pages echoes throughout the text, and the *Autobiography* works to tie Buffalo Bill to the history of the Western frontier at every turn. Although some space is given to purely personal narratives, such as the death of Cody's brother, his early friendships, and his courtship and family life, the book is remarkable for its concentration on public events. It presents an insider's view of historical developments, including the settlement of Kansas, the Civil War, the operation of the pony express, and the Indian wars. It chronicles Cody's relationship with well-known figures, including high-ranking army officers such as Generals Sherman and Sheridan, frontier characters like Wild Bill Hickok and Kit Carson, individuals of public interest such as Grand Duke Alexis and George Armstrong Custer, and notable Indian chiefs like Rain-in-the-Face.

The book's claims to historicity were, however, oddly inflected by occasional reverberations from the conventions of folktale and romance. So, for example, Cody's tone wobbles as he describes one of his great feats of endurance as a scout, a marathon ride carrying dispatches through enemy territory. At times his narrative is reportorial, giving very precise statements about the number of miles he rode and the places he changed horses, yet in the same story he lapses into the realm of tall tale. He insists that he kept a horse from running away by tying its bridle to his belt with a lariat ("he galloped away into the darkness; but when he reached the full length of the lariat, he found that he was picketed to Bison William"), and claims that he had to walk a significant distance behind a mule that ran away and refused to be caught. At the conclusion of the episode, he receives a rich reward in a scene that could have come directly from a fairy tale—or a Horatio Alger novel: "General Sheridan highly complimented me for what I had done. . . . 'Cody,' continued he, 'I have decided to appoint you as guide and chief of scouts with the command. How does that suit you?' 'First-rate, General, and I thank you for the honor,' I replied, as gracefully as I knew how." The promotion has been verified by Cody's biographer, and Sheridan's own memoirs told the same story more formally nearly a decade later: "Such an exhibition of endurance and courage was more than enough to convince me that his services would be extremely valuable in the campaign, so I retained him at Fort Hays till the battalion of the Fifth Cavalry arrived, and then made him chief of scouts for that regiment."[39] But before we leap to the conclusion that Cody's exchange with Sheridan was indeed historically accurate, we should reflect that Sheridan's memoirs were written after Buffalo Bill had become an international celebrity. The general visited the showman often and swapped stories around many a dinner table; it no doubt suited him to make his side of the story match the one Cody had been telling for a decade. Even today, our reading of the *Autobiography* confounds easy distinctions between fact and fiction.

With its hybrid style, now reportorial, now novelistic or folkloric, the *Autobiography* presents Buffalo Bill as both an authentic participant in frontier affairs *and* a consummate showman. Appropriately, his first chapter begins with a theatrical metaphor: "My *debut* upon the world's stage occurred on February 26, 1845." The passage continues with a blend of drama and

Buffalo Bill and the mule, from Cody, *Autobiography*

history. "The scene of this first important event in my adventurous career, being in Scott county, in the State of Iowa. My parents, Isaac and Mary Ann Cody, who were numbered among the pioneers of Iowa, gave to me the name of William Frederick." The writing is simultaneously portentous, comic ("this first important event in my adventurous career"), and winningly ungrammatical. In fact, the hybridity and confusion in the text, even more than the compilation of "insider" information, suggest the fascinating emergence of a public celebrity who would charm audiences with his personality as well as impressing them with his claims to heroic stature. When Cody's manager John Burke drew on the *Autobiography* to produce a biography of his star in 1893, he recast this same passage to fit even more directly the myth of the American hero: "Buffalo Bill made his debut upon the stage of life in a little log cabin situated in the backwoods of Scott County, Iowa. His father and mother were good, honest people, poor in this world's goods, but rich in hope, faith in each other and the result of their efforts, and confidence in the future."[40] Reading Burke's flowery revision helps us to appreciate Cody's own overt struggle for self-definition.

The hybrid tone of the *Autobiography* is especially evident in the scenes that portray Buffalo Bill as an Indian fighter. Cody was never an Indian hater, and he maintained good working relations with Native American collaborators, from the Pawnee scouts who worked for the Fifth Cavalry to the Indians who later performed with his show. The *Autobiography* includes several nuanced encounters, such as the scene in which Chief Rain-in-the-Face declines to harm the injured Cody. But Cody clearly felt it important to establish his credentials as an action hero, and so he included an account of what he says was his first Indian killing. Modern biographers doubt that this incident ever occurred, but the *Autobiography* claims that while he was still a boy, he shot an Indian who menaced a wagon train with which he was traveling. His account of the incident borders on dime-novel heroics while betraying a hint of nightmarish horror, as if the narrator does not know what to make of the experience he describes. The plain, almost childish prose suggests a dreamlike sense of inevitability:

> I being the youngest and smallest of the party, became somewhat tired, and without noticing it I had fallen behind the others for some little distance. It was about ten o'clock and we were keeping very quiet and hugging close to the bank, when I happened to look up to the moon-lit sky and saw the plumed head of an Indian peeping over the bank. Instead of hurrying

Killing My First Indian, from Cody, *Autobiography*

ahead and alarming the men in a quiet way, I instantly aimed my gun at the head and fired. The report rang out sharp and loud on the night air, and was immediately followed by an Indian whoop, and the next moment about six feet of dead Indian came tumbling into the river. I was not only overcome with astonishment, but was badly scared, as I could hardly realize what I had done.

When Burke retold the story in 1893, he made it more conventional and aggressive: "Little Billy showed so much pluck in the dangerous position he occupied that Simpson could not help praising him, and by way of further encouragement he said: 'My brave little man, do you see that Indian on the right, riding out from the party to reconnoiter? . . . Suppose you give him a shot, just by way of experiment.' "[41] Here intrepid Billy unhesitatingly kills his man to the applause of all; there is no wonder or remorse in the spectacle of "six feet of dead Indian" tumbling at his feet. The *Autobiography*'s version suggests Cody's struggle to understand and express the meaning of his own experiences, and to reconcile his desire to be taken seriously as an historical figure with his allegiance to the fictionalized persona that had brought him to public attention.

Cody's style sometimes achieves the dignity to which he aspired. Although it is sprinkled with clichés ("Let us dig out of here quicker than we can say Jack Robinson," "I shot him dead in his tracks"), it also has a kind of direct address to the reader that brings to mind Benjamin Franklin's great autobiography: "I am at my home in North Platte, Nebraska, for the summer; and thus ends the account of my career as far as it has gone." The text clearly aims to position Cody as an adventurous frontiersman, but he usually resists the temptation to exaggerate or sensationalize.

The *Autobiography* has a lively dash of Western humor about it as well. When serving as justice of the peace in Nebraska, for example, Cody is called upon to perform a wedding ceremony. "I had 'braced up' for the occasion by imbibing rather freely of stimulants, and when I arrived at the house, with a copy of the Statutes of Nebraska, which I had recently received, I felt somewhat confused." When he cannot find a sample marriage ceremony, he invents his own, "I now pronounce you to be man and wife, and whomsoever God and Buffalo Bill have joined together let no man put asunder." In describing his perplexity when presented with the script for *Scouts of the*

A Wedding Ceremony,
from Cody,
Autobiography

Prairie, Cody reports that at first he read aloud the entire text, stage directions, cues, and all. Judson admonishes, " 'Tut! Tut!' You're not saying it right. You must stop at the cue.' 'Cue! What the mischief do you mean by the cue? I never saw any cue except in a billiard room,' said I." Writers like Artemus Ward and Mark Twain had already made humor a mark of Western identity, and Cody's autobiography fulfilled expectations in this respect as well as in its historical and heroic voices.

The illustrations likewise helped to define the emerging identity of Buffalo Bill. The eighty illustrations, by several different hands, are varied in quality and style. The publisher obviously reached into a grab bag of available images to produce generic Western scenes (riders on a hillside, army officers in camp, antelope on the plains) and bust-length portrait engravings of various prominent figures mentioned. But the most important illustrations are the ones that chronicle Buffalo Bill's adventures, and the hybridity of these mirrors that of the text. One illustrator consistently pictures him in a faintly comic vein, like a Spanish cavalier or King Charles I, with a sharp nose and exaggeratedly pointed beard. Others show him in a more heroic mode, shooting buffalo or Indians, capturing an outlaw, or, dressed in evening clothes, surrounded by admiring women on his trip East.

By far the most important illustrator who contributed to the *Autobiography* was True Williams, who had worked extensively for Elisha Bliss's American Publishing Company in the previous decade, supplying illustrations for Albert D. Richardson's *Beyond the Mississippi* (1869) and Joaquin Miller's *Unwritten History: Life Amongst the Modocs* (1874), as well as Mark Twain's *The Innocents Abroad* (1869), *Roughing It* (1872), *The Gilded Age* (1873), *Mark Twain's Sketches, New and Old* (1875), and *The Adventures of Tom Sawyer* (1876). The following year Williams would produce thirty-six illustrations for Mark Twain's *A Tramp Abroad,* the book that Frank Bliss lost to his father's firm. For Cody's autobiography, Williams drew at least fifteen clearly signed images, mostly dramatic scenes crucial to the plot, such as Cody's boyish encounter with the Indian he claims to have shot. "A Duel With Chief Yellow Hand," one of Williams's most meticulously rendered and dramatically composed illustrations, gave visual substance to Cody's project of self-authentication and provided a bridge between his plains showmanship of the previous decade and his emerging understanding of the power of self-display and self-creation in new forms of historical entertainment.

By the time Cody published his autobiography, the "duel" with "Yellow Hand," an event that took place in July 1876, had already become an important part of his reputation. His account—and the illustration of it—were bound to be crucial to his autobiographical narrative. The blurring of the boundaries between "fact" and "fiction," and the complexity of Cody's claims to historical authenticity, are perfectly expressed here.

By 1876, Cody had established a pattern of alternating between scouting work on the plains during the summers and theatrical performances during the winters. In early June of that year, Cody joined his old regiment, the Fifth Cavalry, in Cheyenne, Wyoming. Under the command of General Sheridan, the army was attempting to sweep Sioux Indians into the reservations and keep them from joining resistance forces led by Sitting Bull and Crazy Horse. In the field with the Seventh Cavalry, George Armstrong Custer, with whom Cody had served on the hunt arranged for Grand Duke Alexis, unwisely attacked a large Indian encampment at the Little Big Horn River. The deaths of Custer and 215 of his troops on June 25 created a public sensation and impelled Congress to pour more money into the Indian wars; by the end of the summer, the Sioux had been subjugated. [42] Cody carried the message of Custer's death to officers of the Fifth Cavalry, which was conducting a similar search for hostile Indians near the Red Cloud Agency in Nebraska on July 7. This momentous event was very much on Cody's mind ten days later, when he and his regiment moved against a group of Cheyennes attempting to leave their reservation; a battle ensued and a warrior named Yellow Hair was killed. The Indians fled back to the reservation and Cody ended up with the warrior's personal effects, including his scalp. The killing of Yellow Hair was a major act of revenge, Cody declared, the "first scalp for Custer."

Cody's participation in an Indian battle so soon after Custer's Last Stand presented him with an outstanding opportunity for plains showmanship. As soon as he returned to Fort Laramie, Cody began to publicize the incident, persuading Lieutenant Charles King to go to the telegraph office with him and a correspondent from the *New York Herald*, the newspaper of his old hunting friend James Gordon Bennett, to file reports for the Eastern press. The newspaper story asserted that in individual combat Cody had killed the Cheyenne, whose name he misunderstood as "Yellow Hand." Much later this event itself became a battleground in the controversy over Cody's historical truthfulness; his enemies claimed that someone else killed the Cheyenne and that Cody either scalped a long-dead Indian or bought the scalp from a soldier.[43] It is very difficult to assess what did happen, although modern scholars and biographers generally accept that Cody probably shot Yellow Hair during the course of the military engagement.[44] The significance of the killing of Yellow Hair lies not in what "actually" happened but in the uses that Cody made of it and the way the event advanced his claims to historicity throughout his career.

Even before filing the press story, Cody foresaw that this encounter would add luster to his reputation and realized that he had collected tangible evidence to support his claims. Writing to his wife the day after the event, Cody reported:

> We have had a fight. I killed Yellow Hand a Cheyenne Chief in a single-handed fight. You will no doubt hear of it through the papers. I am going as soon as I reach Fort Laramie the place we are heading for now [to] send the war bonnet, shield, bridal [sic], whip, arms and his scalp to Kerngood [owner of a store in Rochester, New York] to put up in his window. I will write Kerngood to bring it up to the house so you can show it to the neighbors. . . . I have only one scalp I can call my own that fellow I fought single handed in sight of our command and the cheers that went up when he fell was deafening.[45]

What is interesting here is his evident pride. Cody already understood the incident as a performance, reporting that it took place in front of a cheering audience of soldiers. Furthermore, it is clear that Cody immediately recognized the value of his trophies, arranging for the display of the artifacts that authenticated his exploit.

Returning to the stage that fall, Cody translated the incident into stage showmanship. He made his strongest historical claim yet with a drama that presented itself as timely news from the front. *The Red Right Hand; Or, Buffalo Bill's First Scalp for Custer* purported to retell the killing of Yellow Hair the summer before. In case audiences had not already heard of the exploit, the playbill made the connection to the Indian wars explicit, advertising Cody and his co-star, Jack Crawford, as "The Renowned Historical Celebrities," and mentioning the well-known names of Generals Terry and Crook. The program reproduced a poem written by Crawford upon hearing of Custer's death, and it also reprinted the *New York Herald* dispatch of July 11, 1876, melodramatically describing Cody's encounter with the Cheyenne warrior. "Yellow Hand, a young Cheyenne brave, came foremost, singling Bill as a foeman worthy of his steel. Cody cooly knelt, and, taking deliberate aim, sent his bullet through the chief's leg and into his horse's head. Down went the two, and, before his friends could reach him, a second shot from Bill's rifle laid the redskin low." Cody had helped to write the news report

George Armstrong Custer, Grand Duke Alexis, Buffalo Bill, c. 1872,
photographic mural by Kaufmand & Fabry Co.

that now was being used to authenticate his dramatization of the event. As if
to cue audience response to the play, the program quoted another *New York
Herald* story about the fervent enthusiasm generated by the "Yellow Hand"
artifacts during the play's New York run. "Broadway was almost blocked yes-
terday in the vicinity of the theatre where Buffalo Bill and his Combination
are holding forth, the cause being the free exhibition in the lobby of the
Scalp, Gun, Bridle, Pistols, &c. &c., worn by the Cheyenne Chief, Yellow
Hand, and captured by the chief of scouts."[46] Within months of a military
engagement, Cody was re-enacting it on stage, quoting his own press
accounts, and displaying trophies of his achievement.

The artifacts not only authenticated his claims to "real" accomplishment
but connected him to a popularly acclaimed military hero. Cody drew on his
association with Custer for the remainder of his career. At some point, he or
his publicists (or a clever photographer acting on his own initiative) merged

two studio portraits from around the time of Grand Duke Alexis's hunt to create a composite image purporting to show Custer, the grand duke, and Cody standing together.[47] Later, with the resources of the Wild West exhibition to draw upon, Cody would re-enact Custer's Last Stand and even propose himself as a near-rescuer of the unfortunate Seventh Cavalry. The scalp and possessions of Yellow Hair traveled with Cody; he displayed them in the theaters where he acted and hung them in his tent when touring with the Wild West. After his death, the artifacts became a part of the collection of the Buffalo Bill Historical Center in Cody, Wyoming, where they remained on exhibit in 1995.

By the time the *Autobiography* was published, Cody had told the story of the killing of Yellow Hand in many ways: in press dispatches and letters, in interviews, and in the lines he spoke in the play written for him by Prentiss Ingraham. Unsurprisingly, his account in the *Autobiography* takes the melodramatic tone of the stage play. The *Herald* dispatch had called the encounter a face-to-face killing, with Yellow Hand felled by Cody's second rifle shot; the *Autobiography* draws out the incident by claiming that the Cheyenne chief uttered a personal challenge to Cody: "I know you, Pa-he-haska; if you want to fight, come ahead and fight me." Leaving aside the question of whether Cody spoke the Cheyenne language, this individualized spoken exchange seems unlikely in light of the recorded memories of other witnesses, who described a quick charge against a small group of Indians, one of whom was shot while the rest retreated.[48] But the aspect of the story on which Cody insisted in the *Autobiography*, and which Williams chose to illustrate, was not the encounter itself but its aftermath, the dramatic display of the Indian's scalp and headdress to his own troops: "As the soldiers came up I swung the Indian chieftain's top-knot and bonnet in the air, and shouted: *'The first scalp for Custer.'* "

Williams's illustration makes explicit the showmanship that lay behind this account. It shows Buffalo Bill in heroic posture, knife in hand, waving aloft a feathered headdress and a (barely recognizable) hair lock from the dead Yellow Hair. In the distance, Indians gallop menacingly toward him, while the dead Indian lies stretched out in the foreground in a pose resembling *The Dying Gaul* or Frederick Pettrich's sculpture *The Dying Tecumseh* (1856). The viewer is in the position of the advancing American soldiers who "came up" to chase the Indians away and to witness Cody's claim of revenge. The figure of Buffalo Bill is meticulously rendered in this carefully executed illustration: everything about his appearance harmonizes with the representations readers could already have seen in his posters and publicity pictures.

A Duel with Chief Yellow Hand, from Cody, *Autobiography*

Buffalo Bill, c. 1875

His costume seems to be taken from one of about the same time: it has the same beaver-trimmed, fringed coat with broad lapels and round buttons, fringed leggings, and broad-brimmed hat that he wore in *The Scouts of the Prairie*.[49] The image that accompanies the *Autobiography*'s most vivid claim to historical authenticity is also its most intensely theatrical.

Autobiographical showmanship, then, staked a strong claim for William Cody's historical authenticity even while it drew upon Buffalo Bill's image and allure as a performer. The voice of the narrative, by turns charming, funny, proud, self-mocking, tedious, and clichéd, purports to represent the "real" William F. Cody, but its purpose is, always, to increase its readers' hunger for representations of the "fictional" Buffalo Bill. And how are we to understand that narrative voice? Did Cody actually write his autobiography? Its style is certainly more grammatical and stylistically smoother than the lurching letters that survive in Cody's own handwriting, more dignified and less sensational than the dime novels he published under his own name. Yet it has some of the qualities of a good yarn that journalists noted when they recorded his lively conversations. Don Russell, Cody's biographer, considered the question and dismissed the claims of the two likeliest ghostwriters, Prentiss Ingraham and Cody's publicist John Burke, believing it is likely that the text was in fact written substantially by Cody, both because of its authentic-sounding details and because of its almost counterproductive modesty. "Who but Cody would have mentioned his brief and unrecorded involvement with Chandler's jayhawkers and horse thieves? Who but Cody would have admitted that he volunteered for Civil War service while so drunk that he didn't know what he was doing? What ghostwriter would have omitted so many of Cody's real claims to distinction while including less creditable episodes?"[50] As with his dime novels, the question of authorship may be tangled and, ultimately, irrelevant. Cody participated in the production of his autobiography in some way, and the text fittingly embodies his hybrid status as showman and historical figure, presenting himself before the public as the performer of his own life story.

"AMERICA'S NATIONAL ENTERTAINMENT"

In 1883, Cody made the move that defined his real contribution to the history of American entertainment and of public interpretation of the frontier experience: he invented the Wild West show, an engaging outdoor display of exotic animals and individuals demonstrating skills and enacting fictions, which his partners soon promoted as "America's National Entertainment." His first decade in show business had built upon the conventions of stage melodrama, even though he had joined other performers in stretching theatrical boundaries by bringing live animals onto the stage, firing guns, and displaying himself and others as "authentic" frontiersmen. The best of these dramas were praised for their stirring excitement, but even the positive reviews categorized them as a barely respectable genre: "lurid Western blood and thunder drama."[51] However, the Wild West exhibition was immediately recognized as a remarkable theatrical innovation, bringing the stage play together with other entertainments such as the circus and sportsmen's exhibitions.

Other performance forms had brought horsemen and animals into show business. P. T. Barnum had staged a buffalo hunt in Hoboken, New Jersey, in 1843, and in August 1872, Wild Bill Hickok participated in a buffalo-hunting performance at Niagara Falls, New York.[52] Since the eighteenth century, circuses had featured equestrian performers, and by the 1830s, they often incorporated wild-animal acts as well. Circuses traveled throughout the country on railroad cars and down the rivers on showboats. Cody probably saw a circus in North Platte, Nebraska, in 1869; he later reported that he incorporated circus tricks into his plains horse-racing showmanship, jumping on and off his running horse while holding its mane.[53] Wild Bill Hickok married the widow of a circus impresario who had become wealthy managing her husband's troupe, and whose daughter was praised as a rider by Hickok's one-time partner Cody.[54] Although Cody's publicists would insist that his show was not a circus, the circus was a model for the riding and animal handling, the staging of parades, and the techniques for moving a theatrical troupe with animals and equipment from one location to another.

The Wild West show represented something new in the history of show

Nate Salsbury

business, but it was also the creature of its historical moment. The historian Lawrence Levine has reminded us that nineteenth-century Americans enjoyed a wide spectrum of high and popular entertainments, from Shakespeare to melodrama, from opera to dog races.[55] It was this kind of polymorphous performativity that Mark Twain would satirize throughout *The Adventures of Huckleberry Finn,* with its public and private posturing (Huck pretending to be a girl, Colonel Grangerford facing down a lynch crowd) and its entertainment troupe par excellence, the King and the Duke. Cody's ten years of stage experience had brought him to think of himself more consistently as an entertainer, and by 1883 he was ready to try something new. In the spring of 1882 his plans were deeply influenced by a fortunate meeting with a lively actor and resourceful theater manager, Nate Salsbury.

Salsbury, an orphan who grew up on an Illinois farm and joined the Union army as a drummer boy, had been touring with a troupe called the Salsbury Troubadours, performing musical comedy and farce. He had traveled to Australia, and had begun to think of staging a riding exhibition that would try to reproduce the horsemanship of the plains in a circuslike setting. He met Cody when they were both performing in Brooklyn, and the two men discussed plans for an outdoor frontier entertainment. However, Salsbury did not have the money to finance such a venture immediately, and Cody decided to move ahead with the plan on his own. He staged an outdoor Fourth of July celebration, the "Old Glory Blowout," in his hometown of North Platte, Nebraska, in the summer of 1882, and then he proposed an entertainment partnership to a successful sharpshooter, William F. "Doc" Carver. Salsbury, invited to invest in this venture, declined on the grounds that "Carver . . . was a fakir in show business and as Cody once expressed it 'Went West on a piano stool.' "[56]

Cody and Carver each put up five thousand dollars for a partnership that was at first called "Cody and Carver's 'Golden West.' "[57] Cody arranged for a group of Pawnee Indians to participate under the leadership of Major Frank North, a widely respected army scout who was Cody's partner in a ranching enterprise near North Platte. He also secured an old stagecoach from the Cheyenne and Black Hills Stage Line and collected the required number of horses, mules, and other livestock. Opening in Omaha in May 1883, the show featured a succession of acts, including marksmanship by Cody, Carver, and another sharpshooter, Captain Adam H. Bogardus; a bareback pony race; a demonstration of pony-express riding techniques; steer roping; "A Grand Hunt on the Plains"; and "The Startling and Soul-Stirring Attack upon the Deadwood Mail Coach."[58] Perhaps most significantly, Cody hired as general manager John Burke, who had handled publicity for *The Scouts of the Prairie* but had stayed with the rest of the cast when Cody formed his own theatrical company. Burke, who served Cody loyally for the rest of his life, wrote much of the program text, smoothed relations with newspaper reporters, and spun the legends that defined the Wild West over the years.

Although the Wild West received some favorable notices during this first season, Cody and Carver found it hard to work together. Each accused the other of malingering and heavy drinking, and by the end of 1883 both were determined to end their partnership. According to Cody's later account, they flipped a coin to divide their assets, and Cody secured the Deadwood stagecoach. Burke stayed with Cody, and Nate Salsbury came on board, bringing show-business experience and financial backing to a partnership that would make them both rich and famous. Soon Cody and Carver were starring in competing performances that jostled for publicity and profit as frontier acts and characters were shuffled and dealt between the two shows. Bogardus and Jack Crawford appeared in Carver's show, then Bogardus joined Cody and Salsbury. Carver used the same format he and Cody had worked out for the outdoor Wild West, with Plains Indians and cowboys performing riding, shooting, and roping acts; he bought another stagecoach and staged a similar attack-and-rescue vignette. Carver took his show on the road throughout the South in the winter of 1883–84 while Cody was working out financial and personnel arrangements for his partnership with Salsbury. At this crucial juncture, it seemed as if Carver might seize the momentum and become identified with the outdoor performances of the Wild West.

However, several crucial factors helped Cody emerge as the premier showman of the Wild West. Although Carver began his independent season using the title "Wild West," Cody executed a maneuver, probably at the suggestion of Salsbury, that helped him make the phrase forever his own. In December 1883, he filed a copyright claim for the script for his Wild West show and also for the use of the name.[59] Although the copyright was not granted until June 1, 1885, Cody and Salsbury's quick thinking gave Cody a powerful weapon in his battle with Carver. John Burke sent out enthusiastic press releases that praised Cody and belittled Carver. His billposters flooded the towns where Carver was scheduled to perform, and handbills claimed that audiences would not see the real Wild West until Cody came to town. Finally, in July 1885, Cody and Salsbury won a legal judgment against Carver that caused him to lose his show. Carver counterattacked, suing for libel, and for weeks the two rival showmen confronted each other in the courts, giving depositions and press interviews accusing each other of fraud and double-dealing.[60] In the end, Cody chose to settle the fifty-thousand-dollar libel suit for a payment of three hundred dollars; Carver had won the battle but lost the war. Bad blood continued between the two showmen; in 1890, cowboys from the two troupes engaged in a shoot-out in Hamburg, Germany, and to the end of his life Carver ranted against Cody as a fraud and a scoundrel.[61]

At the moment of its emergence in the summer season of 1883, the Wild West could have been a star vehicle for any or all of its three featured performers, Cody, Carver, or Bogardus. And Cody's former partners on the dramatic circuit, Jack Crawford, Wild Bill Hickok, and Texas Jack Omohundro, had also shown the potential to emerge as frontier celebrities. It is worth pausing to wonder why Cody's contemporaries and rivals stayed in the ranks of struggling showmen while Buffalo Bill became a singular, world-recognized celebrity.

Wild Bill Hickok was well known in the 1870s as a gunfighter, marshal, and dime-novel hero. Like Cody, he flirted briefly with a stage career, but performance seemed to be foreign to his temperament. Although he traveled with Cody and his company in 1873–74, he did not relish the experience, which gave rise to numerous stories about barroom fights, whiskey drinking, and quarrels with stagehands. According to one account, he annoyed his fellow actors by shooting too close to the legs of supporting cast members; in another incident, he shot out the lights when he was dissatisfied with his share of the spotlight.[62] Hickok's name on the playbill was a great draw, and until he left the cast and was replaced by an actor, the show's publicity could claim *three* genuine scouts on stage, but he did not aspire to the focused show-business career Cody would soon cultivate. He went back to the plains in March 1874, and a little more than two years later he was dead, shot in the back of the head during a poker game.

A more successful journey from the plains to the stage was followed by Texas Jack Omohundro. Like Cody, he was a civilian scout for the U.S. Army after the Civil War, and he too was well grounded in plains showmanship, participating in Grand Duke Alexis's hunt and taking over from Cody when the Earl of Dunraven needed a guide. Cody's friendship may have persuaded him to go to Chicago to be in the first season of *The Scouts of the Prairie*, and then to cast his lot with Cody when the two broke up their partnership with Judson the following year. Omohundro married the most seasoned performer from the first troupe, the Italian ballerina Giuseppina Morlacchi, who added luster to the new Buffalo Bill Combination. By 1876, when Cody and Omohundro parted company after three seasons together (and one in which Cody presented the same play with other actors), Texas Jack was even better placed than Buffalo Bill to succeed in the theater. Judson had written a serial featuring him, Morlacchi was performing in his plays, and the brilliant John Burke continued to work for him as a manager. Over the next four years, Omohundro continued to star in border dramas such as *Texas Jack in the Black Hills*, *The Trapper's Daughter*, and *The Scouts of the Plains*, while Morlacchi appeared with him and also in such vehicles as *The Black Crook*. Their joint earnings allowed them to live comfortably in Massachusetts, and perhaps enabled Omohundro to spend more of his time hunting and less on the stage. He was not so hungry as Cody, not so eager for fame and money, and perhaps that is why he did not pursue his stage career so aggressively; at any rate, he died of pneumonia at the age of thirty-three, in 1880.[63]

Ravenously hungry and fiercely competitive, another "pard" of Cody's, Jack Crawford, tells us more about the dynamics of Buffalo Bill's elevation to fame. Crawford was a fellow army scout who knew Cody on the plains, and he replaced Omohundro in the Buffalo Bill Combination in 1876. Born in Ireland, Crawford had been a young soldier in the Union army, and had learned to read and write at the age of seventeen while recuperating from a war wound.[64] By the time he accepted Cody's offer to appear onstage, he was deeply committed to temperance and to literature, having already composed hundreds of poems, some of which he published in Western newspapers. Although Crawford later took credit for keeping Cody from bankruptcy by convincing him to sign the temperance pledge (a vow Cody did not keep for any length of time), the two men endured a relationship that was competitive and rancorous. They quarreled about money, and after Crawford was injured during a performance in Virginia City they parted company with palpable ill will. Crawford formed his own troupe, the Captain Jack Combination, staging a number of frontier melodramas with mixed success. He continued to move back and forth between theater and frontier activities, searching for wealth in the gold fields of Canada and Alaska, writing and performing plays, and giving poetry readings and temperance lectures. His performances drew their share of enthusiastic comments; one play was called "the best frontier picture play" the reviewer had ever seen, while Crawford was praised for his "fresh individuality and fresh, strong character" in his readings.[65] But Crawford's career never took off. Almost an exact contemporary of Cody's—he was born one year later and died one year later—he traveled widely, performed to packed houses, made cameo appearances in the new medium of film, and, like Cody, used his frontier image to promote American preparedness on the eve of World War I. But he never had a con-

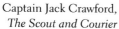

Captain Jack Crawford,
The Scout and Courier

sistent public presentation or a focused promotional campaign, and he never made the leap from the stage to the outdoor arena that became the Wild West show.

Captain Adam Bogardus did not approach Cody's stature as a performer, although he won acclaim as a sharpshooter. Bogardus, who grew up in Elkhart, Illinois, shot birds for sale to commercial markets, and as a young man he competed in pigeon-shooting matches throughout the United States and in England. When passenger pigeons sank into extinction, Bogardus helped to establish a new sport: shooting glass balls, which he manufactured himself. He appeared in many well-publicized competitions sponsored by sporting organizations, and after the initial season with Cody and Carver, performed in various Wild West entertainments and with the Adam Forepaugh Circus. In 1891 he retired from show business and opened a shooting gallery in Lincoln, Illinois. About a dozen years older than Cody, he died in August 1913.

The most interesting of Cody's show-business "pards" was his first Wild West partner, Bogardus's rival sharpshooter, Doc Carver. Carver's early life remains elusive. In 1878 he was giving exhibitions shooting glass balls on

Buffalo Bill and Dr. Carver Rocky Mountain and Prairie Exhibition, 1883 program

Carver's Great Indian Fight on the Republican in 1873, from the Carver scrapbook

foot and on horseback; he had hired an agent who was responsible for a rash of favorable publicity, and he had written an autobiography that narrated a dime-novel-like story of a childhood Indian captivity and daring adventures. Although one modern biographer has believed Carver's claims for his plains adventures, the most thorough scholars consider his stories fabrications, belated attempts to bolster his performing career by casting himself in the role of Western hero.[66] Shooting skill was Carver's main claim to fame. Before joining Cody, he had traveled to England and scored well in shooting competitions staged at sports clubs; his autobiography includes page after page of score sheets indicating hits and misses in various shooting matches. When they performed together, Cody and Carver were both featured as marksmen; after the two separated, each strove to command the audience for the outdoor Wild West entertainment.

The image Carver projected in his publicity deliberately echoed that presented by Cody. In the program for their 1883 show, the two men are virtually indistinguishable, each portrayed as a handsome, longhaired hero with a mustache and broad-brimmed hat. After their rancorous parting, Carver helped himself to some of Cody's most successful visual representations, including an image drawn directly from the famous picture of Buffalo Bill scalping Yellow Hand. In succeeding years, his programs continued to reproduce the very same woodcuts Cody used, including one of a horseman with long flowing hair shooting from a galloping horse. Carver followed Cody's tracks back to the stage, touring with a play entitled *The Scout* and portraying himself in flowing buckskins. Intermingled with stage and Wild

Doc Carver shooting from a horse, from *The Progress of Civilization*,
Combined Wild West and Forepaugh Shows, 1888 program

Buffalo Bill shooting from a horse, *Buffalo Bill's Wild West*, 1884 program

West performances were specialty feats such as shooting sixty thousand lumps of coal in six days and nights.[67] But Carver never understood that exhibitions of skill alone would not bring audiences flocking to him. He lacked charisma and did not convince spectators that he himself embodied the Wild West.

Cody's early competitors continued to search for the magic formula that seemed to come so easily to Buffalo Bill. Both Crawford and Carver outlived their rival, jealous and embittered to the end. Crawford's letter of condolence after Nate Salsbury's death in 1902 turned into a violent screed against Cody, whom he described as "cowardly and cruel," lurching from one insult to another in his fury at his former friend: "But I am so far and away his Peere [sic] socially, physically, morally and intellectually, that I scarcely give him a thought, besides he is not a sincere dealer and Ned Buntline created the most selfish and brutal fake hero ever perpetrated on the American People when he robbed the real Buffalo Bill of his good name and attached it to so unworthy an object."[68] In 1926, Carver wrote to the Copyright Office in

Washington trying yet again to trump his former partner, now nine years dead. At this late date, he wanted to copyright the letterhead and name of "Cody and Carver's Wild West Show. Buffalo Bill and Dr. Carver's Rocky Mountain and Prairie Exhibition." (The request was denied because the assistant registrar of copyrights recognized it as a belated claim.[69]) Carver ended his career as the impresario of a diving-horse act that continued for many years at Atlantic City's Steel Pier (and was recently shown in the film *Wild Hearts Can't Be Broken*).

Perhaps the explanation for Cody's ability to surpass his rivals lies in the fact that only he combined his work as a stage actor and a sportsman, and only he defined his performances as fictions of the frontier (like Jack Crawford and Texas Jack) that were linked to demonstrations of skill (like Bogardus and Carver). He had learned much from his decade in show business, and he took the initiative in assembling the dynamic mixture of elements that made the Wild West such a success. In February and March 1883, Cody was sending a stream of instructions to Carver in preparation for their show: how to paint the coach and what kind of harness to buy, how many Indians to hire, what kind of tents were needed. He showed a keen sense of the kind of publicity such a show needed, urging Carver to have himself photographed in his buckskins ("I was afraid you would be touchy about it, and as you know we have no time to delay") and suggesting that they invest a few hundred dollars cultivating reporters from newspapers in cities such as Chicago and St. Louis, as well as from Bennett's *New York Herald*. In February, Cody favored the title "Cody and Carver's Golden West," commenting that it was "a smooth high toned name" that could "catch the better class of public than Cow Boys & Indians Combination or Yellowstone Combination. The word Combination is so old and so many shows use it. Our entertainment don't want to smack of a show or circus. Must be on a high toned basis. Representations of life in the far west by the originals there [sic] selves."[70] Part of Carver's court case in 1885 turned on the question of who proposed the name "Wild West," but this early letter makes it clear that, whatever the name, Cody anticipated the formula for the show's success: claims of authenticity combined with excitement, the ability to attract a "high toned" crowd and still show them a good time.

Cody's sense of theatricality was strong and canny, but the Wild West would not have become an international sensation without Nate Salsbury's broader show-business experience and John Burke's genius for publicity. Cody's partnership with Salsbury was to extend until the latter's death, in 1902; Burke stayed on the job until Cody died, in 1917. Although the two men sometimes competed for influence and credit, between them they crafted an effective vehicle for their star, and steadied him as he rocketed to worldwide celebrity.

Salsbury had helped Cody envision an outdoor entertainment when they first met, in 1882; picking up the pieces after the unsuccessful season with Carver, he brought to their partnership a strong sense of humor, a trouper's energy, and considerable savvy. As one admiring reporter described him, he was "a man who understands his business, attends to his business and minds his own business . . . shrewd, intelligent and practical off the stage as well as on it."[71] Early on, Salsbury directly addressed the drinking problem that would hover on the edge of control throughout Cody's career. In response to an admonitory letter that berated him for a drinking binge, Cody responded to Salsbury with contrition and the hint of humor that must have made him a delightful companion and exasperating partner:

> Your very sensable [sic] & truly rightful letter has just been read. And it has been the means of showing me just where I stand. And I solemnly promise you that after this you will never see me under the influence of liquor. I may have to take two or three drinks today to brace up on. That will be all as long as we are partners. I appreciate all you have done. Your judgment and business is good and from this on I will do my work to the letter. This drinking surely ends today. And your Pard will be himself. And be on deck all the time.[72]

Although Cody continued to drink heavily (and sometimes baited Salsbury by promising to go on "a drunk that is a drunk. Just to change my luck"), his biographer claims that this did not interfere with his performances.[73]

The first season of the Cody-Salsbury partnership tested everyone's good humor. On its way to an engagement in New Orleans, the boat carrying the Wild West company sank. Luckily no people were injured, but stock and equipment were devastated. According to a frequently retold story, Cody telegraphed for advice to Salsbury, who was in Denver waiting to go onstage with the Troubadours. After asking the orchestra leader to repeat the overture, so he could think, Salsbury sent back the reply, "Go to New Orleans, reorganize, and open on your regular date."[74] This anecdote suggests the resiliency and sense of adventure both men had to have. Cody scrambled to replenish his equipment, but the New Orleans engagement proved extremely disappointing. Days of rain kept audiences away and demoralized the troupe. Cody fulminated to Salsbury: "Fate if there is such a thing is against me. There is not one bit of use trying more the longer we stick at this the worse off we are. The sooner we give this outfit away the better. I am thoroughly discouraged. I am a damn condemned Joner [Jonah] and the sooner you get clear from me the better for you." He apologized for not being more pleasant to someone Salsbury had sent to visit him: "I fear I did not succeed and capture his good opinion, as I really intended doing. But he struck me with the rain and I soon cursing everything from God to a coyote wolf. I will do what I can to entertain him. But really I am in no humor to do so." Salsbury may have found something to smile about in his partner's distress: he labeled the envelope "a charming diatribe." He still had faith in the show, and presumably encouraged Cody, who ended his letter dejectedly reiterating that he was "a damned joner disgusted with my self & the world. There is no *heaven*—if so it can stay there and be damned. Your Pard & take my advice & quit him. Cody."[75]

If Cody was a Jonah, Salsbury led him out of the belly of the whale. Although their first season together was a financial loss and saw a devastating accident that mortally injured the valuable Frank North, the scout who had been their liaison with the Pawnees, the partners reorganized and turned the tide the following year. The season of 1885 added Annie Oakley, who became an instant favorite with audiences because of her remarkable trick shooting and her winning feminine charm. Annie Oakley, in turn, helped Cody and Salsbury recruit the Sioux leader Sitting Bull for part of the season. Sitting Bull had admired her performance in Minneapolis the previous year, and had given her the nickname "Little Sure Shot." Given a tremendous publicity boost by these two new performers, Buffalo Bill's Wild West flourished. In 1886, Salsbury hired an experienced stage writer, Steele MacKaye, to give it a different script, and in 1887 he took the troupe on the European tour he had envisioned from the start, which consolidated its stature and reinforced its preeminence as *the* American Wild West entertainment.

Toward the end of his life, ill and feuding with Cody, Salsbury produced a bitter memoir that he planned to entitle "Sixteen Years in Hell with Buffalo Bill," some of which was published in the 1950s. By no means should this angry reminiscence, which he never planned to make public, be taken as the only word on Salsbury's relationship with Cody. By all accounts, including his own correspondence, the creative years were exciting, satisfying, and fun for Salsbury as well as Cody. But the very qualities that made Cody such an appealing performer could be hard to live with from day to day: he was open-handed and easily distracted, loved a good time, and could be self-indulgent. In his blackest mood, Salsbury put a harsh construction on his relationship with Cody, emphasizing his own importance in shaping the frontiersman's worldwide celebrity.

> There were two of him to me. One the true Cody as he has always been from his birth, and the other was a commercial proposition that I discovered when I invented the Wild West, and picked him out for the Figure Head. Mind you, I am not trying to depreciate his physical courage at all. I have no doubt that he filled his position of Bull Whacker, and Express Rider, perfectly, and a man to do that must have physical hardihood, and courage of a certain kind. But there are others. And there were others, and there will be others, and if any of the three classes had had the good fortune to be good looking, tall, dashing, and the subject of romantic tale telling for a decade, there would have been some other commercial propositions that could have been developed.[76]

Filtering out the bitterness of an aging man who had been suffering from an injury received at the Wild West and who had recently beaten back Cody's effort to drop their partnership and wiggle out of paying his debts, we can still see the justice of Salsbury's claim. The celebrity Buffalo Bill was compounded of the natural man and the constructed hero. He was undoubtedly a "commercial property."

Cody's other lifelong associate, John Burke, had been a newspaperman and theater manager before he worked for Buntline and Cody, writing stories of frontier life and putting together scripts for theatrical groups when needed. He had also managed a touring group of Arabs and Japanese performers. Somewhere along the line he adopted the nickname "Arizona John," began to style himself "Major Burke," and affected the broad-brimmed hat, long hair, and mustache of his frontier stars. As a trade journal wrote of him, "his face is familiar and welcome in every newspaper, railroad and managerial office in the country; . . . everybody knows and likes him."[77] Burke seems to have combined the jobs we would now describe as press agent, advance man, and spokesman; he also wrote copy for the programs and publicity publications, and generated ideas in a steady stream. In the clippings scrapbooks meticulously gathered for each season, article after article in the press hits a common note, comments on the same features, and often uses identical language. By keeping the Wild West "on message" throughout its developmental years, John Burke, publicity coordinator, helped to define the meaning of the Wild West at the moment of its invention.

"BUFFALO BILL'S REALISM"

For the next three decades, Cody and his managers continued to embellish and elaborate on their original conception, and to focus its message, but the essential qualities that made the Wild West an international sensation were present from the very first outdoor season. Like Cody's earlier forms of showmanship, the Wild West succeeded to the extent that it convinced its audience that it was both "authentic" and "entertaining." The early programs insisted on the Wild West's historical accuracy. Promotional material for the 1883 show promised that viewers would see "Many Types of the Pioneers and Vanguard of Civilization. Celebrated Scouts, Veritable Cow-Boys, Mexican Vaqueros. Representatives of THE RUGGED LIFE OF PRIMITIVE MAN! Lassoists, Horsemen, Marksmen, Heroes of the Dug-Out, the Cabin, the Ranch, and the Trail, whose lives have been passed in REALITY ECLIPSING ROMANCE." Inside the program booklet, spectators found educational articles, including biographical profiles of Cody, Carver, and Frank North, a description of Plains Indian buffalo-hunting methods, historical background on the Deadwood stagecoach, information about "The Cow Boys" and the vaqueros, a quotation from Shakespeare, a passage taken from a book about American Indian religion, an essay on the rifle as an "aid to civilization," and a discussion of Indian languages as the sources for names of states.[78]

This historical and educational emphasis dominated the show's printed texts. The 1883 program opened with Burke's "Salutory," signed and dated "North Platte, Neb., May 1, 1883," a pagelong essay that was repeated (and re-dated) year after year. Burke presented the Wild West in a distinctly didactic framework.

> There is probably no field in modern American history more fascinating in the intensity of its interest than that which is presented on our rapidly extending frontier. . . . The story of our country, so far as it concerns life in the vast Rocky Mountain region and on the plains, has never been half told; and romance itself falls far short of the reality when it attempts to

depict the career of the little vanguard of pioneers, trappers, and scouts, who, moving always in front, have paved the way — frequently with their own bodies — for the safe approach of the masses behind.[79]

Here were the main outlines of the Wild West's claim to importance: romance *and* reality, adventure *and* "the story of our country."

The Wild West programs also used a profusion of visual images to position the show at the intersection of entertainment and realism. As early as 1884, covers were decorated with striking color lithographs. An 1885 cover depicts a handsome scout wearing a red fringed scarf around his waist, with long dark hair, a mustache, and a goatee, reining in a black horse and tipping his hat. Birds fly in the background, green grass grows under the horse's feet, and leafy tree branches reach toward the heroic figure. Closer examination shows that the scout is positioned on a decoratively beveled poster, displayed with three-dimensional shading against a background of pine trees and bushes. Indians peek around from behind the poster, while grass on the portrait grows into the background picture space, playfully marrying "reality" and "representation." On the back cover, tall pine trees grow around feath-

Buffalo Bill's Wild West, 1885 program covers

ered banners depicting frontier scenes: buffalo hunting on the plains and target shooting. A portrait of Buffalo Bill in a roundel completes the decorative and colorful cover design.

These brightly tinted covers use the best available color lithography to create an attractive image of the West not as a Great American Desert of empty dry land but as a green and leafy world of colorful Indians, plentiful buffalo, and a handsome scout on a spirited horse. On one cover, Buffalo Bill is on guard, on the next cover he swings a lasso, and on the third he tips his hat. The cover art is both "realistic" and "theatrical." It draws the viewer into a vivid and colorful world that acknowledges its own constructedness; it suggests both work and play, authenticity and performance.

The 1885 program was published by Calhoun Printing of Hartford, in the same city as Cody's publisher, Frank Bliss; he may have cooperated by making engraving plates available. Several illustrations were lifted directly from the *Autobiography*, drawing on its assertions of historical authenticity, and some of the same images were also used for publicity posters. Even more people than read the books or visited the shows saw posters plastered all over barns, commercial buildings, fences, and specially constructed stands. In some seasons, as many as eight thousand sheets were posted for each performance.[80] Images of Cody shooting buffalo, of a galloping stagecoach, of a gun battle with Indians, migrated from the pages of the *Autobiography* to the printed program to the colorful posters; each time the viewer encountered them, the images became more familiar and reinforced the impression that they represented an external "reality."

In the 1885 program, various engravings show Buffalo Bill in different guises. On the title page, a drawing of a bust of Buffalo Bill occupies the center of the heading, flanked on one side by a scout watching over a wagon train and an Indian watching over a settlement of tepees. The bust suggests Buffalo Bill's elevated status (he is described as "the famed scout and guide") and also signals the fact that the show itself is an artifact. In the middle, mediating the conflict between settlers and Indians and presenting the story is Buffalo Bill, already aspiring to iconic status.

Two more portraits of Buffalo Bill greet the program reader. The first is a bust-length engraving, showing the scout with his trademark mustache and goatee and wearing an embroidered shirt; this hovers above the list of twenty-two acts in the Wild West program, as if to give them his approval. On the next page, Buffalo Bill stands commandingly in a coat and boots with spurs, holding a riding whip; the accompanying text gives a brief biography of Cody, quoting praise from General E. A. Carr and General Richard Irving

Buffalo Bill's Wild West, 1885 program, page 1

Buffalo Bill's Wild West, 1885 program, page 2

(*above*) Buffalo Bill's house, *Buffalo Bill's Wild West*, 1885 program, page 7

(*left*) Portrait of Buffalo Bill, *Buffalo Bill's Wild West*, 1885 program, page 4

Dodge: "young, sturdy, a remarkable specimen of manly beauty, with the brain to conceive and the nerve to execute, Buffalo Bill *par excellence* is the exemplar of the strong and unique traits that characterize *a true American frontiersman*." Buffalo Bill is heroic *and* respectable. The text concludes with an engraving of his house in North Platte and an extract from a hometown newspaper describing his success in the "cultured cities of the East" and among "the elite of American society."[81]

The 1885 program also offered a visual image that reinforced Cody's most important historical claim, his account of the fight with Yellow Hand. Unlike True Williams, whose illustration for the *Autobiography* faithfully represented the grassy, open landscape near a river where the skirmish actually took place, the artist who created this program illustration altered the terrain, portraying the action on a high cliff, watched by a group of soldiers below. A gigantic Buffalo Bill towers over the dead Indian, his head in the clouds and his diagonal stance dominating the picture frame. The admiring soldiers have stopped in their tracks to look upward; they stand in for the audience, who would watch the same event enacted during the show. Depicting the "real" event as if it were occurring on a stage, the illustration reinforced the performance's illusion of authenticity. The program illustration is bloodier

Death of Yellow Hand—Cody's First Scalp for Custer,
Buffalo Bill's Wild West, 1884 program

and more graphic than that in the *Autobiography*; the scalp is more clearly identifiable, with skin as well as hair and dripping blood, and the dead Indian lies ignominiously sprawled under Buffalo Bill's feet with a hole in his head.

The show's claim to historicity evoked a powerful response from commentators. "The beauty and worth of this great exhibition of frontier life by Mr. Cody are suggested in the word genuine," gushed one newspaper, probably reflecting the press releases Burke had provided.

> The whole thing is real. There is not a bit of clap-trap about it. It is the picture of frontier life painted in intense realism, each scene standing forth in bold relief—painted, did I say? No, not painted, but acted as it is being acted along the entire frontier line that stretches from the Gulf of Mexico to the Great Slave Lake. It is a place and a scene to visit, therefore, not for mere amusement's sake, but for the sake of studying in a school where all lessons are objective and in which have been gathered materials for observation and instruction which, in the nature of things, are perishable and soon destined to vanish.[82]

Objective, historical representations of a frontier doomed to vanish: this reviewer defined the essence of Buffalo Bill's Wild West as it was to present itself for the next thirty years.

In an article on "Buffalo Bill's Realism," journalist Brick Pomeroy waxed even more eloquent about the Wild West's claims to historical authenticity:

> It is not a show. It is a resurrection, or rather an importation of the honest features of wild Western life and pioneer incidents to the East, that men, women and children may see, realize, understand, and forever remember what the Western pioneers met, encountered, and overcame. It is in secular life what the representation of Christ and the apostles proposed to be in religious life, except that in this case there are no counterfeits but actual, living, powerful, very much alive and in earnest delegates from the West, all of whom have most effectively participated in what they here re-reproduce as a most absorbing educational realism.[83]

Here, the Wild West is not only educational but quasi-religious. Pomeroy thought the show crossed two kinds of barriers: it brought the West to the

East, and it brought the past to the present. Its educational value lay in its historicity, and a Western journalist like Pomeroy could praise it as a "resurrection," a re-creation of a sacred story. No wonder audiences flocked to see it, not only in areas where the West seemed exotic, like the Eastern United States and Europe, but in the West as well. It was becoming a passion play for the American frontier.

Even Mark Twain, who surely understood self-invention, responded to the Wild West's claims of historical authenticity in a letter that the delighted promoters immediately published in the *New York Times*: "I have now seen your Wild West show two days in succession, enjoyed it thoroughly. It brought back to me the breezy, wild life of the Rocky mountains, and stirred me like a war song. The show is genuine, cowboys, vaqueros, Indians, stagecoach, costumes, the same as I saw on the frontier years ago."[84] For Samuel Clemens, too, the Wild West evoked a stirring sense of history. Against all evidence of stagecraft, promoters and observers alike clung to their sense that Buffalo Bill was a historical personage and that the experience of viewing his spectacles offered a "lifelike" glimpse of the history of the American West.

What is the significance of those claims? In the late nineteenth century, the United States was rapidly becoming an urban and industrial nation. The prosperity of the Gilded Age brought increased leisure to a manufacturing elite eager for travel and entertainment; in addition, the swelling population of American cities created an ever-increasing audience for mass amusements. Cody's canny perception that the Wild West should be a "high-toned" entertainment helped him to bridge the economic gap, attracting both wealthy and working-class audiences. The Wild West satisfied a craving for novelty and stimulation that was also answered by vaudeville, burlesque, minstrelsy, melodrama, and seaside resorts; at the same time, it reassured patrons and critics who might be worried about disreputable disorder by insisting on its own instructional value. (Salsbury wisely squelched Cody's idea of offering gambling on the premises.[85]) The "realism" of the Wild West helped to intensify its drama, to heighten the excitement of the wild stagecoach ride or the Indian attack, but "realism" was also key to its educational claims. The Wild West sprang into existence at a crucial moment in the emergence of modern popular entertainment, and it profited from the hunger of a broad audience for amusements that set their pulses racing and also reassured them that the rapidly modernizing world was a safe and stable place. Its enactment of danger and reassurance, its verve and color, and its reliance on a superstar performer whose personal presence became identified with the show itself, made it the harbinger of the modern entertainment spectacle.

Emerging out of a fluid entertainment world and appealing to the popular enthusiasm for the Western frontier that swept the nation after the Indian wars opened the Great Plains for leisure and tourist activities, Buffalo Bill's Wild West caught the crest of a wave that took Cody to stardom. It was his good fortune to join forces with experienced managers who helped him to capitalize on his natural advantages and who created a publicity machine that lifted him out of the world of tawdry entertainment into the heady and exciting realm of celebrity performance.

CHAPTER TWO

THE WILD WEST ABROAD
1887–92

Paradoxically, William Cody's meteoric rise to superstar status received its greatest boost not from the crowds who flocked to see him in American cities and towns but from adulatory audiences all over Europe. When, in 1887, Nate Salsbury and John Burke arranged to take the Wild West, with all its livestock, equipment, and performers, on a European tour, Cody drew capacity crowds, first in England and then in France, Italy, Austria, Germany, and the Netherlands. The enthusiasm of foreign spectators made him a worldwide celebrity and made good his claim to be an iconic national hero.

Cody's personal success also enshrined a particular interpretation of Western—indeed of American—history and culture. Even while his Wild West show amused and entertained its large audiences, it offered Europeans an attractive vision of the American nation, energetic and prosperous after the Civil War. The Wild West's very hybridity—rooted in the most clichéd melodramas and the most grandiose political rhetoric, claiming authenticity and mobilizing show-business glitz—made it powerfully persuasive. Its idea of personal heroism, which sprang from the dime novel, and its belief in the triumph of European civilization in the struggle with savagery, which derived from an amalgam of popular science and imperialist ideology, were as attractive overseas as at home. The Wild West displayed American military and cultural adventurism in a way that seemed familiar to Europeans at the high tide of imperialism. It was another example of the wild world of exotic others brought under the control of white, civilized authority. No wonder the Wild West became synonymous with "America" for millions of people at home and abroad.

TRADITIONS OF THE SPECTACLE

The Wild West's European tour was part of a worldwide circulation of performers of all kinds during the late nineteenth century. American actors and musicians sought wealth and recognition abroad, while European actors, actresses, and opera singers visited the United States, most notably Jenny Lind, Sarah Bernhardt, Henry Irving, and Adelaide Ristori. Nate Salsbury had taken his own theatrical troupe, Salsbury's Troubadours, as far away as Australia. Celebrity authors traveled as well, including Mark Twain, who visited England, and Charles Dickens and Oscar Wilde, who toured the United States to great acclaim. Blackface minstrel groups performed in England, while troupes doing Gilbert and Sullivan operettas came to New York.

But theatrical performances were not the only entertainment spectacles. British audiences for Buffalo Bill's Wild West were accustomed to representations of distant landscapes, natural disasters, wars, and famous people in panoramas, dioramas, wax museums, and automaton exhibitions displayed in specially designed halls and outdoor arenas. At Madame Tussaud's Waxworks in London, spectators could see effigies of guillotined French aristocrats and notorious British criminals, while other exhibitors displayed mechanical wild animals and statues of Napoleon that seemed to breathe, or produced illusions of storms at sea or the eruption of Vesuvius. As early as the 1820s, visitors to Vauxhall Gardens could witness a two-hour re-creation of the Battle of Waterloo complete with horses, cannons, and clashing armies.[1] Circuses and zoos displayed unusual animals, while sideshows exhibited individuals considered to be human oddities—short, tall, or fat people, people with skin discolorations or missing limbs, conjoined twins, muscle men, representatives of distant cultures.

Audiences considered both physical forms of difference and manifestations of unfamiliar cultural practices as exotic. In 1810–11, London audiences flocked with voyeuristic fascination to view Saartjie Baarman, an African woman called "the Hottentot Venus" and acclaimed for the shape of her buttocks. Only a few years later another group of Africans, five San, drew large crowds with their war dances and recitations in their distinctive "click" language.[2]

The American Indians traveling with Buffalo Bill's Wild West evoked particular curiosity throughout Europe, for American natives had long figured in the European imagination. Columbus returned from his first voyage with men, women, and children to display, and more than a century later, Pocohontas visited England and died there of smallpox. Throughout the eighteenth century, delegations of North American natives attracted enormous popular attention from ordinary and eminent Europeans alike, were received by monarchs in France and England, sat for portraits, attended plays and concerts, and were followed by curious crowds through city streets. In 1765, a British showman was criticized for exhibiting two Mohawk warriors for a fee, but by 1818 such spectacles had become acceptable, and a group of Oneida and Seneca Indians performed in theaters in Liverpool and London to great acclaim, advertised as "Wild Indian Savages from the Borders of Lake Erie."[3]

The line between entertainment and education in such exhibitions was always thin. In 1840, the American painter George Catlin, who had traveled extensively in the West and studied native customs in great detail, lectured to the English on American Indian culture. He rented a famous London exhi-

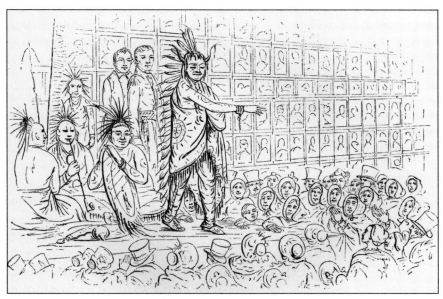

Catlin's Indian Gallery at Egyptian Hall, Smithsonian Report, 1885

bition gallery, the Egyptian Hall in Piccadilly, to display a collection of paintings depicting Native American leaders and Indian life, together with costumes, weapons, and other artifacts, but initial enthusiasm dwindled until he made his exhibition more theatrical. He hired actors to accompany his lectures with Indian dances and chants; then, in 1844, he incorporated the performance of nine Ojibwa Indians who had been brought to England by another showman. After the Ojibwas joined a sideshow, Catlin replaced them with fourteen Iowa Indians, some of whom he had met earlier in the Western territories. Catlin and his Indian performers were received by Queen Victoria, King Louis Philippe of France, and the King of Belgium; they exhibited at the Louvre in Paris and met Victor Hugo, George Sand, and Baron Humboldt.[4] While Catlin's experience abroad was disappointing—his wife and son died of pneumonia during their travels, and his cherished scheme to create a permanent display never materialized—he proved that American Indians exercised a continuing fascination for European audiences.

The American showman P. T. Barnum also walked the line between education and entertainment, ethnographic display and freak show, and he too boosted his career with a well-planned European tour. His most widely acclaimed international success, General Tom Thumb, was both a skilled performer and a physical oddity: when he first began performing with Barnum, dancing and singing American songs like "Yankee Doodle," the five-year-old Charles Stratton was only an inch over two feet and weighed a mere fifteen pounds.[5] Traveling to England in 1844, Barnum created an aura of authenticity for Stratton partly by following directly in Catlin's tracks, renting the same suite in Egyptian Hall and (according to his own account) keeping the Indian portraits and curiosities on the walls during Tom Thumb's shows.[6]

Two years later, Barnum returned to London with an exhibition he tied even more directly to European fascination with Native Americans. William Henry Johnson, an African-American man with an unusual head shape, was described by Barnum as an evolutionary curiosity, a missing link, and a savage. In 1846, hoping to capitalize on Catlin's success, Barnum exhibited Johnson at Egyptian Hall in London as the "Wild Man of the Prairies," claiming that he had been found "in the forests of California."[7] Although he later described Johnson as African, in the decade after Catlin's exhibitions Barnum claimed American Indian status for this performer, whose physical differences he exploited by entitling his exhibition "What Is It?"

Cody and Salsbury were, of course, well aware of the success of Barnum's spectacles—the shriveled mummy known as the Feejee mermaid; Joice Heth, the putative nurse of George Washington; General Tom Thumb; the

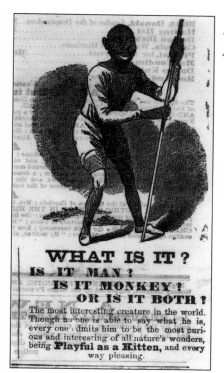

"What Is It?" Barnum's Museum, playbill, April 29, 1861

opera singer Jenny Lind; and a variety of circus acts—and the showman's reputation for entrepreneurial verve. Audiences enjoyed their flirtation with fraud as much as the spectacles themselves, as the historian Neil Harris argued in his 1973 study of Barnum's career.[8] Whether "authentic" or "humbug," these displays had enormous amusement value. Barnum himself had experimented with a form of Wild West enactment in 1843, when he staged a buffalo hunt in Hoboken, New Jersey; but as he explained in his autobiography, the point of this spectacle was not the heroism of the Western plains but the gullibility of New York audiences who paid for a ferry ride across the Hudson to see a "harmless humbug."[9]

Cody rather enjoyed being compared to Barnum; in 1883 he boasted to his sister that "the papers say I am the coming Barnum."[10] Indeed, numerous reviews had invoked the name of the legendary showman, and one biographical sketch of Cody concluded, "Barnum must look well to his laurels."[11] But Nate Salsbury was more cautious about claiming this notorious legacy. The keeper of Buffalo Bill's image was always skittish about presenting the Wild West as a freak show or circus, and insisted that it must be portrayed as an educational enterprise, a "national entertainment." Privately, however, he relished being compared to the master impresario of his age. Salsbury kept in his personal papers a poetic tribute from a friend, written in 1886, praising his management of the Wild West in these terms: "*Barnum* is paralyzed, you say / All other shows must now give way! / So, while the sun shines, make your hay!"[12] On the eve of Cody's departure for England, Barnum visited the Wild West and seemed to give it his blessing. Salsbury's biographer claimed it was the first time in forty years Barnum had attended a show not his own. The aging Barnum told the press that the Wild West did not need spangles to impress its audience, and praised it as "the coming show."[13]

Finally, Buffalo Bill's arrival on old-world shores marked another episode in the continuing story of the self-display of American abroad. United States travelers to Europe had carefully staged their "Americanness" since colonial days. Visiting Rome in the 1760s, the Philadelphia-born painter Benjamin West had called attention to his American identity by comparing the Apollo Belvedere to a Mohawk warrior, and during the American Revolution, Benjamin Franklin had charmed diplomatic and social circles in France by dressing in plain clothes and wearing his hair naturally instead of adopting court dress and a powdered wig. More recently, Mark Twain had inaugurated his literary career proclaiming himself an "innocent abroad," a role he later played with relish during his lecture tours. In 1866, the American humorist Artemus Ward gave a parodic lecture at Egyptian Hall entitled "Artemus Ward Among the Mormons."[14] So Buffalo Bill and all his cast members stepped into an international entertainment scene already prepared to admire their self-display as exotic specimens of New World identity.

By the time the Wild West sailed for England in 1887, the European tradition of spectacle had expanded to include a dramatic new venue for the international display of foreign cultures: the world's fair. In London, the Crystal Palace Exhibition of 1851 had given audiences an opportunity to admire British art, culture, and manufactures, and at the same time invited them to encounter people and products from faraway places. This mixture of commerce and entertainment was so appealing that a Crystal Palace was built in New York just five years later, and world's fairs began to be held throughout Europe in the next few years. As historians and cultural critics have pointed out, these fairs did more than just entertain or sell products. Embodying the imperialistic, bourgeois worldview that supported economic and political colonialism, they laid the peoples and material goods of the world at the feet of European spectators.[15]

In the United States, world's fairs were beginning to serve some of the same functions. The first major American fair, held in Philadelphia in 1876 and celebrating the centennial of national independence, put forward American claims to authority within an international arena. Audiences could sample America's evolving marketplace by viewing its industrial and commercial products—sewing and weaving machines, mass-produced bread, and the telephone—and pay tribute to American patriotism by visiting a model of George Washington's tomb and climbing to the top of the torch from Bartholdi's Statue of Liberty, still under construction. But they could also watch dancing girls in the Turkish café, visit a French restaurant, and, if they were lucky, catch a glimpse of the first foreign head of state to visit the United States, Emperor Dom Pedro of Brazil, who appeared with President Ulysses S. Grant to open the exhibition.

Like most world's fairs, the Centennial Exhibition embodied a theory of cultural hierarchy, and Americans used their own indigenous population for a spectacle of exotic peoples brought under the organizing control of the bourgeois worldview. Museum displays organized by the Smithsonian Institution and live exhibits by performers encamped on the fairgrounds represented American Indians as examples of a primitive culture that contrasted with the modern, industrial power symbolized by the Corliss Engine and other machinery exhibits.[16] In the same year as the Battle of Little Big Horn, this American world's fair already portrayed American Indians as part of a narrative of imperial conquest.

THE WILD WEST AS NATIONAL SPECTACLE

Before departing for Europe, Salsbury, Burke, and Cody had already experimented with linking their show to a world's fair. The New Orleans engagement of 1885 had been planned to coincide with the World's Industrial and Cotton Exposition, the first of the New South fairs. That venture ended in failure because of the steamboat accident that sank their equipment and the constant rain that led Cody to proclaim himself a "Joner."[17] But the fair attracted regional and national attention, and offered an opportunity to bring the Wild West's account of national culture into conjunction with that of the fair itself. The Smithsonian's exhibit, inside the fair's buildings, was viewed by its curators as "a golden opportunity for ethnology," and they deployed an impressive collection of Native American artifacts.[18] Despite the financial failures of the New Orleans engagement, Buffalo Bill's managers had astutely calculated the advantages of associating the Wild West with the imperial vision of a world's fair.

A year later, Nate Salsbury, who had been looking for a way to take the Wild West abroad, scented an outstanding opportunity in an offer to link his show with an international exhibition being planned for London in 1887 that would highlight American manufactures and commercial products. It was timed to coincide with Queen Victoria's Golden Jubilee, the extensive celebrations commemorating the fiftieth anniversary of her ascension to the throne, when festive crowds would be flooding the city in search of entertainment. The Wild West in London, performing on a large tract of land that was easily accessible, would have a convenient platform and a ready-made audience.

In planning the Wild West's London engagement, Cody and Salsbury sought to heighten the show's claims to be not only educational but iconic. That canny performer Mark Twain offered them a boost with a letter of endorsement and also outlined how the Wild West could profit by presenting itself as a national spectacle: "It is often said on the other side of the water that none of the exhibitions which we send to England are purely and distinctively American. If you will take the Wild West show over there you can remove that reproach."[19]

But both Salsbury and Burke worried that Buffalo Bill would not seem dignified enough to Europeans. Although they knew that the Wild West troupe would give lively performances, they feared it would be dismissed as crude. Even in the United States, the performance scene was bifurcated into institutions of high culture such as theaters, museums, and concert halls on the one hand and popular spectacles such as burlesque, music hall, and vaudeville on the other. Thanks to the promotional genius of Burke and Salsbury and to Cody's original perception that his entertainment needed to be "high toned," the Wild West was positioned on a shifting middle ground, a vigorous entertainment that combined the thrills of spectacle and the reassurance of respectability.

To strengthen the latter, Salsbury looked for ways to give the show an added gloss of dignity. A few months before its departure for England, he arranged with the well-known theatrical writer and director Steele MacKaye to create a new narrative for an indoor version of the show to be performed at New York's Madison Square Garden during the winter season of 1886–87. *The Drama of Civilization* continued to feature riding and shooting by Cody, Annie Oakley, and the Indians and acts like the capture of the Deadwood stagecoach, but it embedded these set pieces in a historical and ethnological narrative. It also traded on MacKaye's reputation as a serious dramatic writer and on his theatrical experience to give the actors more professional polish (MacKaye was an expert in the Delsarte method of acting) and to use the latest in scenic design and special-effects engineering. Not coincidentally, MacKaye turned the show into an American historical pageant performed while New York was full of visitors attending the unveiling of the Statue of Liberty.

Theater historians have praised *The Drama of Civilization* for its "pictorial realism," seeing it as the link between early dramas about Native Americans and the motion-picture Western.[20] MacKaye's son Percy, a playwright himself, believed it was a work of genius that "transformed the show's chaotic medley of elements into an organic unity" and brought the "heroic elements of our American background" into theater for the first time.[21] Using a moving cyclorama as a backdrop and supplying comment and continuity through the unifying device of an "orator" who spoke with the aid of an amplifying sounding board, MacKaye's production was divided into "Epochs" tracing the development of the West. "The Primeval Forest" represented America before the settlement of Europeans, and featured Indian dances, battles, and hunting scenes. "The Prairie" included a buffalo hunt, the arrival of an emigrant train, an Indian battle, and a forest fire. "The Cattle Ranch," which showed cowboys riding bucking broncos and lassoing steers, ended with an Indian attack and rescue. "The Mining Camp" introduced shooting, pony-express demonstrations, and the Deadwood stage, and the entire performance ended with a cyclone that whirled all the actors and props away. The individual acts were familiar staples from the Wild West's outdoor performances, but *The Drama of Civilization* gave them a more dignified framework.

Salsbury had admonished MacKaye to avoid comparisons to P. T. Barnum, and instructed him to try to lend the Wild West more dignity. "I don't want any *circusing*," he wrote, and warned the playwright that Cody was "petulant and impulsive, but with good, crude ideas as to what can be evolved from your material."[22] MacKaye took the project to heart. Although Salsbury had advised him not to worry about the acting skills of the troupe— "give them a broad outline of what you want done, and trust them to get up to the level you set"—he knew he could attract press notice by holding acting lessons for cowboys, Indians, settlers, and even mules. "Mr. MacKaye is a deservedly popular actor and dramatic author," read one account, "and he will employ the knowledge obtained abroad by years of study in coaching the Wild West Show."[23]

Meanwhile, MacKaye introduced Cody to influential New Yorkers, hoping to attract society audiences. Writing to Salsbury shortly before the show opened, he described a memorable night on the town with Cody playing the part of a society lion: "I think you will find that without neglecting a single detail that can tend to perfect the presentation of the 'Wild West' in the Garden—I have organized a small army of splendid fellows in the Clubs to advertise with enthusiasm the nobility and grandeur of the 'Wild West' at the Madison Square."[24] In a draft press release, Steele MacKaye praised the show in terms that must have made Salsbury's heart glow: "We owe Mr. Cody not only a new sensation but a new enlightenment. His exhibition rises far above the commonplace for mere amusement, . . . deserving a hearty recognition as much for the dignity of its instructive aim, as for the wonder and beauty of its artistic presentation."[25] The show's promoters declared the Madison Square Garden season a success, in terms both of finances and of publicity. In subsequent seasons, Salsbury would revive *The Drama of Civilization* occasionally when conditions made outdoor performances impractical. Even more significantly, MacKaye's version heightened the promoters' confidence in the show's potential as historical pageant. Some of his emphasis on social evolution went into the program text and some into the publicity, as Burke and Salsbury continued to claim that the Wild West told a heroic story of triumphant conquest. These historical claims were reinforced by appreciative British reviewers: "Civilization itself consents to march onward in the train of Buffalo Bill," they announced.[26]

One more touch completed the upgrading of the Wild West on the eve of its departure for England. Burke and Salsbury correctly realized that Cody's social status would be higher if he were viewed abroad as a military man rather than a showman, and they set out to collect letters of recommendation from American army officers under whom he had served. Significantly, these letters were intended not as private letters of introduction but as part of the public-relations portfolio for the show. They went right into the program text, where they stayed more or less throughout Cody's career, joining excerpts from recent books about the frontier to lend the appearance of documentation to Buffalo Bill's self-presentation.[27] These testimonials were both artificial and authentic: they had been solicited by Cody's press agents, but they did speak in concrete terms of his services on the plains, terms that were shaped, no doubt, by more than a decade of awareness of Buffalo Bill's fictionalized identity. The comments of Generals Merritt and King could have been taken from a dime novel: "He was cool and capable when surrounded by dangers," and "no one has ever shown more bravery on the Western plains than yourself." Many of the letters referred specifically to the Wild West performances: "I regard your exhibition as not only very interesting but practically instructive," commented General Nelson Miles, and General James B. Fry wrote, "I take pleasure in observing your success in depicting in the East the early life of the West." Remembering Cody's anger two years earlier at being considered a "ten cent novel scout" by Jack Crawford, we can see these endorsements as an effective personal justification for Cody as well as useful tools for establishing his credentials.

Finally, John Burke obtained for Cody one thing that his service as a civilian scout did not already provide him: a military title. The governor of Nebraska, John M. Thayer, issued a document commissioning Cody as "aide-de-camp of my staff with the rank of Colonel." As Cody's biographer Don Russell has commented, "it is characteristic of the Buffalo Bill legend that of all the endorsements collected by Burke, the one that was most effective had in it a touch of the phony."[28] This commission was honorary and after the fact, but Cody henceforth became "the Colonel" even to his close friends and associates.[29] It may have been around this time that Burke began calling himself "Major" as well. The patronage of Generals Sheridan and Sherman had clearly helped Cody's business in the United States, but a solid grounding with the U.S. Army seemed to be even more effective abroad. The titles were freely used in publicity and reviews, and Cody's claim to historical significance was conceded even by writers with barbs in their pens. "It is an old joke against Americans, that every citizen of the States considers the safety of the country depends to a great degree upon his own personal prowess," wrote one British reviewer, who went on to attest to his admiration for Buffalo Bill. "Beyond doubt, he is one of the most remarkable characters of his time and country."[30]

For the London engagement, held in an outdoor arena, Cody and Salsbury moved MacKaye's structuring narrative to the program text, keeping its implied historical claims while presenting the show itself in a form closer to its earlier structure, a loose aggregation of individual acts. Following the grand processional and entrance of the performers, the show featured several horseback races; marksmanship by Johnny Baker, the cowboy kid, and the two women trick-shooters, Annie Oakley and Lillian Smith; demonstration of cowboy skills such as riding bucking broncos and roping steers; and enactments of frontier experiences, including a demonstration of pony-express riding techniques, scenes from Indian life, a buffalo hunt, and two dramas of conflict between Indians and settlers, the attack on the emigrant train and the journey of the Deadwood stagecoach. A grand salute ended the performance. Many of the acts had been in the show from the start, and their descriptions were among the items copyrighted by Cody and Salsbury. But unlike the earlier shows, the London performance presented Buffalo Bill as not just another marksman but the central figure, the show's chief symbol. With his newly minted military title, Buffalo Bill seemed to gain stature and personal authority, which only added to his show's credibility as an educational American spectacle.

All of Salsbury's instincts were correct. The Wild West was a smash hit in London, and in fact the American Exhibition would have attracted little attention without it. The fair itself was a lackluster collection of displays such as a diorama of New York Harbor with a replica of the just-installed Statue of Liberty, a switchback railway and tobogganing slide, an exhibition of "Alimentary Products," a fine-arts gallery, and a hall of American hunting trophies, and it drew press notices that ranged from the halfhearted to the scornful. One newspaper proclaimed it a "ghastly failure," an "ill-sorted congeries of uninteresting trifles," while another reported that "the only things that caught our notice were the American Organ, which is very much in evidence [and] an elaborate stall for the vending of the 'Imperial Hair Regenerator.' "[31] All accounts agreed that spectators rushed as quickly as possible from the Exhibition's formal opening ceremonies to the stadium where the Wild West was performed. The Wild West soon surpassed its sponsoring framework and took its place as a spectacle that needed no introduction and no apology.

AT THE FOOT OF THE BRITISH THRONE

When the ship carrying the Wild West (the cleverly chosen *State of Nebraska*, named for Cody's home state) docked at Gravesend on April 16, 1887, it was met by a tugboat flying the Stars and Stripes and carrying a band playing "The Star-Spangled Banner," accompanied by Burke and a gang of reporters.[32] Colorful posters had been slapped on every available surface for an American-style media blitz that took the British press by surprise. One commentator exclaimed,

> *I may walk it, or 'bus it, or hansom it: still*
> *I am faced by the features of Buffalo Bill.*
> *Every hoarding is plastered, from East-end to West,*
> *With his hat, coat, and countenance, lovelocks and vest.*[33]

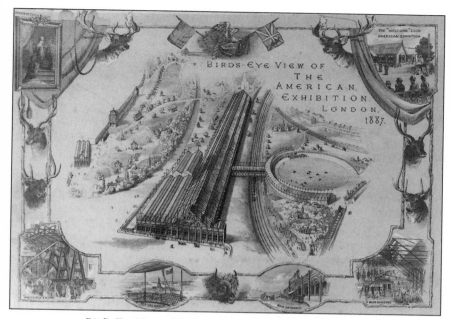

Bird's-Eye View of the American Exhibition, London, 1887

Advance publicity had aroused considerable interest in the show, but the success of the London engagement was secured by an event so remarkable that not even Nate Salsbury and John Burke could have planned it. Four days before the Wild West opened, the Prince of Wales asked to see the show, and less than a week later Queen Victoria herself broke her longstanding custom of declining to appear in public places and attended a command performance. The queen's visit, the resulting publicity, and the show's popularity with royalty from all over Europe who were in town for the Jubilee, made the Wild West a stunning success. As Nate Salsbury wrote in his reminiscences, he had landed Buffalo Bill "at the foot of the Throne of England," and the royal patronage "was enough to secure the attendance of every person in London who desired to be 'it.' "[34] Salsbury estimated that two and a half million people attended the show during its six-month stay in London.

How did this royal patronage come about? What, in addition to the show's intrinsic merits, attracted the Prince of Wales, the queen, and a steady flow of British notables? One track to the throne of England led through the theater, in which, by the late 1880s, influential politicians and the royal family took an interest. Henry Irving, the distinguished actor, had seen the Wild West in New York and endorsed it enthusiastically in a London theatrical paper: "I saw an entertainment in New York, the like of which I had never seen before, which impressed me immensely. . . . I venture to predict that when it comes to London it will take the town by storm."[35] Both the Prince of Wales and the former prime minister, William Gladstone, were regular patrons of Irving's performances (Gladstone, who had many connections among theatrical people, campaigned for Irving's eventual knighthood), so it was not surprising that they took an interest in this highly touted American theatrical entertainment. Soon after the Wild West's arrival in London, Gladstone enjoyed the "marvellous equitation" and regaled the assembled cast with a speech on Anglo-American cordiality.[36]

Gladstone responded to theatrical events with his characteristic moral earnestness, but the Prince of Wales made the pursuit of pleasure a high priority. His love of theatrical spectacle had begun early, and he had been present as a child when Barnum displayed Tom Thumb to the royal family. On a visit to Canada as a young man, he had tried to accept the acrobat Charles Blondin's invitation to carry him across Niagara Falls in a wheelbarrow over a tightrope (the plan was vetoed by his alarmed chaperones).[37] Even in middle age, the future King Edward VII habitually disconcerted his family by fraternizing with theater people and occasionally indulging in notorious sexual liaisons. He also frequented several London clubs where actors mingled with aristocrats.

Additionally, Cody's status as a sportsman and a hunter undoubtedly aroused the interest of English leaders. Hunting was a keenly pursued avocation of the British upper classes, from the royal family to the most provincial country squire. As the historian John M. MacKenzie has argued, the sport of hunting fit perfectly with British military, economic, and political ambition: indeed, it "represented the most perfect expression of global dominance in the late nineteenth century. Hunting required all the most virile attributes of the imperial male—courage, endurance, individualism (adaptable to national ends), sportsmanship (combining the moral etiquette of the sportsman with horsemanship and marksmanship), resourcefulness, a mastery of environmental signs, and a knowledge of natural history."[38] The shapers of the British Empire who sought out explorers and big-game hunters, collected trophies of stuffed heads and animal skins, and sponsored ethnological exhibits, might well have enjoyed Cody's enactment of Anglo-Saxon dominance in the Wild West's display of frontier skills. After all, Cody had presented himself as a plains showman to royals and nobles such as Grand Duke Alexis and Lord Dunraven. Buffalo Bill's exhibition resonated with their own values and concerns.

Even before receiving royal patronage, Cody was welcomed warmly by a coterie of British upper-class hunting enthusiasts and entertained at the Savage Club by its chair, just back from America, and by the Duke of Beaufort, also a renowned sportsman. It was through such contacts that Cody was introduced to the Prince of Wales, who was an avid hunter and regularly sought out hunting opportunities on his foreign journeys. When he visited the United States in 1860, he had gone as far west as St. Louis, joining tobacco-spitting guests dining on buffalo tongues.[39] At the royal estate at Sandringham, tens of thousands of pounds were spent to improve conditions for shooting, and the world's largest larder was built to hold the game brought in.[40] To the prince and to British aristocrats, the Wild West evoked a world of risk and dominance, of virility and exoticism that formed both the amusement and the serious business of the British Empire.

When the heir to the throne accepted an invitation to a rehearsal of the Wild West on May 5, Salsbury, Cody, and Burke understood that this might be their most important performance yet. They hastily improvised a royal box and asked the prince to signal the start of the show. As Cody later recalled the scene,

> My fears of a mishap were dispelled from the moment the Prince gave the signal, and the Indians, yelling like fiends, galloped out from their ambuscade and swept round the enclosure like a whirlwind. . . . The Prince rose from his seat and leaned eagerly over the front of the box, and the whole party seemed thrilled at the spectacle. "Cody," I said to myself, "you have fetched em!"[41]

Like a true sportsman, the Prince of Wales asked to see the stables after the show, commented on Cody's old horse, Charlie, and offered cigarettes to the Indian leader named Red Shirt. The prince's enjoyment of the "wild" and transgressive aspects of the experience might well have been heightened when Annie Oakley, upon being presented, pointedly shook hands with both him and Princess Beatrice, a breach of etiquette she attributed later to her American values and her sympathy for the wife of the unfaithful prince.[42]

But this visit alone was not enough to change the fortunes of the Wild West forever. It was the prince's return six days later with his mother and her entourage that brought the real publicity bonanza. Perhaps he suggested the visit in order to break the tension building before the Golden Jubilee, a royal spectacle designed to ratify Queen Victoria's popularity with her subjects.

Annie Oakley shaking hands with the Prince of Wales, Police Gazette, *1887*

Relatives were arriving from all over Europe, there were endless ceremonies to undergo, and the royal family was struggling with the first intimations of the illness that would prove fatal to the queen's son-in-law, the German emperor Frederick. In the midst of her own demanding schedule, perhaps Queen Victoria welcomed the chance to be a spectator instead of a performer. The queen at first proposed that the Wild West should come to her. Although five years later Cody did stage a command performance at Windsor Castle, on this occasion he and his managers were apprehensive, and so the queen ordered a private performance at Earl's Court on May 11, 1887. Ordinary spectators as well as the press were barred from the grounds, the performance was shortened to fit the royal party's time schedule, and the queen and her entourage drove to the amphitheater after tea.[43]

Queen Victoria maintained a robust interest in exotic lands and peoples; it was during her reign that the term "Empress of India" was added to the English monarch's title. Her husband, Prince Albert, had been identified with international science and education, serving as chancellor of Cambridge University and working to bring about the Crystal Palace Exhibition of 1851. He had also been a devotee of hunting sports, and visits to Balmoral had been a frequent diversion for both of them. The queen felt her husband's absence keenly during the Jubilee festivities. "I sat *alone,*" she wrote of the ceremony in Westminster Abbey on June 21, 1887, "oh! Without my beloved husband, for whom this would have been such a proud day!"[44]

By all accounts, the queen was gracious and attentive at the Wild West, and she made a remarkable gesture that Burke and Salsbury were glad to publicize. When a horseman rode into the arena carrying an American flag, the queen rose and bowed, followed by all the members of her court. This mark of respect to the national emblem, only twenty-six years after England had considered intervening in the Civil War on the side of the Confederacy, was viewed as a turning point in Anglo-American relations. Or at least so the publicists of the Wild West claimed. "It was a great event," Cody's memoirs said. "For the first time in history, since the Declaration of Independence, a sovereign of Great Britain had saluted the star spangled banner, and that banner was carried by a member of Buffalo Bill's Wild West! . . . We felt that the hatchet was buried at last and the Wild West had been at the funeral."[45] The queen's journal recorded her sense of the spectacles' exoticism: "All the different people, wild, painted Red Indians from America, on their wild bare backed horses, of different tribes,—cow boys, Mexicans, &c., all came tearing round at full speed, shrieking & screaming, which had the weirdest effect."[46]

The royal visits brought a flood of distinguished patronage. On June 20, the very date of the fiftieth anniversary of Queen Victoria's ascension to the throne and the day before the ceremony at Westminster Abbey, the Prince of Wales escorted a group of royal visitors to a morning performance of the Wild West. On this occasion, the rulers of Belgium, Denmark, Greece, and Saxony rode in the Deadwood stage, together with the Prince of Wales. Cody and his publicists would tell and retell the witticism Buffalo Bill exchanged with the prince: "Colonel, you never held four kings like these before," said the prince. "I've held four kings, but four kings and the Prince of Wales makes a royal flush, such as no man ever held before."[47] Poker was still an exotic game in England, introduced by American diplomats, and both the showman and the prince may have enjoyed this lowbrow reference, so difficult to explain to the royal relatives.

The royal family's patronage gave Cody an undreamed-of boost. Nate Salsbury could not help gloating, "The success of the London Season was of the phenomenal kind that brings cheer to the heart of the Showman. In our case it was especially gratifying, because we had been warned of the doom that awaited us, by those who had been there before and FAILED."[48] The publicity agent Lew Parker kept a daily record of "distinguished personages" who visited the Wild West, proclaiming that "the annals of show business have no record approximating in any degree such a marvelous success."[49] Burke and Salsbury soon produced a pair of engravings to be used as posters and later reproduced in program booklets: "Distinguished Visitors to Buffalo Bill's Wild West, London, 1887." Each shows a bust-length portrait of Buffalo Bill surrounded by similar portraits of visiting notables, one recording men (five kings, the Prince of Wales, a general, a member of Parliament, and a former prime minister) and the other women visitors, with Her Majesty the Queen predictably at the top, surrounded by her daughters, daughter-in-law, and other dignitaries. The Wild West had discovered a rich vein of celebrity endorsement. Less than two years after John Burke gave away free barbecue dinners in the hope of attracting a bit of press coverage and Cody waged a buffoonish set of court battles with Doc Carver, the Wild West was performing for the crowned heads of Europe and Cody was hiring a social secretary to ensure that he kept his appointments with influential politicians, businessmen, and titled aristocrats.

The success of the London season permanently transformed the Wild West's stature, its claims to public attention, and the way in which Salsbury, Burke, and Cody understood what they were doing. No longer one showman among many, Buffalo Bill now thought of himself—and others thought of him—as a unique and uniquely successful representative of the American spirit. Salsbury's claim that the Wild West represented "America's National Entertainment" took on a second meaning: not just an entertainment that appealed to Americans, but one that represented the United States to the world.

Distinguished Visitors to Buffalo Bill's Wild West, London, 1887, lithograph, posters by A. Hoen & Co.

WORLD'S WONDROUS VOYAGES

The engagement at the American Exhibition ended in October 1887, and the Wild West traveled to Birmingham and Manchester before returning for a brief season in the United States in the summer of 1888. The homecoming was short lived: foreign travel had been so successful that Burke and Salsbury lost no time in arranging a series of European tours that would keep the Wild West abroad for the next four years. In May 1889, again reaching for association with a world's fair, the show began a five-month engagement at the Exposition Universelle in Paris, the ambitious commemoration of the centennial of the French Revolution, for which the Eiffel Tower had been built. Then, gaining confidence, Salsbury and Burke took the company on a series of tours through southern France, to Barcelona, Sardinia, and Corsica; to Naples, Rome, Florence, and other Italian cities; and through Austria and Germany in 1889 and 1890. In 1891 the Wild West went to Germany, Holland, Belgium, and cities in England, Wales, and Scotland, concluding with another London engagement in the summer of 1892. Over these four years, the Wild West presented itself in a number of different guises—as a long-running arena show, a short-stay touring company, and a revival of the Steele MacKaye pageant for the stage during wintry weather; and it also experimented with new acts, expanding its cast of international horsemen. Still, the show's experiences in Europe solidified its presentation of its subject matter and sharpened its image. Cody and his managers developed a more consistent interpretation of who they were and what story they were trying to tell.

Cody's earlier career had traded on his familiarity to audiences, but the European tour helped him learn how to present himself as an exotic spectacle. As a plains showman, he had been a guide to spectators who shared with him a sense of place and who experienced a spectacle that in a certain sense worked independently of his performance. Even the touring Easterners in James Gordon Bennett's party, fortified with champagne and surrounded by luxury, could see the prairie around them. They slept in tents, rode on horses, and had at least some direct contact with the landscape and animals whose story Buffalo Bill helped to tell. As a stage showman, Buffalo Bill still assumed prior knowledge (from dime novels or newspaper accounts) and traded on the evidence of his physical person to link his show to a pre-existing set of experiences. Later, the Wild West mobilized a whole arena full of animals and people purporting to re-create a Western experience that was part of the everyday life of his audience when he performed in Western cities like Omaha and Denver. But in Eastern cities and more especially in Europe, Cody's spectacle was very different from the world around it. For audiences there the Wild West existed nowhere but in the arena. The more clearly the show's managers understood this, the more successfully they could define their enterprise.

Despite their claims to authenticity and historicity, and despite John Burke's efforts to secure Cody a military title, in Europe Buffalo Bill and his troupe seemed to come from a distant world and were, as fascinating to audiences as Tom Thumb, Catlin's Indians, or the African warriors being exhibited in zoos, exhibitions, and sideshows. In Europe, the Wild West had to accept—and to learn to trade upon—its own exoticism and its underlying fictionality. Although the American press continued to cover its doings (and Burke worked hard to place a string of stories that would remind Americans of its existence) and Americans abroad flocked to it, the audience was chiefly composed of people with little or no prior knowledge of the West but with an enormous appetite for the thrilling story Buffalo Bill had to tell. By the time Cody and his troupe had returned from Europe, the Wild West they enacted had become more remote even in the United States, and the coherent fictionality that was the legacy of the European tours served them well as they took their show into the twentieth century.

The Wild West's second European tour helped further to sharpen its image. Cody and his troupe sailed for France in April 1889 amid a carefully orchestrated blitz of publicity. Reminding Americans that this was in some sense *their* show, newspapers reported that the cowboy band played "Hail Columbia," "The Girl I Left Behind Me," "Yankee Doodle," and "Auld Lang Syne," and that the Indians cheered and whooped on deck when the ship left the dock in New York.[50] Burke's advance team had also worked hard to create a sense of anticipation in France, papering Paris with posters, to the dismay of some French journalists, who complained, "Have we had enough of this Buffalo Bill for the past fifteen days?" "*L'Ouest sauvage de Guillaume Bison*," promoted through countless portraits of a man who "looks at the same time like a warrior and a tenor," seemed to some observers to be in danger of publicity overkill.[51] But the exhibition won over its critics and charmed the public. "*Eh bien!* All that ingenious and bold American advertising enterprise has proved to be as honest as our tame [publicity] ever was. Nothing has been pictured or said too much. It is a splendid living illustration," declared *Le Temps*, echoing the show's own claims to authenticity.[52] In France as in England, audiences were intrigued by the way in which the show seemed to bring to life an exotic world of fictional characters, to be a "splendid living illustration" of American identity. Newspapers reported that ten thousand Parisians stood outside on opening day and fifteen thousand spectators competed for twelve thousand seats in the arena. The president of France attended the opening performance, and Buffalo Bill and Annie Oakley charmed visitors at a reception following the show.

The publicity was designed not only to bring in paying customers but to articulate once again the meaning its organizers hoped the Wild West would convey to audiences. To a gathering of French reporters, John Burke, wearing a tricolored handkerchief in honor of the French republic, explained Buffalo Bill's Wild West in terms of American identity and historical memory. He was reported as asserting:

> The object of the show was not to present a circus performance, but to give a true picture of American frontier life with real characters who had played their part in the history of a portion of the American continent which would soon be a thing of the past. "Even the buffaloes," said the Major, "are the last of the race. In a few years they will live but in history. This is why our show is of real interest. In ten years people who read of buffalo hunts will recollect what we have shown and what they will never again have a chance of seeing."[53]

No better expression could be found for the Wild West's self-definition at the intersection of history, drama, and nostalgia. Burke demonstrated that Buffalo Bill's business was the creation of memory. He knew that the Wild West's task was to make the memory of this entertainment spectacle become, for its audiences, the memory of the real thing.

The way in which the Wild West produced imagined memories for its audiences is well illustrated in the most compelling set of artifacts from the European tour. While in Paris, Cody met the distinguished French painter Rosa Bonheur, well known in America and Europe for her animal paintings. *The Horse Fair* (1853), a painting admired by Queen Victoria and French emperor Louis Napoleon, had been owned by a series of American collectors including A. T. Stewart and Cornelius Vanderbilt, and engraved reproductions of it had secured her fame and fortune.[54] Bonheur was already interested in the animals and people of the American West, for she owned a copy of Catlin's album of North American Indian lithographs, and she probably saw his exhibition in Paris in 1845. When the Wild West took up residence in Paris, she invited Cody to visit her at her country home, and he permitted her to sketch his troupe as often as she wished. "I was thus able to examine their tents at my ease," she wrote. "I was present at family scenes. I conversed as best I could with warriors and their wives and children. I made studies of the bisons, horses, and arms. I have a veritable passion, you know, for this unfortunate race and I deplore that it is disappearing before the White usurpers."[55] Bonheur expressed exactly the interpretation of the Wild West that Burke was working so hard to disseminate: that it gave audiences a truthful glimpse of a vanishing reality. From her sketches, Bonheur produced at least seventeen paintings, many of which represent, not scenes of entertainment, but scenes of Plains Indian life *as if she had been present on the frontier.* For example, *Rocky Bear and Red Shirt* (1890) shows two American Indians riding on their horses through a field and *Buffalo Hunt* (1889) portrays an Indian hunter on a galloping horse, pulling alongside a running bison with bow and arrow poised to shoot. As Burke had predicted, the memory of the

Rosa Bonheur,
Col. W. F. Cody,
1889, oil on canvas

Wild West was transformed into an impression of a buffalo hunt on the plains.

Rosa Bonheur provided the same service for Cody himself. Her portrait of *Col. W. F. Cody* (1889) shows a confident, virile horseman and his spirited mount, Tucker. Like the American Indians she painted, Cody is pictured not in a performance arena but riding through a landscape (although the dirt path and soft green trees could represent a French park as well as a Western plain). The painting seemed to testify that seeing Buffalo Bill's Wild West in performance was the same as seeing the men and animals of the West in their natural setting. Cody valued this image of himself, perhaps considering it a heroic, high-culture tribute. His sister reported that when his house caught fire in November 1890, he telegraphed, "Save Rosa Bonheur's picture, and the house may go to blazes."[56] The painting also served as a part of the Wild West's publicity, appearing in a poster used to promote the show's next trip in France (in 1905).

Another poster, first produced in 1894 and often reprinted, used Bonheur's portrait to make Buffalo Bill's claims to historical importance and authenticity even more striking. Under a banner announcing his show, two figures on white horses pose before a demure and distinguished-looking Bonheur, seated at her easel. On the left, a flabby-looking Napoleon gazes

Art Perpetuating Fame, Rosa Bonheur Painting Buffalo Bill, poster

Buffalo Bill at the Vatican, from an 1890 scrapbook

morosely ahead, while on the right noble Buffalo Bill sits erect, alertly scanning the horizon, and Bonheur gazes intently at him. "Art Perpetuating Fame," announced the poster. "Rosa Bonheur Painting Buffalo Bill—Paris 1889." Like the judge in a contest, the French painter gives the laurel wreath (also represented in the caption) to the virile American hero. Buffalo Bill is compared to Napoleon, whom the poster identifies as "The Man on Horse of 1796." The modern "Man on Horse," Buffalo Bill, boasts not military conquests but show-business triumphs: "From the Yellowstone to the Danube. From Vesuvius to Ben Nevis." Bonheur provides a kind of celebrity endorsement: to be commemorated by a famous French painter is to be ranked with a famous French general. The poster also suggests how the Wild West produced its own history: it created an illusion of time travel, so that European viewers could be persuaded they had experienced the old American West, and Buffalo Bill himself seemed to become coeval with military heroes of the European past.

Buffalo Bill had become, by the end of his European tours, an American national hero. During his brief New York season of 1888, newspapers reported, "Buffalo Bill is probably the best known man in New York. Wherever he goes he is recognized and pointed out by the crowd. . . . What a candidate for Vice President he would make to help out a chilly ticket."[57] By

"The Only Indians Ever in Venice," hand-colored photograph by Paolo Salvaiti

Buffalo Bill and Members of the Wild West in Arena, Mount Vesuvius, Italy, 1890

World's Wondrous Voyages, c. 1892, color lithograph, poster

1890, another newspaper was marveling that Cody's reputation had been transformed by his enthusiastic reception abroad: Although his "fellow-citizens in the United States have never taken him quite seriously . . . Americans in Europe grow as enthusiastic over the Deadwood coach *et al.*, as the Europeans, and finally look upon the Colonel as one of the characters of the age."[58] After his second trip to Europe, Cody had been received by Queen Victoria twice, had led the Wild West to an audience with the Pope at the Vatican, and had hosted countless members of the European aristocracy, many of whom had ridden in the Deadwood stage during his performances. European success had transformed Cody's stature in the eyes of his country-men.

From this time onward, publicity for the Wild West hearkened back to the glorious European tours. Like any returning tourist, the Wild West had a scrapbook full of travel photographs, and many of them became standard fixtures in program booklets until the end of Cody's career. Images of Cody and the Indians from his show in a Venetian gondola, at St. Peter's in Rome, in front of Mount Vesuvius, at Land's End in England, all appeared regularly. In 1894, a poster celebrated the "World's Wondrous Voyages" of the Wild West: "From Prairie to Palace, Camping on Two Continents, Distance Travelled, 63,000 Miles or Nearly Three Times Round the Globe." Maps with colored lines traced the company's travels from a curiously flattened U.S. sea-coast to a carefully delineated Europe. Around the margins, postcardlike images celebrated famous places and people (cowboy on a bucking bronco, Buffalo Bill posing in his thigh-high boots with a stuffed head of a buffalo, Indians in the Venetian gondola and at Earl's Court) that showed the troupe's presence in distant lands. The same image was used, as well, as a back cover for the show's program in 1895. The most extravagant claims John Burke could formulate seemed, at the pinnacle of Cody's success, to be corroborated by a worldwide audience.

[CHAPTER THREE]

AT THE COLUMBIAN EXPOSITION
1893

Emboldened by his enthusiastic reception in Europe, Buffalo Bill brought the Wild West back to America with even stronger assertions of its signifi-cance. Its showmanship was polished, its printed materials were attractive and well executed, and its publicity strategies were finely honed. Cody had outmaneuvered his rivals among frontier showmen and achieved worldwide recognition as a symbol for the American nation itself. During the decade since he had premiered his hybrid frontier entertainment, the United States had accelerated its rush toward modernity: industrialization was shaping a new South; the end of the Indian wars opened the West for economic devel-opment and tourism; and the cities of the North and East, swelled by immi-gration, were enjoying new forms of mass culture and entertainment. With the mystique of international endorsement for its presentation of America's fast-fading past, Buffalo Bill's Wild West was ideally suited for American audi-ences hungry to celebrate their national identity.[1]

Its 1893 season was brilliantly planned. Performing on a tract of land just outside the gates of the World's Columbian Exposition in Chicago, it attracted huge crowds of spectators attending the fair. The juxtaposition was one of those perfect opportunities that cultural historians dream about, revealing much about the deep structure of this popular entertainment and highlighting its relationship to American culture in its time and our own.

The millions of spectators who visited the Wild West and the Columbian Exposition believed that they experienced, and understood, a crucial step in America's passage to modernity.

CULTURE AND SHOWBIZ AT THE WHITE CITY

The World's Columbian Exposition was a triumph of show business, economic boosterism, and national self-congratulation. A metropolis within a metropolis whose dazzling buildings earned it the nickname "the White City," the 633-acre fair drew more than twenty-seven million spectators during its six months of operation. Chicago had won the right to host the fair after intense competition with New York. Millions of dollars in financial support from a coalition of merchants and bankers, combined with the political success of its lobbyists, brought this bonanza to Chicago at a time when the

View Across West End of the Main Basin, World's Columbian Exposition, Chicago, 1893, photograph by C. D. Arnold

city was reinventing itself after the ravages of the great fire of 1871 and making a bid for national prominence. But if the world's fair took place in a location that Easterners like Henry Adams identified as "the Northwest," its planners were careful to avoid any regional flavor and to stake their claims to a grander heritage. A cadre of academically trained architects and sculptors was employed to design a monumental, dignified pleasure ground that would visually suggest the majesty of past civilizations and at the same time display American expertise in areas ranging from science and technology through art, architecture, music, and handicrafts. A barrage of publicity heightened spectators' interest, and the fair drew visitors from all parts of the country, from many foreign lands, and, to some degree, from a social and economic cross-section of the nation. There were serious gaps: Sunday closings made it difficult for working-class visitors to attend, and prominent African-American spokesmen decried the racial exclusivity of the managing boards as well as the lack of attention paid in programs and exhibits to the accomplishments of nonwhite Americans. Nonetheless, the fair tried to attract customers with special events such as Chicago Day, Italian Day, German Day, and Colored People's Day at the fair.

The Exposition was relentlessly high minded and didactic; as Henry Adams sarcastically commented, "Education ran riot at Chicago, at least for retarded minds which had never faced in concrete form so many matters of which they were ignorant."[2] Many other institutions of high culture — such as art museums and symphony orchestras — were just coming into existence in major American cities, and in Chicago they were supported by some of the same businessmen who bankrolled the fair. Yet the planners also reached into the less respectable, more hybrid world of low culture, attaching to the fair a milelong strip of carnival-like attractions, the Midway Plaisance. Under a thin veneer of education, with the label "ethnological exhibits," the Midway offered fairgoers a kaleidoscope of different displays that would have elicited cheers from P. T. Barnum: re-creations of villages from Java, Cairo, Tunis, Lapland, Dahomey, and Ireland; an Old Vienna exhibit; an Eskimo exhibit; an Indian bazaar; a cyclorama of a Hawaiian volcano; an electric theater; and the World Congress of Beauty of the International Dress and Costume Company; all accompanied by food concessions, a trained-animal show, and various rides including, most memorably, the 260-foot-high Ferris wheel. Many analysts claim that the Midway became the financial salvation of the Columbian Exposition. Certainly, it gave the public a chance to dilute the didacticism of the fair proper.

In its own time and ever since, the Columbian Exposition has been

Ferris Wheel and Moorish Palace, World's Columbian Exposition, Chicago, 1893 (photographer unknown)

viewed as an event rich in cultural significance. The Midwestern writer Hamlin Garland remembered that he was "amazed at the grandeur of 'The White City,' " and he immediately urged his aging parents to leave their Dakota farm and come to the city. "Sell the cookstove if necessary and come. You *must* see this fair," he declared, hoping—vainly, as he later admitted— that the feast of sights and experiences would "make up in a few hours for all their past deprivations." In fact his parents, overwhelmed, soon begged to return home.[3] Many other observers registered wonder and amazement, like a Denver attorney who wrote in his diary, "I am dazzled, captivated and bewildered, and return to my room, tired in mind, eyes, ears and body, so much to think about, so much to entice you on from place to place, until your knees clatter and you fall into a chair completely exhausted."[4] Henry Adams found himself sitting and brooding, too, but with a more specific question in mind: "Chicago asked in 1893 for the first time the question whether the American people knew where they were driving."[5]

Like Adams, modern historians have asked whether the fair answered that question.[6] Alan Trachtenberg suggests that the White City should be taken as "a pedagogy, a model and a lesson," important for both what it asserted and what it kept hidden about the sources of power and influence in turn-of-the-century America.[7] Warren Susman considered the fair a national "rite of passage" to a new consumer-oriented society, and many recent scholars have commented on not only the promotion of manufactured products but the fair's suggestion that exotic peoples of the world could be fixed in place, viewed, and "consumed" by American elites.[8]

The White City also propounded a theory of history. Designed to commemorate the four hundredth anniversary of Christopher Columbus's first voyage to North America (even though planners could not, as they had originally hoped, open it in 1892), it celebrated not only that event but a series of assumptions about its meaning. The Columbian voyage was thoroughly heroic in this interpretation, heralding the worldwide dominance of an unquestionably superior Western civilization. Replicas of Columbus's three ships, which were built in Spain and sailed across the Atlantic for display at the fair, represented the tangible link between the triumphant past, the self-satisfied present, and the splendid future. In this view, the United States emerged as the heir of all the ages, the pinnacle of a glorious Western heritage. The fair's neoclassical buildings expressed America's claim to the mantle of Western civilization, while the miracle of their rapid construction suggested modern speed, efficiency, and ingenuity. In the space of a few

The Statue of the Republic,
World's Columbian
Exposition, Chicago, 1893
(photographer unknown)

years, the fair proclaimed, Americans could build a city rivaling the great monuments of Europe—never mind the fact that what appeared to be gleaming marble was really a lightweight mixture of plaster, cement, and jute called "staff," painted white with compressed-air squirt guns.

The fair's intention to link contemporary America with the heritage of Western culture and world dominance could be seen at every turn. Inside the exhibit halls, displays touted American advances in science and engineering, manufacturing and technology, and in its massive public spaces the fair linked the glorious present with the monumental past. At its symbolic heart, the Court of Honor, the fair's architects placed two sculptures: Daniel Chester French's sixty-five-foot-high gilded statue of the *Republic* holding aloft a globe and a lance, and, facing it across the water-filled Basin, Frederick MacMonnies's *Columbian Fountain*, in which an allegorical figure of Columbia traveled on a barge rowed by the arts, sciences, and industries, guided by the figure of Victory at its prow. Both sculptures used symbols and images drawn from the history of Western art to figure the United States as a New World empire. The "primitive" peoples and displays on the Midway Plaisance were spread out at the feet of the *Republic* like captives paraded before a Roman emperor. In its architecture as in the content of its exhibits, the Columbian Exposition dazzled viewers with a vision of the power of the American economic and industrial order and proclaimed that power to be the natural result of the forces of historical inevitability and racial determinism.

Cody and his managers were inspired to bring their show to the gates of the Columbian Exposition for many of the same reasons that had brought it to Rome, Paris, and London. The series of performances in Roman amphitheaters, on the grounds of Windsor Castle, and at the foot of Mount Vesuvius had given Cody and his publicists ample occasion to reflect on the course of Western history. By the time they arrived in Chicago, John Burke was ready to make Buffalo Bill's claims to the tradition of Columbus explicit: "As Columbus was the pilot across the seas to discover a new world, such heroes as Boone, Fremont, Crockett, Kit Carson, and last, but by no means least, Cody, were the guides to the New World of the mighty West, and their names will go down in history as 'Among the few, the immortal names / That were not born to die.' "[9] The stationery used by the Wild West during its Chicago season featured matching portraits of Columbus and Cody, the first captioned "Pilot of the Ocean, 15th Century—the First Pioneer," and the second labeled "Guide of the Prairie, 19th Century—the Last Pioneer."[10] The colorful, polyglot, high-energy performance of the Wild West seemed to contrast sharply with the hierarchical, serious-minded display of the White City, but the two shared like historical assumptions—and show-business ambitions.

THE WILD WEST IN CHICAGO

When Nate Salsbury could not secure a spot inside the Chicago fairgrounds, he leased a tract of land between Sixty-second and Sixty-third Streets, just opposite the entrance to the fair. Cody's mangers had long understood the benefits of traveling in the wake of another crowd-pleasing attraction, a point that was not lost on other impresarios such as Florenz Ziegfeld, who staged shows during the world's fair, too. The Wild West's Chicago season has been called "the most successful year in outdoor-show history," earning profits of up to a million dollars for the Cody-Salsbury partnership.[11]

As it turned out, the Wild West's separate location outside the fair's gates was probably an advantage. On the Midway Plaisance, the Wild West would have had to compete with other attractions, and its claims to special status would have been harder to sustain. Located as it was, just opposite the elevated railroad station on the roof of the Transportation Building annex, which gave many visitors their entryway to the fair, the Wild West was a clear alternative to the labyrinthine fairgrounds. The Wild West was identified on the official fair map, and it took a full-page ad in Rand, McNally's guidebook. "All roads lead to Buffalo Bill's Wild West," it proclaimed. In a logo used throughout the season, the guidebook ad pictured a key, for the Wild West promised to be the key event. [12]

The Wild West succeeded on many levels in Chicago. From the moment of his arrival, Cody was honored as a dignitary. Daniel Burnham, the Columbian Exposition's director of works, included him in a ceremonial breakfast on opening day, where he mingled with fair officials and high-culture exponents such as the architect Frederick Law Olmstead and the conductor Theodore Thomas. Cody was the only private citizen invited to join two thousand legislators, judges, and foreign commissioners watching President Grover Cleveland push the button that switched on the electric power for the fair at the opening ceremony. And the following day, he arranged a meeting with the President for a delegation of his American Indian performers. The local press treated Cody like a king: *Chicago Daily News* reporter Amy Leslie found him to be "one of the most imposing men

*All Roads Lead to Buffalo Bill's Wild West, from Rand, McNally,
Hand Book of the World's Columbian Exposition*

in appearance" but "the kindliest, most benign gentleman, as simple as a village priest and learned as a savant of Chartreuse." Newspapers ran interviews with Cody, Salsbury, Burke, and as many Indians as they could find. Meanwhile, advertisements described the Wild West in terms that competed directly with the White City's monumental claims:

> The biggest outdoor animated amusement exploit extant or known, either ancient or modern. Life, action, skill, daring, danger defied; one thousand animated pictures in two hours given by flesh and blood; creation's greatest handiwork, nature's noblest mechanism, too natural and colossal for canvas or building. The grassy sward our carpet, heaven's blue canopy our covering. . . . An affair of magnitude second to none in novel enjoyment, instruction, interest and educative merit.[13]

In Burke and Salsbury's promotional rhetoric, the Wild West was not merely an adjunct to the fair but "second to none," a competitor that enlisted the effects of nature itself ("heaven's blue canopy"). And, as a display that was limited in time and could be seen sitting down, it was far less fatiguing.

The long Chicago season refined the publicity skills of the Wild West's now-considerable staff. During the European tour, Burke and Parker had produced stories about the Wild West, translated into local languages, that preceded the show everywhere, and simultaneously, had supplied American newspapers with running updates on the Wild West's successes. Their meticulous scrapbooks record a variety of publicity strategies; some newspaper clippings are annotated with the words *press agent* in colored pencil; similar versions of the same story, run in one newspaper after another, are shown. The scrapbooks for the Chicago season are different, however, for most of the stories circle back to the same Chicago and New York papers. Staying in the same place for six months required a different kind of tactic. Burke had to give reporters "news" about the Wild West so they would keep writing about it and stimulating public interest, so he had to find new ways to explicate its significance.

One approach that had proved its merit during the first London season was to issue regular report on visitors to the Wild West. In England, as we have seen, visits by royalty and aristocracy had been newsworthy indeed, and had constituted a sort of celebrity endorsement for the Wild West. In Chicago, where there was no such hierarchy of visitors, reports tracked the eclecticism of the Wild West's appeal rather than its patronage by any single group. On May 29, newspapers reported that Julian Hawthorne, the son of the great novelist, attended the Wild West's performance; they speculated that he was planning a novel with Buffalo Bill as central figure. Susan B. Anthony visited the Wild West on June 11 and was interviewed by avid reporters: "Miss Anthony was so much entertained that she remained through the performance despite the chilly air. She said the riding was a revelation and an education in the ways of many lands." In July, news stories reported that "all dignitaries within reach avail themselves of the opportunity to see [Buffalo Bill's] performance. Today the program will be enjoyed by the world's fair directors, the national commission, the foreign commissioners, and the officers of the caravels and the steamers Johnson, Blake, and Michigan." Around the same time, the Board of Lady Managers attended the performance and presented Cody with a souvenir coin. A group of editors from Indiana visited the Wild West, as did the Maharajah of Kapurthala; the evangelist George Francis Train; a group of West Point cadets; eight hundred newsboys and a party of deaf-mutes from Philadelphia; Cardinal Gibbons; the sculptor of the Statue of Liberty, Frédéric Bartholdi; a delegation of Mormon bishops; and Miss Alice Shaw, the celebrated whistler.[14] The audience for the Wild West was as polyglot and various as the show itself, reinforcing its claim to represent an American national entertainment. By September, Wild West publicity was advertising the sale of photographs made by a new process: visitors could order an extra-large picture of the grandstand on the day of their visit, "showing distinctly every occupant of a seat."[15] Not only could purchasers record their own visit, but perhaps they might take home a photograph of a celebrity visitor as well.

During the Chicago season Cody's love for children became an important publicity theme. In July, Columbian Exposition organizers had tried to promote "poor children's day" at the fair. The event was originally planned to bring ten thousand "waifs" to the White City, where they would parade through the Exposition grounds, eat lunch, visit the Wild West, then enjoy an afternoon of sports. Not to lose sight of the children's economic niche, fair organizers had promised that "a rapid trip will be made to the city in time to let the newsboys hustle the afternoon papers." However, the Exposition's president, Harlow Higinbotham, a Chicago businessman, apparently worried that a crowd of poor children would keep away paying customers, and refused to give them free admission. In a brilliant publicity move, Buffalo Bill stepped into the breach, paying for a picnic, a parade, and a day at the Wild West for children from a number of Chicago charitable institutions, including the Waif's Mission, the Chicago Hebrew Mission, the Unity

Church Industrial School, the Home for the Friendless, the Chicago Nursery and Half-Orphan Asylum, and the Jewish Training School. He was rewarded with a flood of favorable news stories. The *Manitoba Free Press* proclaimed, "Bravo! Buffalo Bill. He entertained Chicago's Poverty-Stricken Children When the Haughty Fair Directors Refused Them Admission." Another newspaper mused,

> Colonel Cody is a true philanthropist. He does not distribute tracts, but sandwiches; he does not inculcate any high moral lessons, but he smoothes the rugged pathway of the children of the streets for at least one day by taking them away from their squalid surroundings. So, too, shall Colonel Cody's trail toward the happy hunting grounds be made easy and fringed with prairie flowers because he has done thus much to brighten the lives of others.

The papers reported enthusiastic praise from the children themselves as well as from officials at the institutions. " 'We wanted to see Buffalo Bill's show, anyhow,' said one of the newsboys, 'and we wuzn't stuck on seein' dem big houses in de fair nohow. President Higinbotham kin keep his ole fair for all I care.' " The Superintendent of the Waif's Mission observed that "my poor little boys took more pleasure in President Higinbotham's refusal to admit them to the fair than he did in repulsing them." The fair's reputation for exclusivity could not have been helped by the press coverage of the children parading with banners that read: "We are workers, not paupers," and "We are trying to make a living, why not help us."[16] But Cody emerged as a hero. Charity performances for children became a staple of the Wild West practice—and publicity—for the rest of his life.

Some of the publicity schemes were less successful. In June the Wild West sponsored a "cowboy race" on horseback from Chadron, Nebraska, to Chicago. Buffalo Bill put up some of the prize money and promised to greet the winner at the Wild West. But humane societies criticized the race's grueling pace; the Society for the Prevention of Cruelty to Animals posted a reward of five hundred dollars for the arrest and conviction of anyone participating, and soon Burke produced a flood of articles attempting to put distance between Cody and the questionable aspects of the race. Buffalo Bill had only reluctantly agreed to end the race at the Wild West, he claimed. "This permission was not so readily granted as one might suppose. Buffalo Bill is one of the most humane men in the country and at the outset said plainly that he would have nothing to do with the race if it was conducted after the style of the German army officers' race from Berlin to Vienna." The article went on to say that Cody was a life member of the Humane Society who had long ago suggested using clay pigeons in shooting matches as a substitute for live birds. In the end the race was held, supervised by the Humane Society, and despite various allegations of cheating and some confusion about who had won, the Wild West gamely tried to make the most of it. Burke took out ads on the day the race was due to end:

> Will Arrive Today,
> *at Buffalo Bill's Wild West*
> the contestants in the Cowboy 1,000
> Mile Race.
> An Equine Race Humanely Run,
> Humanely Won,
> Under Supervision of the Society
> for the Prevention of Cruelty to Animals.
> The Contestants and Steeds Will Be
> Introduced as They Arrive Today.
> See Latest Telegraph News in Press.

Other press stories reported the event differently: "At some uncertain hour to-day it is expected that a small, wiry bronco bearing a yelling cowboy will dash madly into the enclosure of the Wild West show and win the cowboy race. The ubiquitous advance agent of the Cody show is not asleep."[17]

Cody's advance agents, it seemed, were never asleep. The Chicago season placed new demands on the show's promoters and pushed them to adopt new forms of publicity. The story told by the show's advertising was no longer simple; Buffalo Bill had the advantage of celebrity, but his promoters had to find ways to keep his name in the news and to elaborate on his message. Cody was no longer a novelty, an "authentic" scout straight from the plains; now he was a famous figure, and Burke and Salsbury had to pique curiosity about someone whom the public thought it knew. Cody's publicity could connect him with events (like the waifs' picnic or the cowboy race); and it could also exploit the public's interest in his private life. Articles about his wife and daughters, his ranch and development interests, appeared frequently, and interviews with Buffalo Bill often touched on military and political events in the outside world. For years Cody had given statements about the Indian situation, and in the year after the Chicago season he was also quoted in favor of women's suffrage. By the mid-1890s, Cody's publicity team had taken on now-familiar tasks of image creation, spin-doctoring, and, sometimes, damage control.

STAKING A CLAIM TO HISTORY

The clearest articulation of the Wild West's aspirations was, of course, always found in the program booklet. By 1893, Burke and his team were producing a booklet sixty-four pages long (twice the size of that for 1885), crammed with articles on virtually every aspect of the show. Together they made the case for Buffalo Bill's importance as an authentic American hero and expressed the delicate balance between fictionality and authenticity in the Wild West's performance.

The cover for the booklet features colorful lithographs placing Buffalo Bill in the center of a sequence of authentic-looking frontier scenes. On the

1893 program, cover

1893 program, back cover

front, a head-and-shoulders portrait of Cody is surrounded by three vignettes: a hunter shooting two buffalo, Buffalo Bill aiming a pistol from a running horse, and, across the bottom of the page, the Deadwood stage under attack by Indians, with Buffalo Bill and the cowboys riding up to save it. These three dramatic scenes could be interpreted as actual occurrences in Cody's own history and also as scenes from the Wild West performance. A dignified Buffalo Bill is presiding over the sort of historically evocative "action pictures" the Wild West's advertisements promised.[18] The back cover shows a very different scene, one that could not be duplicated in the arena: a rocky landscape seen from a distance, with an Indian encampment on a plateau, and two tiny figures starting up a long, steep path toward it. The caption credits a periodical source, the *Illustrated American* of January 10, 1891, and identifies this scene as "Sioux on the War-Path: Stronghold in the Bad Lands of the Hostile Indians, Chiefs, 'Short Bull' and 'Kicking Bear.'" So the back cover represents the "real" West that exists independent of its fictional enactment. But unlike the playful trompe l'oeil covers of 1884, 1885, and 1886, these lithographs stake strong claims for their own representational power. The show that had convinced Europeans they had seen the authentic West and inspired Rosa Bonheur to paint as if she had visited the Great Plains framed its program booklet with images that linked staged representation with the "real" Wild West.

The text embraces both performance and the world outside the arena, and the language of fiction jostles against the apparatus of authentication. Burke's opening message, "Salutatory," written for the first season in 1883 and reprised with only a few changes, mobilizes the extravagant formulations of frontier romance. Extolling "the little vanguard of pioneers, trappers, and scouts, who, moving always in front, have paved the way—frequently with their own bodies—for the safe approach of the masses behind," it echoes the closing lines of James Fenimore Cooper's *The Pioneers*, which had helped to create the frontier myth in 1823 when it described Natty Bumppo as "the foremost in that band of Pioneers, who are opening the way for the march of our nation across the continent."[19] The booklet also includes romanticized poetry, such as "Cody's Corral; or, the Scouts and the Sioux," reprinted from the dime-novel publication *Beadle's Weekly* and part of the program booklet since at least 1885: "And loudly rings the war-cry of fearless Buffalo Bill / And loudly rings [sic] the savage yells, which make the blood run chill!" But the sensational tone of these passages is juxtaposed with the serious-minded items documenting Buffalo Bill's offstage importance: facsimiles of Cody's 1889 commission as brigadier general in the National Guard of Nebraska and of a set of letters from January 1891 in which the governor of Nebraska orders Cody to undertake special service and Major General Nelson Miles of the U.S. Army informs him about the state of Indian hostilities. The letters of recommendation solicited by Burke before Cody's departure for London are quoted at length, and newspapers and books about the frontier are cited to authenticate Cody's service on the plains. The booklet draws on the resources of both romance and realism, showing Buffalo Bill is an

Facsimile of Cody's commission, 1893 program, inside front cover

Shooting buffalo, 1893
program, page 13

Bringing Meat Into
Camp, from Cody,
Autobiography

unabashedly fictionalized hero yet at the same time documenting his place
in history.

The copious illustrations reflect this blend of highly colored romance
and solemnly invoked claims to factuality. Some of the images are line
engravings in the exuberant spirit of novel illustration, while others are dignified, posed photographs. A few of the engravings had been part of Cody's
repertory for nearly fifteen years: for example, an illustration showing Cody
pursuing a running buffalo amid covered wagons and tents is a slight rework-
ing of "Bringing Meat into Camp," an illustration in his Autobiography
(1879). An image of an Indian on horseback peering into the distance was
taken from a poster circulated as early as 1885. The booklet also contains
some very familiar visual materials in slightly altered versions, including the
scalping of Yellow Hand, the image of Cody on a running horse shooting

The Former Foe—Present Friend, The American, 1893 program, page 10

Death of Yellow Hand,
1893 program, page 48

A Practical "All-Round Shot," 1893 program, page 14

Attack on the stagecoach, 1893 program, page 23

glass balls tossed in the air by an Indian, and the attack on a stagecoach. Such images connect the Wild West performance with its sources in the dime novel and other forms of popular literature.

But photographs in the program booklet also connect the Wild West spectacle with an emerging documentary tradition. Cody had used souvenir and carte de visite photographs for publicity since his earliest days as an entertainer, but when the Wild West returned from Europe, photographs blossomed in the program booklet as well. The halftone process, which made it possible to print photographs and words on the same page, had revolutionized American publishing starting in the 1880s, and by the 1890s many books and popular magazines included illustrative photographs. Photographs emphasized the "real" in books as diverse as Civil War albums and travel books, while urban reformers were using photographs to authenticate the claims of their texts. *Harper's Monthly, Century,* and *Collier's* included many photographs, especially accompanying nonfiction articles.[20] The photographs in the Wild West booklet follow this same logic: portraits of show

Buffalo Bill's Home,
1893 program,
page 19

personnel, a view of cattle and horses grazing at Cody's Scout's Rest Ranch, a full-page photograph of Cody on horseback with General Miles. A lengthy section on American Indian culture is illustrated with posed photographs of carefully identified individuals, including chiefs and children. The last few pages are filled with photographs from the Wild West's European tour. The remarkable picture of Cody and several of his costumed Indian performers in a gondola in Venice receives a full page, and a photograph of the encampment at Earl's Court in London is also included.

But this deployment of images blurs the boundaries between "real" photographs and "imaginary" drawings. Some of the illustrations combine the two in a manipulated "realistic" image. Sketches of the Wild West performers are added to what appears to be a photograph of the Colosseum in Rome, and similarly, the company is drawn into a photographic image of St. Peter's. Like the show itself, the images lay claim to overlapping realms of fictionality and "truth," insisting on the interrelatedness of performance and the "real" West.

The program booklet also blended fact and fiction in its portrayal of the show's growing international element. By 1893, the Wild West proudly advertised a wide variety of acts from around the globe. The Congress of Rough Riders of the World included an impressive number of riding and military acts: Mexican vaqueros, Syrian and Arabian horsemen, Russian cossacks, Argentinean gauchos, and military units from Germany, England, and France. The booklet gave educational, historical, and descriptive information about these performers in words transplanted, perhaps, from press releases. At the same time, the international horsemen enacted a romantic and theatrical extravaganza that became ever more central to the show. When these colorful riders galloped into the arena, audiences were treated to

Colosseum, Rome,
1893 program, page 59

*St. Peter's and Vatican,
Rome,* 1893 program,
page 58

a dream of exotic lands, and perhaps also a vision of American imperialism extending, not just across the Western plains, but throughout the world as well.

The very structure of the Wild West's program projected this careful balance between romance and fact. The content had remained remarkably consistent since Cody and Salsbury filed their copyright papers in 1883: a processional introducing the show's personnel was followed by the different acts—races, demonstrations of skill, and narrative segments that embedded fictional representations of historical events in an authenticating frame of real animals, real guns, real frontier characters. Annie Oakley's shooting act was now firmly placed at the beginning of the show, for experience had proved that audiences who felt nervous when confronted with the noise and smoke of gunfire felt reassured when they saw a petite, attractive woman shooting first. Furthermore, both her shooting skill and her physical presence helped to establish the show's credibility, as if to vouch for the fictive acts to follow. Several other segments claimed historical and ethnographic authenticity, including a demonstration of pony-express riding techniques, a buffalo hunt, and a demonstration of "Life Customs of the Indians." In the last two, American Indian performers appeared in a sympathetic light, but at least three other segments cast them as villains in staged narratives: the "Prairie Emigrant Train Crossing the Plains," the "Capture of the Deadwood Mail Coach by the Indians," and the "Attack on a Settler's Cabin."

In the midst of the 1893 season, Cody and his managers made one change in the program that intensified the Wild West's claim to historical significance and at the same time complicated its promise of a happy ending to the civilizing process. In August, the Wild West replaced the standard "Attack on a Settler's Cabin" with "The Battle of Little Big Horn, or Custer's Last Charge." Cody had always traded on the powerful emotions stirred up by Custer's death. He had mounted an enactment of this incident in London, and now he added it to the Chicago season, perhaps to stimulate a burst of return visitors halfway through his six-month engagement. Publicity releases announced that the act would include three Indians who had actually been in the fight, Plenty Horses, Painted Horse, and Rocky Bear; and a large party of army officers attended its first performance. By presenting an episode from frontier history that did not end happily, the Wild West risked contradicting its promise of triumphant conquest. Yet in the show as in the battle itself, the death of Custer gave advocates of expansionism a martyr whose death could justify their cause. And Custer's death did not end the performance: Buffalo Bill galloped in, too late to rescue Custer but poised to continue the work of conquest.

Reviews of this new Custer sequence, like those for the Wild West as a whole, reinforced the show's historical claims. An enthusiast reported, "those who had 'been thar' said it was a faithful representation of the scene." The conjunction of Custer and Cody, which came solely from dime-novel accounts and not from the historical record, seemed by 1893 to be entirely appropriate. "Colonel Cody rode down to the grandstand, waved his hat, his old army friends whooped for him and the satisfied crowd filed out of the arena."[21] The stage Custer was fictional, the army officers were real, and Colonel Cody linked them together, satisfying the crowds who believed they had seen history in the making.

The Battle of Little Big Horn was a fitting close to the Wild West performance. Factual and fictive segments of the program worked together to make explicit the show's overriding message: the memory of the Wild West was one of heroic conquest. Dangerous wildness, in the form of hostile Indians, would be subdued by those who, like Buffalo Bill and the Rough Riders, had turned wildness into a skill or tool. The Wild West promised that the march of civilization would be exciting and fun (more fun than the solemn White City), and that the forces of law and order, of Western civilization, would still triumph.

THE WILD WEST AND THE FRONTIER THESIS

Cody, Burke, and Salsbury were not the only ones thinking about the role of the West in American history during the summer of 1893. As other commentators have pointed out, an important juxtaposition occurred when Frederick Jackson Turner delivered his influential scholarly essay, "The Significance of the Frontier in American History," at a meeting of the American Historical Association held in conjunction with the World's Columbian Exposition in July 1893.[22] Although the paper attracted little attention at the time, it became a widely cited statement about the importance of the westward movement in the formation of American identity, as well as a marker of the moment when that movement radically changed character. Both of these matters were at the heart of Buffalo Bill's performances in 1893. Academic history and popular-culture history were thus, curiously, entwined.

Turner was not the first historian, of course, to stress the significance of the West in American development. Before the Civil War, Francis Parkman had undertaken a rigorous trip on the Oregon trail to provide the experiences underpinning his great project, eight volumes on the history of European settlement in North America, the last of which was published in 1892. Like George Bancroft before him, Parkman worked within a framework that celebrated the triumph of Anglo-Saxon conquest and saw English, and later American, domination of North America as a story of the progress of civilization over savagery and the extension of freedom over the continent.

Both Bancroft and Parkman lived into the 1890s, long enough to see the impact of their ideas on a historian-politician who would articulate a powerful interpretation of the West in American life and then express it in war and politics: Theodore Roosevelt. The Harvard-educated Roosevelt was already a published historian and an influential New York politician when he traveled to the Dakota Badlands for an extended stay in 1884. His sojourn in the West was an escape from personal disasters that had overwhelmed him over the course of several months: in February 1884 his mother and his wife died suddenly on the same night, and by the following summer he had become embroiled in a destructive political struggle. Roosevelt went west in search of physical, emotional, and intellectual refreshment. Riding and hunting while managing a cattle ranch, he turned his energies to writing history and memoirs: in 1888, he produced a travel memoir, *Ranch Life and the Hunting Trail*, and, beginning in 1889, a four-volume historical work, *The Winning of the West*.

Like Bancroft and Parkman, Roosevelt considered the story of the American empire as a triumphant narrative that he located firmly in the context of European imperialism. "During the past three centuries," *The Winning of the West* begins, "the spread of the English-speaking peoples over the world's waste spaces has been not only the most striking feature in the world's history, but also the event of all others most far-reaching in its effects and its importance." Roosevelt followed in some detail the different patterns of the settlement and conquest of North America in Atlantic, Northwest, Southwest, and Midwestern regions, insisting that territorial expansion was the "great work" of the nation, the force that produced a national life. "All other questions, save those of the preservation of the Union itself and of the emancipation of the blacks, have been of subordinate importance when compared with the great question of how rapidly and how completely they were to subjugate that part of their continent lying between the eastern mountains and the Pacific." In a preface added in 1894, he made his claim for the significance of the West in American history even stronger: the success of Western settlement "determined whether we should become a mighty nation, or a mere snarl of weak and quarrelsome little commonwealths."[23]

Much of *The Winning of the West* consists of heroic accounts of settlement, focusing on leaders such as Daniel Boone and George Rogers Clark but also discussing unknown hunters and settlers who followed "the instincts working half blindly within their breasts, spurred ever onwards by the fierce desires of their eager hearts." Both leaders and followers, though, are imagined by Roosevelt as heroes, men who *created* the national destiny by their own deeds. This heroic narrative, of course, resembles the narrative of Western settlement told in dime novels and border dramas and then, compellingly after 1883, by the Wild West. Roosevelt's description of Daniel Boone could have been transferred from one of John Burke's descriptions of Buffalo Bill: "His self-command and patience, his daring, restless love of adventure, and, in time of danger, his absolute trust in his own powers and resources, all combined to render him peculiarly fitted to follow the career of which he was so fond."[24] Roosevelt infused history with the narrative drive and descriptive conventions of romance in a way that was not too different from John Burke's program booklet.

In fact, one could argue that popular representations of the West had been significant in convincing Roosevelt that the Badlands could be a place of healing and a stage on which to live out his version of the strenuous life. During his first summer in the West, Roosevelt was still searching for a suitable costume and language for his Western experiences: acquaintances were said to be amused by his Eastern locutions, such as his orders to cowboys during a roundup, "Hasten forward quickly there!" He wrote to a friend describing his frontier outfit: "my broad sombrero hat, fringed and beaded buckskin shirt, horsehide chaparajos or riding trousers, and cowboy boots, with braided bridle and silver spurs."[25] Where did he get his ideas of proper cowboy garb? Buffalo Bill had been described in such clothing as early as the Sheridan dude hunt; stage and arena appearances by Cody and his cast of cowboys had already made this costume synonymous with the Wild West.

Not only did Roosevelt present the West in a theatrical manner that

Theodore Roosevelt in cowboy garb

recalled Buffalo Bill's Wild West, but his accounts, both the history volumes and *Ranch Life and the Hunting Trail*, were tinged with the same anticipatory nostalgia, the sense that the life of the frontier was quickly vanishing, that flooded the Wild West presentations from their earliest days. The preface to *The Winning of the West* describes the book as "a labor of love" and emphasizes Roosevelt's own connection with Western scenes, which, he writes, are disappearing. "The men who have shared in the fast-vanishing frontier life of the present feel a peculiar sympathy with the already long-vanished frontier life of the past." In *Ranch Life and the Hunting Trail* he frequently notes that the scenes he is describing are changing "before the onward march of our people; and we who have felt the charm of the life, and have exulted in its abounding vigor and its bold, restless freedom, will not only regret its passing for our own sakes, but must also feel real sorrow that those who come after us are not to see, as we have seen, what is perhaps the pleasantest, healthiest, and most exciting phase of American existence."[26] Roosevelt adopts and transmits a heroic vision of the West, and a sense of its transitoriness, that Buffalo Bill and his publicists had already absorbed and were circulating.

So the stage had been set when Frederick Jackson Turner stepped forward to deliver an academic paper in Chicago in the summer of 1893. Popular works of history had emphasized the importance of Western settlement for generations, and dime novels, stage shows, and the riveting, hybrid Wild West performances had provided vicarious frontier experiences for a broad public. Turner's paper, like his subsequent work about the frontier, brought to historical writing some of the vivid imagery and compelling energy of the Wild West performance itself, and placed the Western frontier at the forefront of historical discussions of national identity.

Turner drew upon some of the images of the frontier that had flowed through Buffalo Bill's performances as well as the historical writing of Roosevelt, Parkman, and Bancroft. Like Roosevelt and Buffalo Bill, Turner saw westward movement as central to the history of the United States. "American history has been in a large degree the history of the colonization of the Great West," he wrote, and, even more forcefully, "The true point of view in the history of this nation is not the Atlantic coast, it is the Great West." And like all of them, he imagined that the westward movement exemplified a struggle between "savagery and civilization."[27] Roosevelt believed that Turner's essay merely restated well-established theories. He wrote to Turner congratulating him on his "first class ideas," and said that he had put "into shape a good deal of thought that has been floating around rather loosely."[28]

Buffalo Bill, full length, in Indian clothing holding a rifle, c. 1878

But the familiarity of Turner's characterization of the frontier masked some very important differences in his approach. Far from thinking that the conquering civilization stayed intact while transforming the "wild" land and peoples it encountered, Turner argued that the confrontation with wilderness changed the colonizers. He put it in sober historical terms: "In the settlement of America we have to observe how European life entered the continent, and how America modified and developed that life, and reacted on Europe." His language could also be vivid, metaphorical, performative: "The wilderness masters the colonist. It finds him a European in dress, industries, tools, modes of travel, and thought. It takes him from the railroad car and puts him in the birch canoe. It strips off the garments of civilization, and arrays him in the hunting shirt and the moccasin . . . The fact is, that here is a new product that is American."[29] As the historian Ray Allen Billington has argued, Turner "had moved far toward a modern understanding of historical processes."[30] By stressing the transformative power of the Western frontier, Turner overthrew the reigning metaphor of heroic conquest in favor of a much more complex, conflicted one of change and evolution. Although

"The Race of Races," *Buffalo Bill's Wild West and
Congress of Rough Riders of the World,* poster

later historians have questioned Turner's view of progressive evolution, and
debated such issues as the conflicts of cultures and dynamics of change in
the natural environment, there is no denying the power of Turner's proposition that American settlers on the frontier underwent changes in their political and economic institutions as well as in their intellectual and moral
traits.

How did this proposition relate to the story told by Buffalo Bill's Wild
West? On one hand, it ran counter to the Wild West's apparent narrative of
triumph, its happy-ending legacy drawn from the dime novel and the stage
melodrama. Part of the pleasure of the Wild West was its reassurance that, no
matter how noisy the gunfire or how loud the Indian war whoops, Buffalo
Bill would always ride in to save the day, and that Buffalo Bill would remain
recognizable, stable, identifiable. He would never be tempted to "go native."
There is only one known photograph of Buffalo Bill wearing an Indian costume, dating from one of the early stage plays when the plot called upon him
to disguise himself and sneak into the Indian camp. The structure of the
Wild West, and its increasing reliance on the Congress of Rough Riders of
the World, reinforced the show's underlying premise: in "the race of races,"
the juxtaposition between different peoples of the world, the viewers could
always tell the cowboys from the Indians.

But one element in Turner's thesis did support the message so successfully conveyed by Buffalo Bill's Wild West: his observation that by now, the
frontier should be considered a phenomenon of the past rather than a continuing fact of American life. The famous beginning of "The Significance of
the Frontier in American History" cites the superintendent of the census for
1890 to the effect that an unbroken line of settlement—a clear demarcation
between the "wild" and the "civilized," once a characteristic feature of Amer-

ican demographics—no longer existed. "This brief official statement marks the closing of a great historic movement," Turner maintained. The essay ended by restating his belief that the era of the frontier had now passed away forever: "And now, four centuries from the discovery of America, at the end of a hundred years of life under the Constitution, the frontier has gone, and with its going has closed the first period of American history."[31] This was exactly the stance Buffalo Bill's Wild West had taken by 1893. Burke began the program booklet by quoting his own words from 1883, describing the frontiersman as "a class that is rapidly disappearing from our country." He ended it by expressing the hope that "in presenting our rough pictures of a 'history almost passed away,' we may have done some moiety of good in simplifying the work of the historian, the romancer, the painter, and the student of the future."[32]

At the White City, the Wild West reached out to historians quite specifically. The management invited participants in the American Historical Association conference to attend the show on the afternoon of July 12. Turner was not present, since he was hard at work completing the speech he would give that very night, but at least some of the historians who heard him deliver it had gunfire and Indian war whoops ringing in their ears, smoke or dust from the Wild West still on their clothes.[33] Buffalo Bill's dramatic claims to historicity formed part of the context and the rationale for the reception of Turner's historical analysis.

BUFFALO BILL REBORN

During its six-month season in 1893, Buffalo Bill's Wild West reached probably six million American spectators with a colorful, focused, well-defined show. Whatever a performance by Buffalo Bill had meant before, by now the Wild West was firmly entrenched as a dynamic show-business spectacle with strong appeal to audiences of different ages, regions, affiliations, and occupations. Cody and Salsbury had succeeded in creating an entertainment for a mass audience that was not a circus, not a burlesque, not a freak show; like vaudeville, it called on a variety of resources from high and low culture. It claimed "serious" historical significance and at the same time energetically deployed melodramatic conventions; it demonstrated feats of skill and also told stories. It used music, colorful costumes, and the display of "exotic" peoples. But in contrast to the more fluid Barnum-infected entertainment world where it started, the 1893 Wild West had found a place for itself in the increasingly hierarchical cultural milieu of modernizing America.

By 1893, urbanization, industrialization, and an ever more bifurcated social and economic structure took large areas of the United States far from their rural, relatively open and fluid past. The nostalgic tone that had been part of the Wild West's presentation from the start allied it with other forms of what T. J. Jackson Lears has named "antimodernism," including medievalism, Orientalism, and a renewed fascination with strenuous activities and sports.[34] Henry Adams returned from Chicago even more convinced that the coming of the twentieth century was sweeping away the America his family had helped to shape, and contemporary writers like Theodore Dreiser and Frank Norris were beginning to sketch a harsh new vision of the urban wilderness that was replacing it. While realists and naturalists portrayed a threatening world that could overcome a hapless victim, the Wild West continued to celebrate the heroic individual's ability to triumph over danger. The very qualities that seemed scarce in turn-of-the-century culture—optimism and national and personal self-confidence—were found in abundance in the colorful, dramatic, and thoroughly spectacular world of Buffalo Bill.

CHAPTER FOUR

BUFFALO BILL
AND MODERN CELEBRITY

Buffalo Bill's success was at its height in 1893. He was a celebrity in the modern sense of the word: a well-known figure who attracted public attention as much because of who he was as for any particular deeds or accomplishments. But even as he reached the peak of his career, his highly crafted persona began to take on a reality of its own, and the human being was, increasingly, hard put to keep his life in harmony with his public image. While Buffalo Bill reassured his audiences that the old values of individual heroism could tame the wildness of emerging modernity, William Cody struggled with problems of excess and chaos in his personal finances, his marriage and love life, and his corporate identity.

GILDED AGE BUSINESSMAN

Cody was a Gilded Age businessman who loved to portray himself as a rags-to-riches hero. His financial aspirations had been formed in a time and place of great economic volatility: the American West right after the Civil War. Land rushes, mining strikes, the expansion of the railroad and of shipping lines that opened the West for tourism and commerce, all held out the promise of prosperity. Horace Tabor (1830–1899) and Charles Ingalls (1836–1902) were just two of Cody's contemporaries who experienced the booms and busts of the frontier economy. Tabor made a great fortune in silver mines and became Colorado's lieutenant governor and briefly a senator, but lost everything and died destitute. He was a legend in his own time and became the tragic subject of a twentieth-century American opera, Douglas Moore's *The Ballad of Baby Doe*. Ingalls, a homesteader who moved his family from farm to farm and suffered losses from grasshoppers, hard winters, and changes in government policy, also worked as a carpenter, butcher, hotel manager, and railroad manager. His daughter, Laura Ingalls Wilder, memorialized him as the warm and nurturing "Pa" in the *Little House* books, but he never led his family to financial success. Despite the myth of endless opportunity nurtured by speculative fever, the postbellum West brought ruin and heartbreak to many.

Cody, like others of his generation, had hungered after wealth and respectability in the old, restless days on the Great Plains. His *Autobiography* described an early venture in land development, a half-interest in a city grandiosely named Rome along the route of the Kansas Pacific Railroad. Although he could joke about the failed scheme, ruefully titling that chapter "A Millionaire," he yearned to strike it rich in land, cattle, or mining. In 1877, when he had begun to amass some money from his theatrical ventures, he went into the cattle business with Frank North, and although he immediately called himself a rancher, this venture did not require the purchase of land; the partners used open range for grazing, building minimal structures to house themselves and their workers, and selling the cattle for a profit in roundup season. Meanwhile, Cody began acquiring land in North Platte, Nebraska, and in 1878 built a house there for his wife, Louisa, and his two daughters, Arta and Orra; eventually he bought land for a ranch north of town as well. During his years as a stage showman, he became North Platte's most illustrious citizen and involved himself in numerous civic activities when he came home between tours.[1]

Even in the days when his prosperity was tenuous, Cody spent money generously, according to the recollections of his friends and neighbors, throwing parties and staging hunts for visitors, sponsoring dances and theatrical events, and paying the admission for long lines of town boys to the latest shows at the local opera house. North Platte knew him as a devoted family man. He bought expensive clothing and household furnishings for his wife and doted on his children. He never ceased to grieve for his little son, Kit Carson Cody, who had died in 1876. In 1883 his pleasure at the birth of another daughter, Irma Louise, was shadowed by the death of eleven-year-old Orra. Cody looked after his four sisters as well, bringing them to North Platte for family parties and arranging business opportunities for their husbands. He took his nephew Ed Goodman on tour with him, and he expanded his family by reaching out to a starstruck North Platte boy, Johnny Baker, who traveled with the Wild West as the "Cowboy Kid" and became a loyal friend who Cody called his "adopted son." Even while he was making himself famous as an extraordinary individual, a manly frontier hero, Cody also wanted to be a respected member of his family and community.

As Cody tried to modulate his dime-novel reputation and move toward greater respectability during the 1870s, he began to portray himself publicly in terms of wealth and community status. His press interviews in the 1870s stressed his non-show-business financial interests. In 1879, he boasted that he had cleared thirty-eight thousand dollars on his stage ventures that season, and declared, "I am now in the cattle business in Nebraska." Another interview from around the same time described his "fine farm improved by an elegant mansion."[2] Although he and his managers insisted that he was, authentically, a scout, he stressed that he was also a businessman. Like many other public figures of his age, including Mark Twain and P. T. Barnum, he envisioned himself as both an entertainment star and a prosperous gentleman of the Gilded Age. Cody embodied this image of himself in a photograph taken in 1876 in the Naegeli studio on Union Square, in New York. Posed like a rich businessman, with one hand on his hip in a commanding stance, he wears a fur-trimmed coat with suit, tie, and gold watch chain. The frontier scout could also be a solid citizen.

But Cody's respectability was always at risk to his impulsive openhandedness. Even as he began sending his earliest theatrical earnings home, his wife, Louisa, put the land she purchased in her own name because she feared he would lose everything in a lawsuit that he was financing for his sisters over a claim to some property in Cleveland.[3] Indeed, the lawsuit dragged on for years at great expense, with Cody always hoping he would hit the jackpot. "My Cleveland case is costing me a good deal of ready money," he wrote to a friend who had asked him for money, "besides I had to place in the Bank there several thousand for security for costs of suits. We had to bring suit against 113 different occupants each suit I had to put up cash for security for. But we will make it come our way you bet. Then I will have money to throw to the birds."[4] According to one account, he refused an offer of three hundred thousand dollars to settle the suit, declining a large sum in hopes of an enormous fortune.[5] The suit failed, and the money he spent pursuing it was lost.

William F. Cody, c. 1876,
photograph by Naegeli

If Cody had been more of a reader, he might have been sobered in his optimistic pursuit of the lucky strike by reading Mark Twain and Charles Dudley Warner's *The Gilded Age*, published at the end of 1873. The character of Colonel Beriah Sellers, dreamer, speculator, get-rich-quick addict, was based on a distant cousin of Clemens's in Louisa Cody's hometown, St. Louis, who, like Cody, jumped at every chance the postwar West offered for financial bonanza. The fictional Sellers plans a railroad that would run through the towns of Slouchburg, Doodleville, and Hallelujah to the newly established Corruptionville; he glories in the easy credit that allows his pipe dreams to flourish, and, chillingly, he ends up a bankrupt. Even though Cody probably never read the novel, he may have been familiar with its dramatic adaptation starring John T. Raymond as Colonel Sellers, which earned large profits during the heyday of Cody's own stage career in the 1870s.[6] Cody's increasing prosperity delivered him into an economic culture permeated by speculative fever.

Cody was always saying that great wealth was just around the corner. In

1883, he told his sister Julia he had "the foundation laid for a fortune before long," but six weeks later he admitted, "I have had a hard summer's work and have not made much money as my expenses have been big. . . . I am a little pushed for ready cash right now."[7] In 1886, he boasted to his old partner Jack Crawford, "My success here has been the greatest ever known in the amusement business. The receipts greater. And New York is wild over the show. I am taking about $40,000 a week, something never heard of before." At around the same time, he wrote to Julia, "My Dear Sister I think our poor days are over."[8] Elated by his success, Cody lost no time spending the profits from the 1885 and 1886 season on a new house and barn for his North Platte ranch, managed by Julia and Al Goodman, as well as expensive stock (three Thoroughbred stallions rumored to have cost five thousand dollars each), and social events for his wife and daughters.[9]

The London season of 1887 only fueled Cody's sense of grandeur; his income was substantial, but his expectations skyrocketed even faster. The patronage of the royal family and dinner invitations from important business and political leaders led to a heady round of socializing and a good deal of loose talk. "There is lots of money to be had in this country for 3 percent," he wrote to his brother-in-law, "and if you hear of a big syndicate that has got a good honest thing that requires lots of money, I believe I could float it over here. I am running with such men as the Rothschilds now. I have been offered a million dollars for the Wild West providing I stay with it three years."[10] Nate Salsbury feared that Cody was making a fool of himself, and some journalists were inclined to agree: "A few years ago W. F. Cody was shooting buffalo and dodging Indians and playing 7-up and drinking bad whiskey in western Kansas. Then everybody called him Buffalo Bill. Now he is the social lion in London and Lords and Ladies are running over each other to get an introduction to him and they call him 'Colonel, the Hon. William F. Cody.' "[11] Cody spent the money even faster than he made it. He and his family sponsored performances at the North Platte opera house and entertained performers and guests with parties; he contributed money to a fire company named in his honor, bought fancy new uniforms for the town band, and imported for his family an enormous British coach, a fourteen-passenger vehicle that caused a stir whenever he drove it around North Platte.[12] But Cody wrote from Paris in 1889 to complain to Julia that the pace was wearing him down and that he was feeling pressured by debt: "Today I am off my feed—I am like you I can't stand so much as I used to and I am not all well this summer. Now as we are getting old we must not kick at our breaking down, it can't be helped, but I don't want to break down until I get

North Platte band
uniforms

Cody's coach,
the Tallyho

out of debt and ahead of the hounds far enough to take it easy."[13] And the
sense of pressure was no illusion: the builder of his house sued him for failing to pay his bills.

Cody's finances fluctuated during the European tour. His company
arrived in Barcelona in the middle of an epidemic, and he lost money when
cast members became ill and quarantine laws prevented them from perform-

ing (several Indians and his announcer, Frank Richmond, died). Back in North Platte, his daughter Arta was married in an elaborate wedding; newspaper reports stated that the bride's father gave the young couple the deed to a home and five thousand dollars. During the winter of 1890–91, the Cody home in North Platte burned to the ground; although his possessions were saved, the house had been underinsured, and Cody lost more money.[14]

The season at the World's Columbian Exposition was a tremendous success, and newspapers reported that the Cody-Salsbury partnership had earned a million dollars. In North Platte, Cody was more generous than ever, giving hundreds of dollars to the town's churches and installing a stained-glass window in the sanctuary of the Episcopal church in memory of his two children who had died, Kit Carson Cody in 1876 and Orra Maude Cody in 1883. He brought the finest house in town as a gift to his wife and furnished it handsomely. When he discovered an old employer impoverished in Denver, he helped him publish his autobiography and set up an allowance for his support. And all the while, old and new friends and acquaintances besieged him with offers for investment schemes, which cost the most of all.

With an old frontier chum, Dr. Frank Powell, Cody set up a company to manufacture a cereal-based coffee substitute in La Crosse, Wisconsin. Powell also involved him in a patent medicine, "White Beaver's Cough Cream, the Great Lung Healer," purportedly based on American Indian herbal remedies. Around the same time, Cody became deeply involved in land and

Cody's North Platte home, Welcome Wigwam

development schemes in the Big Horn Basin of Wyoming. He helped to fur-
nish a luxury hotel in the town of Sheridan, the terminus of the Burlington
and Missouri River Railroad line, and invested ten thousand dollars, plus the
cost of land, in digging an irrigation canal from the North Platte River to his
ranch. He made plans to start a colony of Quaker settlers and contracted for
the planting of crops on his irrigated lands. But his North Platte ranch was
heavily mortgaged, and his other investments suffered from the drought and
financial downturn of 1893. A year after the end of his million-dollar season,
according to one of his biographers, he was near bankruptcy.[15]

For the remainder of Cody's career, he continued to act like a tycoon yet
hover on the brink of financial ruin. He poured more money into the
Wyoming lands. The town of Cody was named for him, and his nephew Ed
Goodman was appointed its first postmaster in August 1896. He brought
herds of cattle to the land he was buying and established the TE Ranch.
Thanks to his influence, the Burlington Railroad extended a branch to Cody,
the government built a road from Yellowstone Park, and an enormous water
project resulted in the building of the Shoshone Dam, the highest in the
world when it was completed in 1910. Cody invested in numerous projects
aimed to attract tourists to the area, including a line of stagecoaches; a hunting lodge, Pahaska Tepee, at the Yellowstone entrance; the Cody Military
College and International Academy of Rough Riders; and the Irma Hotel in
Cody, named for his daughter. All these enterprises were advertised in the
Wild West programs, with the hope that the show would turn spectators into
tourists. Cody's vision of cashing in on his fame through an integrated net-
work of tourist attractions was plausible, even farsighted. But he spread himself too thin, and his grip on his overall financial situation seemed tenuous.
In an 1896 interview, he airily told a reporter, "I have lost several fortunes in
outside adventures. I am now in almost a multitude of enterprises." Yet he
claimed that he planned to retire from show business four years later, after a
season at the Paris World's Exposition in 1900, and he estimated that he was
worth five million dollars.[16] Nate Salsbury remembered that he surrounded
himself with "Old Timers" who preyed on his hospitality; the businesslike
manager wrung his hands at Cody's improvidence.[17] Yet even the prudent
Salsbury invested in the Wyoming land venture, as well as a development in
Long Branch, New Jersey, called "The Reservation," which rented holiday
cottages with colorful Indian names.[18] Cody had bad luck with timing (the
Irma was too big for the town when it opened, and reportedly lost five hundred dollars a month on operating expenses) and lacked the financial
reserves to wait for the tourist trade to come into its own.

Cody's most disastrous investment was not the land-development scheme, however, but a mining operation he bought into around the time the Irma Hotel opened. The Cody-Dyer Mining and Milling Company was looking for tungsten, gold, and lead at a site in Arizona. Despite glowing reports from surveyors, his investment in land and equipment was fruitless, and the mine never yielded any valuable ore. Don Russell estimated that Cody lost half a million dollars on the mining project alone.[19]

Thus, despite the lavish entertainment, the generosity to friends and relatives, the kindly habit of filling his pockets with silver dollars to give away, the triumphal tours and glittering receptions, Cody never had the resources to match his style of living. He wrote to Nate Salsbury in 1895 begging for help in keeping out of debt:

> It's wrong to trouble you. But I am in a tight place. And if I had a little time to go on I am sure that I could push through and make a loan on my property. . . . Will you go on my note with Stokes for $5000. Nate this is to keep my credit good that I ask this. And if I fail to make money next summer I will sell everything I have and pay you and others I owe. And start in fresh. This being pushed to the wall. I will not starve. Nothing hurts me more than to be in debt.[20]

But the correspondence goes on teeming with complaints that money is slipping through his fingers, as in this letter to a Wyoming friend some months later:

> You tell me to put on the brake and quit giving up to every one. Say I have lost the brake entirely and from looks of things the dam team is running away, for I am making $50,000 a month and the whole world is after me for money. I have always been considered a sucker and I guess I am for they talk me out of my drawers.[21]

Salsbury claimed he lent Cody "over a Hundred Thousand Dollars at a time without a scrap of paper between us," and in the absence of clear records his widow, Rachel Salsbury, ultimately accepted a financial settlement after her husband's death that her brother thought woefully inadequate.[22] Cody's venture into the world of big money had brought luxury and pleasure, but carried a heavy price in anxiety and debt, making him vulnerable to exploitation.

LOVE AND MARRIAGE

The public prominence of the modern celebrity, which had made him so vulnerable in financial matters, enmeshed Cody in other temptations as well. From the beginning, his success in show business was founded on his personal magnetism, his extraordinary body displayed for admiring audiences; yet Salsbury and Burke had understood the importance of framing this display of virility and power in didactic terms, as a family entertainment, an educational spectacle. Cody's marriage, his educated daughters, and the middle-class respectability of his home in North Platte were all important parts of his public image, guarantors of propriety that gave spectators a sense of safety, just as the cowboy band and the lady performers made it safe to contemplate the spirited animals and exotic performers of the Wild West. Assertions of Cody's respectability allowed audiences to respond, in acknowledged or buried ways, to Buffalo Bill's sexual magnetism. But that power was a dangerous and volatile commodity, one that the lionized and admired Cody found difficult to control.

During the summer of 1894, John Burke highlighted his star's personal charms, arranging for two different female reporters to interview Cody, and producing newspaper copy that played to stereotyped images of both the women and the celebrity about whom they wrote. Did these reporters drench themselves in conventional women's rhetoric in order to gain a foothold in the masculine preserve of the Wild West? "Women are all romantic, you know, and impressionable," wrote one, who took the name of Henry James's impulsive, doomed heroine, "Daisy Miller." Did her nom de plume undercut her apparent hero worship? "I immediately enshrined the hero of the plains in the recesses of my heart, and felt that the very atmosphere he breathed must necessarily bespeak romance."[23] Another female reporter, who signed herself "J.M.W.," wrote an interview headlined "Colonel Cody Talks," illustrated by a sketch of a diminutive lady reporter sitting at the feet of a gigantically proportioned Buffalo Bill, who gazes down on her in regal splendor. Not only the illustration but the text accepted the "feminine perspective" to the point of self-parody. "Big men are always gentle to women," gushed the reporter, "so I was not afraid to interview Buffalo Bill." Did he think, she went on provocatively, that a frontier hero like himself "is a pet with the women?" John Burke, impresario of the interview, called attention to the question by seeming to turn it aside. "The Major, who was, perhaps, afraid that the Colonel might give himself away . . . said that it would make a man look like an egotist to talk about a woman's attentions to

Buffalo Bill Talks to the Reporter, from an 1894 scrapbook

him." Playing her role to the hilt, the reporter ended by addressing her presumably female readers directly: "If he isn't a pet with the women he ought to be. Don't you think so?"[24] Such publicity went far beyond the goal of making women comfortable with the noise and dust of the Wild West. It came close to naming—and even enacting—the unspoken basis for Buffalo Bill's charm: his sex appeal.

Cody's own attitude toward women was a complex one. He always wrote and spoke respectfully of his mother, who managed the family after his father's death in 1857 and whom he credited with persuading him to leave the disreputable Kansas irregular raiders at the outbreak of the Civil War. As a boy, he had lived in a woman-centered household, surrounded by four sisters and a half sister (two brothers died young), all of whom negotiated the hardships of frontier life and made more or less successful marriages. His half sister Martha, nine years older than he, married when Cody was twelve years old and died soon after. As he became famous, Cody remained resolutely loyal to his four surviving sisters, aiding them financially and becoming entangled in their mutual quarrels and jealousies. Julia, two years his senior, married Al Goodman and took over the task of raising the younger siblings after their mother's death in 1863. Cody corresponded with her throughout his life, trusted her and her husband to manage his ranch, and later asked Julia to run the Irma Hotel. His sister Eliza married George Myers and lived until 1902; Helen married twice, writing a book about her famous brother and running a newspaper after her second husband's death. May Cody, who had been the subject of one of Buffalo Bill's melodramas, also survived two

Buffalo Bill and
his sisters

husbands, living in Denver. During his prosperous years, Cody shared his wealth with his sisters, sponsoring family reunions like the one that produced a photograph of Cody in coat and tie, sitting straight and holding his Stetson hat politely on his knee, surrounded by four black-clad middle-aged women looking sternly at the camera with hands folded. It is an arresting image: the virile hero of the Wild West tamed and subdued by powerful women; and it suggests the claustrophobic domestic world of hard work and respectability to which the Wild West formed an appealing alternative for his audiences and, perhaps, himself.

When the young William Cody left home for work in the fluid, masculine world of the frontier, he encountered many women quite different from his mother and sisters, including the "ladies" who entertained the Sheridan hunting party with dancing and champagne, the Native American women who had married traders and scouts, and the showgirls who traveled with the Buffalo Bill Combination. Cody was a convivial companion, and must have been popular with women as well as men from his teenage years on.

Perhaps it is surprising that Cody married so young—just a few days after his twentieth birthday. Many of his "pards" of the plains, like Wild Bill Hickok, married late or not at all. His father had married for the first time at the age of twenty-three, although he could hardly have been said to settle down, roaming from Ohio to Missouri to Iowa to Kansas; he was thirty-four when William Cody was born to his third wife. Settled domesticity held little charm for Cody, who as a teenager had repeatedly left home to ride with wagon trains, messenger services, hunting parties, and the Union army. Why, then, did he rush to marry Louisa Frederici, whom he had met when army duty took him to St. Louis at the close of the Civil War? It was probably his first time in a big city, the farthest east he had been except in military campaigns. Louisa Cody's ghostwritten memoir spins an unlikely story of romantic parlor flirtations, while Buffalo Bill's *Autobiography* spends little time on his courtship except to declare, "I now adored [Miss Frederici] above any other young lady I had ever seen."[25] Cody later claimed that she had pestered him with letters after his return to Kansas, insisting that an offhand remark was a proposal of marriage and that he married her to keep his word. "Boy-like, I thought it very smart to be engaged," he explained later, when the marriage had begun to seem like a mistake to him.[26] His own motivations, and Louisa's, may be hard to discern when their versions of the story were all written in retrospect, in the context of Buffalo Bill's celebrity. The marriage was certainly a quick one, sandwiched between a series of scouting and horse-driving jobs for Cody, and followed immediately by their departure for Kansas. The birth of their first child, Arta, followed the wedding by almost exactly nine months, but by this time, Cody had given up domestic life as a

Louisa Cody

hotel-keeper and had returned to scouting, sending his wife to live with relatives. Louisa's Catholic family had agreed to her hasty marriage after a short courtship to a man with very unsettled prospects, for Cody appeared to have no clear plans to settle down and raise a family. It is at least worth speculating that Cody's sexual magnetism may have hurried him into an early and ill-considered marriage that was fully rewarding for neither husband nor wife.

By their first anniversary, Cody and his wife had established the pattern their marriage would take: Louisa stayed home with the children, while Cody centered his life on hunting, scouting, and, later, show business. In his first stage season, he enjoyed her occasional visits to the theater, calling out to her from the stage, "Oh, Mamma, I'm a bad actor," and at least once bringing her up on the stage, to her great embarrassment.[27] But as Cody became a star entertainer, his relationship with Louisa grew more distant. She rarely visited the Wild West and had little to do with the visitors who followed her husband to his Western home. She seemed to take very little interest in his public life, and Cody was apparently content to let her represent domestic respectability while he played the role of convivial scrapegrace. Louisa's ghostwriter commented disparagingly to Don Russell, "The poor old woman hardly knew the parade had gone by — Buffalo Bill's life was largely a haze to her."[28] Although Cody appeared at family events and established Louisa in finer and finer residences as he prospered, their relationship showed strains from an early period. In 1883, Cody was referring to his wife

An Embarrassing Situation, from Cody, *Autobiography*

as "that woman" in letters to his sister, and in 1887 his nephew Ed Goodman was reassuring his father that he didn't talk about "family troubles" to other Wild West cast members.[29] Louisa's letters do not survive.

At least some of Cody's problems with his wife arose over real or imagined infidelity. Cody and Louisa had a quarrel in 1877 over a farewell party for his theatrical troupe that ended with his being kissed goodbye by four actresses. Cody later insisted there was nothing wrong with this demonstration of affection: "I think [most women] would have been rather proud of a husband who had six or seven months work with a party of people who were in his employ, to know and feel that they were on a kindly footing with their late manager."[30] In 1893, Louisa made an unannounced visit to Chicago and was shown to "Mr. and Mrs. Cody's" hotel suite; one of Cody's assistants, remembering the incident, reflected, "It was only natural; any man would have done the same, the way women ran after him."[31]

Cody's rising fame in show business provided ample opportunities for romantic entanglements. In the 1879 autobiography, he professed himself embarrassed by the "throng of beautiful ladies" who surrounded him on his trip east, but an illustration showing him the center of doting attention at a ball probably captures the spirit of his successes. Cody met many women, from society matrons to showgirls, who found him fascinating. And, as he began to prosper, and to represent himself as financially successful, the terms of his relations with women changed even more.

The actresses who kissed him goodbye in 1877 were part of a world in which emotion and sexuality were more overt than in bourgeois society. That Cody understood this was shown in his defense of the incident years later: "Actresses are not a narrow-minded people. They do not go off behind the door or to some dark room if they want to kiss a man. They boldly walk up to him and with their enthusiasm, they are willing to let the world know that they like him and do not hesitate to show it in their voice and by their lips."[32] But, even at this early date, Cody was not just another member of the risqué theatrical world; he provided its financial underpinnings. And the kiss of the actresses could be seen not only as a tribute to his personal attractions but as an acknowledgment of his power and a bid for favors that his money and celebrity could supply.

Ten years later Cody began an entanglement with an actress that sheds some light on the complicated relationships among love, money, and power in the life of a celebrity. He met a young American actress, Katherine Clemmons, during his first London engagement and agreed to finance her stage career. Ultimately he spent fifty thousand dollars sending her on tours of

Katherine Clemmons in
A *Lady of Venice*

England and later of the United States, but her plays lost money. In 1893 he argued publicly with her manager; she was the object of Louisa's suspicions in Chicago; in 1894 he got into a fight about her in a Washington restaurant.[33]

Perhaps Cody could see a bit of himself in Clemmons, a frontier girl who was trying to succeed in legitimate theater. She was an accomplished horsewoman and a good drinking companion who also yearned for respectability. In a play Cody financed, A *Lady of Venice*, she played a young wife who disguises herself as a man and fights a duel; but her part also involved more conventionally feminine behavior. Her costumes included sumptuous gowns which critics described as "dreams of loveliness in the dress-maker's art." A *Lady of Venice* was panned by critics in Boston and New York in 1894, though Cody's considerable investment was recognized in the critics' praise for the "luxurious" sets and costumes. Kindly comments were made about her "youth, beauty, talent and intelligence," but the actress was described as amateurish, her delivery of blank verse as "monotonous" and "wearisome." During the run, publicity stories emphasized Clemmons's frontier background, suggesting that she had been rescued by Buffalo Bill from an Indian attack as a little girl, and that he supported her career out of loyalty to her mother.[34]

A few years later, Clemmons left behind her own frontier origins as well as her association with Buffalo Bill when she allied herself to a celebrity of a different kind. In 1898 she married the multimillionaire Howard Gould, son of the financier Jay Gould, and the press reported that her husband risked losing five million dollars of his inheritance by choosing a wife of whom his family did not approve. Publicity stories about her marriage reinvented a more genteel background for her: prominent ancestors, studies in Europe, and the encouragement of fashionable patrons of the arts. But when the marriage turned sour ten years later and Gould accused the actress of habitual drunkenness and sexual misconduct with several men, Clemmons was again linked with Cody in a way that was damaging to both.[35] Gould reportedly offered Cody fifty thousand dollars to bolster his case by testifying against Clemmons in court, but Cody refused, although he was desperate for money at the time. Cody's effort to keep to the high ground did not protect him from the scandal, however, for its allegations of sexual and financial profligacy contradicted the image so carefully nurtured by Buffalo Bill's public-relations team and upset the Wild West's delicate balance between risk and safety, personal magnetism and respectability. The glimpse of an all-too-human Buffalo Bill undermined the stability of his public persona.

The greatest damage to Buffalo Bill's status as a hero was largely of his own making, however, the result of the divorce suit he filed against his wife, Louisa, in 1904. The separate lives they had been living, the jealousies and competitions between and among Cody's sisters, their husbands and children, and his wife, had led to considerable friction over the years. Cody's letters about domestic matters are by turns exasperated and conciliatory. In 1891, he had already instructed his brother-in-law to take care of Louisa's property, writing, "I often feel sorry for her. She is a strange woman but don't mind her—remember she is my wife—and let it go at that. If she gets cranky just laugh at it, she can't help it."[36] But other letters express his frustrations with her and mention the possibility of divorce. In March 1902, he complained to his sister Julia that his life with his wife was "a false lie," and declared his determination to get her to agree to a "quiet legal separation," threatening that if she refused, "then it's war and publicity."[37] But Cody had a false sense of his own ability to manage publicity in private warfare. Divorce was considered scandalous, and the resulting depositions and court testimony threatened to destroy the underpinnings of respectability that had allowed Buffalo Bill to frame his entertainment as "high toned" and, despite the illusion of danger, safe for bourgeois society.

When Cody filed suit for divorce, he opened private areas of his life to an intense scrutiny that unsettled his role as a public hero. Nellie Snyder Yost, who based her biography of Cody on the records and reminiscences of his neighbors in North Platte, reported that as the divorce proceeded, the towns-people felt obliged to take sides, and even as late as the 1960s some were still trading stories of the sisters' jealousies, Cody's alleged infidelities, and Louisa's excesses.[38] Newspapers covered the suit with relish. "WE'RE LIABLE TO HEAR NAUGHTY THINGS," croaked the *North Platte Telegraph*, while other papers East and West made fun of Cody's predicament. Since Cody wanted the divorce and Louisa wanted to maintain the marriage, he had to prove that she made life "intolerable" for him, so he complained that she was rude to his friends and that "she grumbled and kicked" and displayed ill temper. The *Denver Post* reported that Cody wanted to divorce his wife for "nagging," while the *Baltimore American* printed a poem mocking Cody's claims that his wife drove away his friends by imagining that she tried to stop Indians from scalping the cook and cowboys from shooting the chandeliers.[39]

Cody filed his initial complaint and gave depositions in March 1904. After various postponements, Louisa answered the complaints in January 1905, and the case went to trial in February. Witnesses testified about Cody's drinking and womanizing and Louisa's fits of rage. Cody had accused his wife of trying to poison him and of intentionally killing some of his dogs. One witness testified that Louisa was jealous of her husband's relations with Queen Victoria and Queen Alexandria of England. Husband and wife agreed that they had quarreled violently when their adult daughter Arta died the year before, shortly after Cody filed divorce papers; Louisa had accused him of killing their child by breaking her heart. The judge hearing the case required that some of the more extravagant claims be stricken from the record and then found in favor of Mrs. Cody. Cody could not end the mar-riage, and he had dragged his most private quarrels into the public eye. His local Masonic lodge discussed ejecting him from the order, to which he had belonged since 1869, because of the unseemliness of the divorce proceed-ings.[40] Newspapers wondered at the hero's feet of clay. "What's the Matter with Buffalo Bill?" asked one article in March 1905, and answered its own question by blaming the star-making process itself. "Adulation corrupted his staunch manhood; laces and graces made him over again in a newer but very much commoner mould. . . . It is unpleasant to see a national idol fall from its pedestal. But why worship at a shrine that has no illusion left or that has been desecrated by the idol itself?"[41]

The Cody divorce scandal threatened to undo all of Nate Salsbury and John Burke's careful efforts to craft Buffalo Bill's public image. Because Cody had witnessed the triumph of public relations in so many settings, he might have thought that he could handle "war and publicity" in this matter as well, but just as he erred so often in financial matters, in managing his romantic affairs he miscalculated his own control over his public persona. Buffalo Bill the celebrity had a life of its own, and when Cody complained that his wife nagged him, he created a dissonance with the image of himself he had collaborated in creating. Living the life of a national symbol gave him opportunities and temptations in the overlapping worlds of love and money, but his pursuit of private desires undermined the public approval that made him a symbol in the first place. Like so many others, Cody learned that a twentieth-century celebrity could be discredited by the very same public acclaim that had elevated him.

THE PARTNERSHIP PROBLEM

Cody was made and undone as a celebrity not only by the audiences that responded to his performances and news releases, but also by the business partners who helped him to achieve success. At every stage of his career, Cody drew on the financial acumen and public-relations skills of one or more collaborators. The charm and personal magnetism were his own, and he proved that he was a comfortable and canny showman. But the rise and fall of his fortunes depended to a large extent on the fit between his talents and abilities, on the one hand, and the judgment and experience of his partners, on the other. One indication of the modernity of Cody's stardom is that it rested on powerful behind-the-scenes work. The financial debacle of Cody's last decades was largely a result of his unwise investments and entanglements, but his visibility made him ever more vulnerable to exploitation by self-interested partners.

Collaboration was an essential element in Cody's career. Propelled on his course by Ned Buntline, supplied with material during his theatrical days by the writer Prentiss Ingraham, stimulated as well as irritated by Doc Carver, Cody had made good use of other talents as he carved out his public persona and rose to stardom. But the crucial element in the Wild West success was

Cody's partnership with Nate Salsbury. Salsbury's experience made all the difference: he knew about routes and bookings, envisioned the European tour, broadened the Wild West's program to include international riding acts, and provided the hard work behind the scenes that allowed Cody to appear in public as a delightful drinking companion, fascinating yarn-spinner, and handsome showstopper. Salsbury's management created the environment in which Cody's natural dramatic abilities and personal warmth could flourish.

Salsbury's character and qualities as a partner are nowhere better represented than in some of the anecdotes of his unpublished "Reminiscences." Although he angrily details his grievances against Cody, elsewhere he gives delightfully witty accounts of his deep involvement in the Wild West's greatest triumphs. When he masterminded a command performance for Queen Victoria at Windsor Castle in 1892, he was invited to view the show from the royal pavilion in order to answer any questions the queen might have. Salsbury humorously pictured himself as a representative of his own democratic nation holding his own in the encounter with royal snobs. As the show's international riding act made its entrance, younger members of the royal family were not impressed.

Mr. Salsbury at His Desk,
from an 1894 scrapbook

The Royal Party Watching the Performance from the Terrace, from an 1892 scrapbook

Prince Battenberg, who was standing in the rear of the pavilion, said to the Queen in German, "Mamma, do you think
[the Russian riders] are really Cossacks?" Before the Queen
had time to reply to him, I said, "I beg to assure you, sir, that
everything and everybody you see in this entertainment, are
exactly what we represent it or them to be." Her Majesty
turned to the Prince and said, "Prince, I think we had better
speak English for the rest of the afternoon."

Even if the diction of the last line does not ring quite true, the anecdote
allows Salsbury to portray himself as the witty Brother Jonathan sparring
with presumptuous Europeans who look down on their American cousin.
He gave the story what Mark Twain would call a "snapper" by adding one
more twist, recalling that he had proved that he could understand a second European language when he answered Princess Beatrice's gibe to her
husband in flawed but recognizable French. "Princess Beatrice, who was
sitting beside the Queen, was much amused at her husband's discomfi-
ture, and smilingly said to him [sic], 'Mon chere, vous avez recu votre pre-

miere lecon Americane.' I immediately replied, 'Oh, Madame, j'espere [que] non.' "[42]

Perhaps it was no coincidence that the beginnings of Cody's financial difficulties came at the time that his best partner was forced to step back from active management of the show. In 1894, the Wild West performed all summer at Ambrose Park in Brooklyn. Salsbury began to suffer from ill health; although he lived for eight more years, he was unable to travel with the Wild West again. His papers show that his canny entertainment sense continued to serve Cody despite his physical ailments. "At the close of our season at Ambrose Park I was stricken down with the trouble that made me an invalid for years," he wrote in his "Reminiscences." "My plan for the coming season was to go on the road with a plant the same as we used in Europe and Great Britain." To accomplish his arduous schedule, Salsbury struck a bargain with James A. Bailey, formerly the partner of P. T. Barnum, and since Barnum's death, in 1891, the proprietor of the two largest American circuses. The arrangement had great advantages, since Bailey knew how to run a touring company and manage all the crucial logistical arrangements: hiring and supervising traveling support staff such as cooks, animal handlers, matrons, and even barbers; overseeing the advance agents and canvassers who posted bills ahead of the troupe's arrival; arranging and maintaining railroad cars; buying provisions; and booking performance sites. In negotiating the initial contract, Salsbury was careful to define Bailey's role as a subcontractor rather than a partner: "I looked upon the opportunity as a good one to share the trouble and worry of getting a plant together with somebody else. . . . His connection with the Wild West was the exact one of being a speculator in the results of the road."[43]

In his first year of work with Salsbury and Cody, Bailey was appointed local manager in each town, while Salsbury retained the supervision of a second entertainment in which he and Cody were investing. Before his illness, Salsbury had arranged to produce Black America, a Wild West–like entertainment featuring African-American performers, on the show grounds they had fitted up at Ambrose Park, in Brooklyn; contracting for Bailey's services permitted him to cut his responsibilities in half. But Salsbury's illness worsened and Black America lost money. According to the reminiscences of a staff member, it finally ground to a halt: "Mr. Salsbury was taken sick and things went wrong so the show was disbanded."[44] Later Cody castigated Salsbury for losing seventy-eight thousand dollars on Black America, and Salsbury complained that Cody insisted they keep it open when he had wanted to cut his losses and close it earlier.[45]

The arrangement with Bailey had several consequences that neither Salsbury nor Cody foresaw. For one thing, it made the Wild West more like a circus. After years being presented as an educational exhibition, the show began to have sideshow attractions, and the press reported on the itinerant hawkers of beer, lemonade, peanuts, and "gawdy looking souvenirs" who followed the show.[46] The show also became the target of pickpockets and grifters of all sorts who preyed on circus customers, although Cody and his staff worked to chase away such unwanted elements.[47] The Wild West's printed program took on a more commercial look and added advertising: in 1895, spectators were urged to buy remedies for eczema, men's suits, Mrs. Winslow's soothing

Advertising Car No. 1, from Buffalo Bill's Wild West Route Book Season of 1896

Canvasmen, from Buffalo Bill's Wild West Route Book Season of 1896

syrup for teething, the Liberty bicycle, Bicycle playing cards, Phoenix horse shoes, Horse Shoe plug tobacco, Dr. T. Felix Gouraud's Oriental Cream, Beeman's Pepsin gum, the Rochester Lamp, Cushing liquors ("for medicinal purposes"), and many other products aimed at men, women, and children.[48] The circuslike management made the Wild West's schedule more hectic, as well. Salsbury had already planned to tour in 1895, but Bailey's experience in scheduling one-night stands may have speeded up the pace even more. That year the company gave 333 performances in 203 days, including 156 one-night stands, traveling more than ten thousand miles.[49] Over the next decade, Bailey's preference for touring dominated the Wild West's scheduling, and Cody and his company found themselves following a very different routine from the long-term engagements of 1893 in Chicago and 1894 in Brooklyn.

Bailey also coordinated the Wild West movements in a way that kept it out of competition with his own businesses, the Barnum and Bailey Circus and the Adam Forepaugh and Sells Brothers Circus, in which he eventually shared an interest with his other competitor, the Ringling Brothers. When Barnum and Bailey returned from a European tour in 1902, Bailey planned a foreign tour for Buffalo Bill's Wild West. Although one early biography of Cody, written with the assistance of Nate Salsbury's son Milton, claimed that Bailey kept the Wild West abroad and subjected it to money-losing policies in order to help his circuses, the later biographer Don Russell concluded that it was in Bailey's interest to see the Wild West prosper, and the lackluster results of the European tours were not his fault.[50]

Another unintended consequence of the arrangement with Bailey was a deep and damaging rift between Cody and Salsbury. By September 1899, Bailey was completing his fifth season managing Buffalo Bill's Wild West, and Cody was deeply involved in his expensive Wyoming development scheme. Always in need of more money to support his burgeoning enterprises, Cody must have been a receptive audience for Bailey's proposal for a new business arrangement. Perhaps the new plan was conveyed through Bailey's assistant, Louis Cooke, whom Salsbury described as "a good talker and the cleverest man that Bailey ever had in his employ."[51] Cody had always left the details of the business to Salsbury, and in his enthusiasm for Bailey's schemes, he forgot that Buffalo Bill's Wild West Company was a legal entity, incorporated under the laws of New Jersey in 1887, and that Salsbury was vice president, treasurer, and a 50 percent stockholder.[52] On September 7, 1899, he wrote to tell Salsbury that he wanted to re-examine the "conditions for continuing as partners." He congratulated himself on his loyalty to Salsbury during the latter's illness:

You know that when you fell sick and these five years have been sick I didn't just quit you as many thought I would and that I had a right to do—as in this world most every one looks out for himself first. But not me I have stood by the ship and when not worried have tried to give you cheer—and let you rest and get well—And as you are now on the fair way to recovery I think it is more than right that we should fully understand how we do stand.

But, he went on, probably reflecting the flattering speeches he had heard from Cooke, his success had been his own and he was entitled to make the most of it with different business arrangements:

You know that I spent years of my life and every dollar I had or could make to make myself what I am and now that there is money in my name and my work. Not only do I know it—but our books show it. And men with capital are willing to speculate on it. And have been all this time you have been sick. And I said no—But you know that I have done the work & made the money.[53]

In a second letter, Cody detailed the offer Bailey had made: if he broke with Salsbury, Bailey would pay him fifty thousand dollars immediately and one thousand dollars a week salary. Cody defended his proposed defection by saying that he had earned three hundred thousand dollars for Salsbury, and now deserved a chance to make his own plans. Furthermore, he suggested that the debts he owed his former partner should be canceled because of the money lost by Black America.[54]

Salsbury exploded. He reminded Cody that Buffalo Bill's Wild West was a corporation, that use of its name was controlled by legal agreements, that Salsbury was entitled to 50 percent of the profits, and that Cody owned him money. He hotly disputed Cody's claim to have been doing all the work, remonstrating that he had always traveled with the show before he became ill, and that he had shaped the Wild West in its present form after the failure of Cody's partnership with Carver. "I will remind you," he exclaimed, stung by Cody's accusations, "that for seven months of every year, sick or well, I have been in charge of the business and of the concern, and I have staid on deck in the interest of the Wild West solely." Finally, he implied, Cody had taken money from the treasury for his own other projects, while in contrast,

"I have not used my money to promote any other schemes." He offered to dissolve their business association and threatened a lawsuit if Cody did not respect the terms of the Wild West charter.[55]

This exchange of furious letters ended with a plan for the two men to meet in New York, which apparently resulted in some sort of compromise agreement, because their business relationship did continue for another three years, until Salsbury's death on Christmas Eve, 1902, just before the Wild West's opening performance in England that year. But Salsbury's papers contain lists of his grievances against Cody, presumably drawn up in response to this quarrel, and the bitter statements about Cody's shortcomings in his "Reminiscences" were intended to give his family and friends ammunition with which to counter any accusations that might be lodged against him later. Their correspondence contains more charges and counter-charges—Salsbury told Cody that his Wyoming projects were ill conceived, and Cody accused Salsbury of sending spies to look into his affairs—yet

The Visit of Their Majesties, 1903, lithograph poster by Stafford and Co.

apparently the two men planned to make a break with Bailey and resume their direct partnership after the London season. Salsbury had advanced Cody twenty-five thousand dollars of his own money, secured by the assignment to him of all the remaining stock in the company, in order to finance the show's voyage to England. And Salsbury's last letter to Cody urges him not to worry about their past friction, declaring that "in three weeks and a little more we will be done with Bailey and Cole forever, and a new order of things will begin."[56] But after Salsbury's death, his widow was unable to recover the twenty-five thousand dollars and sent another ten thousand dollars after it to try to keep the show afloat during a disappointing season.[57] Eventually, Nate Salsbury, Jr., reached a settlement with Cody, against the advice of his mother's brother, in which Cody paid his debts, Mrs. Salsbury was released from the contract with Bailey, and the Salsbury family relinquished all shares of stock in Buffalo Bill's Wild West without any compensation.[58] It was a melancholy end to a remarkably creative partnership.

A week after hearing of Salsbury's death, Cody wrote to a friend in Denver, "It was to [sic] bad about poor Nate Salsbury. He was a good true man. I am all alone now and have all the responsibility. And more of the proffits [sic]."[59] To another friend he echoed, "with the death of my partner I have all the more to do—& more responsibility," adding a few months later, "every day year in and year out is a rush day for me. I cannot get even one hour to my self to quiet my nerves. Some one wants my time all the time. I have to attend to my own business—and receive company at the same time—say nothing of the letters I am compelled to write."[60] Though he continued to rely on James Bailey for management expertise, Cody often felt overwhelmed. And the show's European tour was financially challenging. Bad weather curtailed many performances, competition with a rival Wild West show was costly, and the show sustained a devastating loss when an outbreak of glanders forced the destruction of two-thirds of the show's horses. Although Cody's publicists could brag about royal visitors to the Wild West, including the Shah of Persia and the King of England, and crowds formed in many locations, the show failed to arouse the mass excitement it had generated a decade and a half earlier. Finally, just as the season of 1906 was ending and Cody was preparing to return to the United States, James Bailey died, depriving him of another collaborator and entangling him in negotiations with the Bailey estate that drove him even deeper into financial crisis.

Until Salsbury's death, Bailey had worked under a contract to manage the Wild West's operations. His hard-driving showmanship had shaped the practices and, to some extent, the content of the show in the years after Salsbury withdrew from its active management. An admirer of Bailey's called him "the little Napoleon of show business" and stressed his deep dedication to his work: "When Bailey picked up a newspaper he did not first turn to the base-ball score, nor did he stop to read the news of the day until he had first scanned the market reports and ascertained the price of cattle, hogs, flour, potatoes, cotton, tobacco, butter, eggs, etc. That told him more than the most thrilling headline."[61] Salsbury, respectful but less enthusiastic, also commented on Bailey's drivenness:

> Bailey's capacity for work is enormous, or at least it seems so to me, for I never heard of his devoting any time to anything but work. He has told me himself, that he cared for nothing but to make a success of his business at any cost. I never heard of his taking any sort of social pleasure. I do not believe he ever attended a theatre, or any other form of amusement for the sake of the amusement.[62]

Salsbury's blend of earnestness and lively humor had served Cody well; Bailey's focused ambition might have supported Buffalo Bill's financial aspirations if he had lived longer or if the Wild West had been his only business concern. As it was, Bailey's services came at a high price. After his death, Cody did not regain full control of his show, and the long, painful downward slide of his finances accelerated.

Although Cody's sympathetic biographer Don Russell insists that "the Colonel was fully capable of managing his own affairs when necessity arose," Cody was careless about many details. At some point he signed a note for twelve thousand dollars to James Bailey, and although he claimed he had repaid it, he kept no records; after Bailey's death he had no receipt for the money.[63] When Cody opened the 1907 season at Madison Square Garden, he was deeply in debt, and Bailey's heirs had taken over a controlling interest in the Wild West. John Burke threw himself into the task of making Cody's return home profitable; a newspaper cartoon shows him accosting an editor with a handful of publicity notices. The promotional booklet opened with "An Emphatic Statement" signed by Cody insisting that his show was the "ORIGINAL and the ONLY morally and RIGHTFULLY entitled 'WILD WEST AND CONGRESS OF ROUGH RIDERS OF THE WORLD,'" suggesting that he felt the pressure from the rival Wild West entertainments that had sprung up over the years. "With ripened experience to aid a faithful

Maj. Burke Gets the Drop on the Editor— With a Wad of Press Notices, from a 1907 scrapbook

desire to instruct, as well as to please, I guarantee energetic attention to all details of production, genuineness of the personalities of the races and nations announced and everything possible to be accomplished by personal supervision and presence, to add to the comfort and enjoyment of the visitor."[64] Cody's writers struck the familiar notes of authenticity and education, but the strain of his precarious finances had begun to show.

Pressed hard by the Bailey estate and eager to clear up his affairs, Cody agreed to the most visible partnership of his career. Starting in 1909, he merged Buffalo Bill's Wild West with a rival entertainment headed by Major Gordon W. Lillie, also known as Pawnee Bill. Lillie, who had once taught school at a Pawnee agency, had served as interpreter for the Pawnees in Cody and Carver's 1883 show. He organized a Wild West show of his own, which received a boost when Annie Oakley joined it for about a month in 1888. By 1893 he was touring with Pawnee Bill's Historical Wild West, Mexican Hippodrome, Indian Museum, and Grand Fireworks Exhibition, which looked remarkably like Buffalo Bill's Wild West, calling itself "Historic" and "America's National Entertainment," mounting pony-express exhibitions and featuring a stagecoach attack.[65]

As a showman, Lillie had seen successes and failures in the United States and Europe. In the early years of the century, he had benefited by Cody's absence from the American circuit to exploit the popular taste for Wild West exhibitions. At the same time, he had competed more directly with circuses by including a variety of exotic people and animals. During the 1907 season, Pawnee Bill's show included a miraculously growing mango tree, a Hindu escape artist, a snake handler, and dancing girls, as well as performers from Africa, Australia, and South America, in combination with acts representing a Western train robbery, Indian battles, and the lynching of a horse thief.[66]

Lillie's show also featured performances by his wife, May Manning Lillie, who (unlike Louisa Cody) involved herself in every aspect of her husband's business. The couple invested in Oklahoma land and helped to develop the town of Pawnee; Lillie was vice president of the Arkansas Valley Bank. But their investments were cautious. They put their money into land and live-stock, and Lillie kept in close contact with his banking partners. His discretion and May Lillie's involvement perhaps protected Pawnee Bill from the speculative fever that made Cody so vulnerable.

The partnership of the two Bills was a complicated one, and it high-lighted the changes that had overtaken Cody after the deaths of Salsbury and Bailey. Lillie was fifteen years younger than Cody—he lived until 1942—and wrote an account of his own life twenty-one years after Cody's death, in which he was still wrestling with his attitudes toward the rival, mentor, and model in whose shadow he had spent his career. Lillie recalled that he grew up reading Ned Buntline's novels (he was nine years old when the first Buf-falo Bill dime novel was published) and idolizing Buffalo Bill. As a teenager, he was thrilled to see Cody, Texas Jack Omohundro, and Wild Bill Hickok in *The Scouts of the Plains*, and he credited these experiences with inspiring him to go west in search of adventure. But he took pains to puncture Buffalo Bill's heroic public image by recalling some of Cody's drunken exploits, such as his attempt to ride a wild buffalo during the first Wild West season. On first joining the Wild West, Lillie claimed, he was shocked to find that the famous celebrity had feet of clay: "I never was so disappointed in my life. He had been sleeping on the floor of a tent in some hay, his fur coat was missing, his hair was all matted and he was drunk."

As he became a rival showman, Lillie was painfully aware of the difficul-ties in competing with a rising star whose celebrity was so painstakingly nur-tured by a brilliant public-relations team. In 1888, Lillie had been stung by Cody and Salsbury's fierce billposting onslaught against his show, and it must have rankled deeply that his money-losing European tour of 1894 followed on the heels of Cody's successes abroad and at the Columbian Exposition. So the opportunity to unite with his old rival under profoundly changed cir-cumstances would have offered Lillie a complicated satisfaction. Lillie recalled that he won Cody over to the idea of merger in 1908 by demonstrat-ing a superior knowledge of the entertainment business, predicting that Cody's show would do badly in New England but well in Michigan. Even while seeking Cody's cooperation, he marshaled the power that made the merger inevitable, enlisting the support of the Bailey heirs, with their con-trolling interest in Buffalo Bill's Wild West. Pawnee Bill's enthusiasm for the merger was not entirely grounded in business considerations. According to his memoir, the practical-minded May Lillie opposed the move and declined to perform in the combined show. The motive for a partnership with Buffalo Bill, then, lay deep in his own reaction to Cody's star status. "Here is my reason—the only one I have," he claimed to have told his wife. "I want this combination of the two biggest Wild West shows in the world to take place, with myself as owner and general manager, so that these same people, who threw their hats in the air [when his earlier show failed], and worked so hard to down me, will have to come to me and receive their check from my hand."[67]

Cody's partnership with Lillie was, like the one with Salsbury, based on the commercial value of Buffalo Bill's celebrity, but with the ironic difference that Cody was now a figurehead with little hope of realizing his own ambitious financial goals. Lillie hoped to profit by the new arrangement, but he did not need the money as desperately as Cody did, and he clearly enjoyed his new power. His memoirs claim that the Bailey management pressured him to fire John Burke, who had done so much for Buffalo Bill, and that he saved his former tormentor's job out of loyalty to Cody. Midway through the 1909 season, Lillie bought the Bailey estate's remaining two-thirds interest in the show for $66,666.66 (having previously paid it fifty thousand dollars for the first third). He was now sole owner of Buffalo Bill's Wild West, although he maintained the fiction that he and Cody were equal partners, with Cody's share of the show advanced to him as a loan by Lillie; Lillie's memoir reveals the satisfaction he took in these small acts of generosity. As part of the purchase agreement with the Bailey estate, he obtained the twelve-thousand-dollar note Cody had claimed to have paid and delivered it as a gift to the older showman. "That's bully, Major!" he reported Cody as exclaiming. "You have made me as happy as a man with a pair of twins." Cody was equally grateful when Pawnee Bill paid off another note for him: "I thank you! I thank you! I will never forget you for this—you have greatly relieved my mind."[68] Throughout his memoir, Lillie comments disdainfully on Cody's lack of business sense, noting that he always fell prey to demands for money from his mining partner: "Col. Cody, to me was more like a child in his business dealings, he apparently cared nothing for money, except when he wanted, or needed it to spend, then if he did not have it, or could not borrow it, it made him sick; he would go to bed."[69] His closing remarks on Buffalo Bill cast him once again in the role of hapless child and asserted the reversed power relationship between the two Bills: "Buffalo Bill died my friend. He was just an irresponsible boy."[70] Behind the mask of friendship and generosity, Lillie gloried in his ability to condescend to the world's most famous showman.

A publicity photograph of the two men shows them seated opposite each other across a small table. Cody, bareheaded, turns majestically toward the camera, while Lillie, with his hat on, leans forward, eyes downcast, as he writes something on a piece of paper. Perhaps unwittingly, the photograph captures the essence of the partnership: Cody is the public attraction while Lillie wields economic control. The new show presented both men in Western garb, but it identified Cody with the Wild West and Lillie with the circuslike Oriental acts. "Buffalo Bill's Wild West Combined with Pawnee Bill's Far East" included the classic Wild West set pieces together with an act called "A Dream of the Orient," featuring camels, elephants, and dancing girls. In 1910, the show began to advertise that Buffalo Bill was contemplating retirement, and the two Bills planned a three-year circuit that would allow them to present "farewell" appearances in different parts of the country. Lillie's careful management and Cody's celebrity brought four hundred thousand dollars in profits to the partnership, and Cody began to pay off his debts to Lillie, even while continuing to sink money into the Arizona mines.[71]

In January 1913, Cody once again yielded to the temptation to change partners, with disastrous results. Harry Tammen, a Denver businessman who controlled a newspaper (the *Denver Post*) and a circus (Sells-Floto), had met Cody in Denver when Cody was visiting his sister May Decker. Tammen, described by Don Russell as "amoral and unscrupulous," probably flattered Cody as Bailey's agents had years before, and once again Cody conveniently forgot that Buffalo Bill's Wild West was a corporation and not his own private property. He owed Lillie twenty thousand dollars for the expenses for wintering the show, and rather than borrow from his partner against the next season's earnings, as he had done in the past, he accepted a loan from Tammen for that amount, signing a note with the show property as collateral and promising to leave the Two Bills show at the end of the season in order to appear with Sells-Floto. The 1913 season was financially unsuccessful, and when Tammen's note came due in July, the show was in debt for feed and lithography. Tammen's own lawyers helped the lithographers sue the show, and the publisher had the show attached in accordance with the terms of Cody's twenty-thousand-dollar note. Although Lillie had money to pay off the note, his anger at Cody's betrayal and Tammen's quick maneuvering thwarted him. Lillie's own savings, including the mortgages he held on Cody's property, were not threatened, but the show was forced into bankruptcy and its assets sold. The public auction of September 15, 1913, was

Buffalo Bill and Pawnee Bill

Buffalo Bill's Wild West Combined with Pawnee Bill's Far East, 1911 program, back cover

widely reported, another painful consequence of Cody's fame. Two friends bought his horse, Isham, and sent it to his ranch as a gift; but no gestures could change the electrifying news that the internationally famous Buffalo Bill was now a bankrupt.[72]

Gordon Lillie gave up the Wild West business and returned to his ranch, but Cody tried desperately to reinvigorate his career while carrying out the commitments he had made to Harry Tammen. His final partnership with Tammen is hard to see in any other light than as the exploitation of a celebrity by a cunning profiteer. In 1914 Cody toured with the Sells-Floto Circus, now ironically embedded in the very entertainment form he and Salsbury had always scorned. Headlined as "Buffalo Bill (Himself)," as if spectators might justifiably doubt that the old scout would ride in a three-ring circus, Cody's initial appearance followed Fred Biggs, "the funniest female impersonator who ever caricatured the feminine sex," and preceded a display of trick ponies and lady riders weaving a maypole on horseback.[73] Cody received one hundred dollars a day and 40 percent of receipts over

Story Book and Program,
Sells-Floto Circus, cover

three thousand dollars; he toured with the circus for two seasons, but when he tried to leave it Tammen sent him a letter claiming he still owed him twenty thousand dollars. Cody refused to continue with Sells-Floto, claiming that its shabby equipment endangered the lives of spectators, but Tammen announced that Cody had signed over the right to use the name "Buffalo Bill" and would have to pay him five thousand dollars if he appeared with any other show.

Although Cody performed for one more season in a show called "Buffalo Bill (Himself) and 101 Ranch Wild West Combined with the Military Pageant 'Preparedness,' " his affairs continued to totter. One biographer depicts the faithful John Burke spending his breakfast money on newspapers to trace Cody's activities. Cody wrote to the U.S. government to see whether his Congressional Medal of Honor entitled him to a ten-dollar monthly pension, but he continued to write hopefully in letters to friends, "I am climbing for another fortune."[74] A little more than two months after the season ended, he became ill and died at his sister's house in Denver, on January 10, 1917, just short of his seventy-first birthday.

It seems likely that, after his death, Cody's last and most unscrupulous partner seized control of one more asset: Buffalo Bill's own mortal remains. Although his will had stipulated that he wished to be buried in Cody, Wyoming, and authorized ten thousand dollars for the building of a monument there, Louisa Cody agreed to a burial site outside Denver, on Lookout Mountain. Cody's biographers have speculated that Tammen cut a deal with the confused and grieving widow. Perhaps she, too, had expected that Cody was climbing to another fortune and was shocked to find out how impoverished his death left her. The appraisal of Cody's estate shows few assets of any kind, certainly nothing approaching ten thousand dollars to build a monument in Wyoming, and no money or property for his widow; but the executors note that Louisa Cody is to be paid a legacy of one thousand dollars per year.[75] Did these funds come from the pockets of the Denver publisher? One report suggested that Tammen paid Mrs. Cody ten thousand dollars to give his city the distinction of hosting Buffalo Bill's grave and claiming him in death as a perpetual tourist attraction.[76] At any rate, Tammen's newspaper, the *Denver Post*, derived much copy from the choice of grave site, a fund drive to raise money from schoolchildren for the monument, and the elaborate funeral. "Magnificent Dome Will Cover the Resting Place of Colonel Cody, Beloved Plainsman and Scout," announced the newspaper. "Scene from Towering Structure Builded upon Great Mountain Height Is of Vast Grandeur."[77]

Cody's body lay in state at the Colorado capitol, where a crowd of twenty-five thousand filed past. The funeral brought the governors of Colorado and Wyoming, the lieutenant governor of Nebraska, delegations from three state legislatures, Elks, Boy Scouts, veterans of the Civil War and Spanish-American War, representatives of the Showmen's League, as well as other organizations that claimed Buffalo Bill as their own. The governing council of the Oglala Sioux of Pine Ridge sent a message of condolence, declaring that "the Oglalas found in Buffalo Bill a warm and lasting friend; that our hearts are sad from the heavy burden of his passing, lightening only in the belief of our meeting before the presence of our Wakan Tanka in the great hunting ground."[78] Colonel John W. Springer of Denver delivered one of the eulogies, praising Cody's "real, true, and progressive Americanism": "the spirit of William Frederick Cody shall live and dwell with us like a sweet benediction, forever and forever."[79] A second ceremony was held five months later when the grave site at Lookout Mountain was ready. Both events were widely reported and drew throngs of spectators.[80]

During Cody's last years, the face of the fallible mortal had often appeared behind the visage of the international celebrity. His marital and financial failures had disappointed his admirers, and the embattled remains of his publicity machine had struggled to hold on to the shreds and tatters of his myth. Perhaps he had believed in his own heroic stature, hoping until it was too late that his Midas touch would not desert him. Or perhaps he had simply failed to grasp how the notion of his celebrity, which he had done so much to create, was continually destabilized by the messy facts of human fallibility. But his death changed all that. When he died, the narrative of Buffalo Bill's life was complete, and the "last of the great scouts" returned to the pantheon of legendary national champions. Buffalo Bill was buried and memorialized as the hero he had aspired to be.

[PART TWO]

PERSPECTIVES

Frederic Remington, sketches from Buffalo Bill's Wild West,
Harper's Weekly, September 3, 1892

CHAPTER FIVE

AMERICAN INDIAN PERFORMERS IN THE WILD WEST

From the beginning of Cody's career, his relationship with American Indians defined and authenticated his public role. Audiences were interested in his sharpshooting abilities and prowess as a buffalo hunter, but as the mediocre showing of some of his earlier competitors like Jack Crawford and Doc Carver suggests, demonstrations of skill and displays of animals were not enough to elicit the passionate sense of national identification that Cody achieved. He became part of a story of struggle and conquest on the American frontier that stretched from the novels of James Fenimore Cooper through the histories of Theodore Roosevelt to the film Westerns of the twentieth century. This drama evoked the oldest epic formula, the struggle of a hero against the forces of evil. In his triumph over danger, such a hero affirmed for the spectators, who associated his plight with their own hopes and fears, their own power and goodness. In its crude form as dime novel or melodrama, and in its more sophisticated form in the animated outdoor drama, this Wild West story reached for the power of myth. And to attain this mythic level, it required an enemy, a counter-force against which the hero displayed his virtues. American Indians were consistently cast in this role.

At the same time, the audiences who came to the Wild West were impressed by the very presence of American Indians in it. Seeing them parade through town, visiting their encampments, watching their skillful riding, and thrilling to their colorful costumes, spectators ranging from young children to writers, painters, and photographers responded excitedly to these simultaneously exotic and accessible people. The Wild West's great achievement—giving audiences excitement and adventure in a safe, secure context—was made possible largely through the contribution of the American Indian performers.

To consider the ways the American Indians were represented by Cody and his handlers and how they were received by the audiences is to tell only part of the story, however. At the end of the twentieth century, we are drawn to the irony—if not tragedy—of the dilemma of those American Indian performers enacting a drama in which their fictional demonization had profound implications for their own lives and the future of their people. Stage actors can walk away from the parts they play, but the Wild West confounded distinctions between "reality" and "representation," and just as Cody was considered a "real" hero because of his dramatic enactments, the American Indians in his company were identified with the villainous roles they played in the show. When the Wild West traveled, its American Indian performers were encouraged to walk about the streets in costumes. In a Venetian gondola or a New York opera house, these men and women in blankets and feathers were a walking advertisement for the show, and the fact that they appeared the same whether on- or offstage seemed to endorse the Wild West's claims to authenticity and its view of history.

But what of the performers' own interpretations? How can we move closer to their point of view? To assess Cody's understanding of himself is difficult enough, and requires careful reading of texts and images whose meaning is rarely straightforward or unmediated. The American Indian performers left texts and images, too—contracts, letters, autobiographies, interviews with reporters, drawings and photographs of themselves—but these records are problematic. Autobiographical narratives were sometimes written for a predominantly white audience, like Luther Standing Bear's *My People the Sioux*, or told after the fact to a white interpreter, like *Black Elk Speaks* ("as told through John G. Neihardt"), or largely fabricated, like *The Memoirs of Chief Red Fox*. Photographs were inflected by the commercial, publicity, and artistic imperatives of the photographers. Artifacts such as costumes, tepees, and weapons might have one meaning to their possessor and another to those who viewed and displayed them. Yet, the complexity and mediated nature of these sources should not prevent us from trying to understand them.

PERFORMING INDIANS

Who were the American Indians who cooperated with Cody, and how might they have understood their situation? In his own time and since, Cody was criticized by people who found his exhibition of American Indians exploitative and demeaning. In 1914, a Sioux spokesman named Chauncey Yellow Robe protested against what he called the "evil and degrading influence of commercializing the Indian before the world" in Wild West shows.[1] Writers of our day, looking for the origins of stereotypical views of American Indians in the Western film, have also criticized Cody.[2] Turning the dramatic medium against one of its greatest practitioners, Arthur Kopit's play *Indians* (1969) and the Robert Altman film elaborating on it, *Buffalo Bill and the Indians, or Sitting Bull's History Lesson* (1976), portrayed Cody as a shallow, drunken exploiter of the Native Americans whose culture he was helping to eradicate. And yet, many American Indian performers spoke positively of their experiences with Buffalo Bill's Wild West, and they voted with their feet as well, signing up for performance tours year after year.

The Native American historian Vine Deloria has suggested that the performing Indians had much to gain from participating in shows such as Cody's. As he points out, American Indians in Buffalo Bill's Wild West performed many roles, of which stage villain was only one: they also displayed skills that reflected positively on Plains Indian culture, such as horsemanship, and their dances, songs, and games gave audiences a more nuanced sense of Indian life. Work with the Wild West offered reasonable pay, a chance to travel, and an opportunity to interact with a large variety of non-Indian people. For some, work in the Wild West was, literally, an alternative to imprisonment, for Cody's reputation as an Indian fighter allowed him to get permission to employ individuals who were widely viewed as dangerous. "Many Indian agents and Army officers would have preferred to see these characters in the stockade," Deloria comments. "Touring with Buffalo Bill probably saved some of the chiefs from undue pressure and persecution by the government at home." Furthermore, Cody's performers were treated with dignity offstage, and few restrictions were placed on their movements. The Indian performers were thus able to encounter other aspects of America—and the wider world—than those represented by the military and missionary forces they encountered on their reservations. "The freedom these Indians experienced with Buffalo Bill, and the chance to learn about the rest of the world, held sufficient appeal to lure many of the chiefs away from the reservation," Deloria says, adding that "as a transitional educational device wherein Indians were able to observe American society and draw their own conclusions, the Wild West was worth more than every school built by the government on any of the reservations."[3]

Our ability to understand in detail the perspective of the American Indian performers in the Wild West has been greatly aided by the historian L. G. Moses's carefully researched study *Wild West Shows and the Images of American Indians* (1996). Using documents from the files of the Commissioner of Indian Affairs as well as reservation and agency records, Moses demarcated a group of American Indians who identified themselves and were identified by others as "show Indians." Cody was their most famous employer, and his dealings with them set the pattern for others. Moses, diligent and creative in searching for evidence of the Indian performers' own attitudes toward their work, offers an intriguing perspective on the criticism Cody and other Wild West entrepreneurs attracted in his own day and since.

As Moses points out, many turn-of-the-century critics who attacked the Wild West performances for degrading their American Indian participants were firmly committed to assimilation as the solution to the Indian "problem." The Dawes Act of 1887 which offered citizenship to American Indians at the cost of radical changes in their culture, mandated the dissolution of their traditional forms of land ownership and undermined their systems of tribal governance. Groups that cared about the Indians' welfare were often spearheaded by missionaries who pushed for their Christianization as the price for their obtaining political rights. Institutions such as the Carlisle Indian Industrial School in Pennsylvania had long tried to "Americanize" natives by removing children from their families before teaching them trades, deportment, and the English language, trying to transform their customs, religious practices, forms of dress, and points of view in order to erase difference. When Chauncey Yellow Robe said the Wild West shows were degrading, he specifically criticized their *encouragement* of native traditions. "The white man is persistently perpetuating the tribal habits and customs," he observed, protesting that Wild West shows teach audiences "that the Indian is only a savage being."[4] Advocates of assimilation disliked the Wild West performances because their images of American Indians were ones they considered "savage" and inferior. Yet, Moses argues, the performances actually helped to preserve traditional native culture, even while acquiescing in its transformation into a popularization—even parody—of itself. Other commentators have warned against too easy a celebration of this theme, yet Moses has helped enormously to expand the debate about the meaning of performance by American Indians during Cody's heyday.[5]

Of course, the meaning of American Indian performance changed enormously in the forty-five years from Cody's first ventures in plains showmanship in the early 1870s to his death in 1917. Rapid settlement of the West, accelerating pressure on American Indian lands, the disappearance of the buffalo, and the last, overpowering push to defeat native military resistance and enforce reservation boundaries all profoundly transformed Indian life. Whether for performers or audiences, dramatized scenes of warfare had quite a different meaning when they were a counterpoint to death and dying on the battlefield (before 1890) and when they evoked a fictionalized memory (by the turn of the century).

BEFORE THE WILD WEST: INDIAN ALLIES

Cody's first attempt to stage a live American Indian performance occurred during his scouting years, when he negotiated the cooperation of a group of Brulé Sioux under Spotted Tail to ride on the 1872 hunt with Grand Duke Alexis and to entertain the visitors with songs and dances around the campfire. Just as Cody's own performance as a guide blurred the boundaries between fact and fiction, the Sioux performance replicated actual practices while showing spectators something they already anticipated. A report on the grand duke's hunting party in *Frank Leslie's* magazine mentioned "Indian festivities" in a way that suggested that readers would already have an image in their minds: the grand duke had "shaken hands with partially-tamed Indian warriors and smoked the pipe of friendship in ancient style. . . . The red men have appeared in a grand pow-wow and war-dance, and indulged in arrow-practice for his particular benefit."[6] It is clear that by 1872 Cody was beginning to see how he could profit by staging versions of his own scouting exploits, but why should Native American leaders have wanted to participate?

By the late 1860s, Spotted Tail was one of a group of Sioux leaders along the North and South Platte Rivers who were seeking accommodation with the United States government. In 1870, a new agency was established for his band in the White River area, and Spotted Tail used all his diplomatic skills to negotiate better terms for his people and to contain the impatience of resistance leaders like Crazy Horse. (After the Battle of the Little Big Horn in 1876, he was marked as the Sioux leader with whom the white government preferred to negotiate. In 1877, he carried messages to Crazy Horse from

General George Crook that helped to convince the independence leader to surrender.) Assisting with the buffalo hunt for the grand duke in 1872, a project important to the powerful General Sheridan, made sense as a part of his larger strategy, by which Spotted Tail hoped to avoid further loss of lives and land for his people.

A few months after the grand duke's hunt, Cody began his stage career, and he continued to seek performers among American Indians who, like Spotted Tail, had a pattern of cooperation with U.S. military forces. These included chiefs and leaders who saw the American army as one more player in the shifting political and military situation on the plains, and who hoped to gain advantage over traditional rivals through their alliances with powerful outsiders.

Tribal politics had affected relationships between Europeans and native peoples since the seventeenth century. Through trading relationships and military agreements, native peoples had struggled to retain territory and power, and different groups had formed alliances with French, Spanish, English, and later American interests as they battled with other tribes and bands. Narragansetts had allied with English settlers in their struggle against the Pequots in 1637; the Iroquois League, for the most part, supported the English in their wars with the French. Choctaws and Cherokees aided Andrew Jackson during the War of 1812; and Creeks helped the U.S. government in the Second Seminole War of 1835–42. When white settlers pushed into Indian lands in Texas and the Southwest, the Great Plains, California, and the Northwest, Indian tribes could be found on both sides of the resulting conflicts, as native leaders sought to capitalize on the weaknesses of their traditional enemies. After the Civil War, the rapid transformation of the Great Plains put pressure on all the Indian peoples, competing with each other as with white settlers for land and food; intertribal warfare continued to be a major preoccupation of many leaders.[7] The army units Cody served had a long history of working with Indian allies, and they gave him contacts he could draw on.

Cody's early frontier dramas employed both real and fake Indians. Advertisements for *The Scouts of the Prairie*, in 1872, promised "genuine red men of the woods," and the playbill showed "Pawnee and Indian Chiefs" played by "Grassy Chief," "Prairie Dog," "Water Chief," "Big Elk," "Great River," and "Seven Stars," but Cody wrote in his autobiography that the production had employed " 'supers' dressed as Indians."[8] When he first staged *The Red Right Hand; Or, Buffalo Bill's First Scalp for Custer* during 1876–77, the program made no pretense about the fact that the Indian roles were played by non-native actors. However, the following season, Cody hired performers from the Red Cloud Agency for *May Cody; Or, Lost and Won*; according to his biographer Don Russell, this was the first time he used reservation Indians in his show.[9] The American Indians who joined him may have had a good reason, since the Red Cloud Agency was just in the process of being relocated: in the fall of 1877, followers of Red Cloud were evicted from their former lands in Nebraska and forced to move to the Pine Ridge Agency inside the Sioux reservation. Cody's recruitment coincided with a period of change and dislocation among Plains Indian communities that may have made such ventures into the outside world more attractive for reservation dwellers.

Among the Sioux on Cody's 1877–78 tour was Two Bears, a Lakota leader experienced in crossings between native communities and the white world. In 1865 he had allied with the U.S. Army to repel Indian raids on Fort Rice, on the upper Missouri River. Three years later, he traveled with Father De Smet on a peace mission on behalf of the Fort Laramie Treaty, visiting Hunkpapa villages and attending a ceremonial council with tribal chiefs under the banner of the Virgin Mary. Later he was to be regarded as a protégé by the Indian agent James McLaughlin at the Standing Rock Agency, where he deployed his forces in support of the land cession treaty of 1889.[10]

Touring with Cody may have seemed to Two Bears an extension of his own plains career as a government ally. Certainly he helped to create the prototype of the show Indian and was complicit in the pretense of bringing the dangerous life of the frontier to the safe confines of the stage. The playbill for *May Cody* reassured audiences that Two Bears cooperated with whites: "This Sioux chief, who accompanies the Combination, will be found very social, and an attentive listener to any and all who wish to communicate with him." He was an exotic specimen, but he was also a "good Indian": "He was one of the first to accept the conditions offered by the Great Father at Washington in the late conference, and anxiously hopes a reconciliation will be made with 'Sitting Bull' and all the hostile tribes now at war." In the turn that so infuriated Indian reformers, the program assured viewers that despite his sociability and cooperation, Two Bears represented a people who were and always would be defined by their "savage" ways. "Every effort has been exhausted to lift the American aborigine or red man into a higher condition, and to encourage him to assume the privileges and responsibilities of full citizenship, but in vain. His Maker evidently never intended him to become a citizen anywhere."[11] Despite this demeaning and patronizing tone, the terms of Two Bears's employment in Cody's entertainment spectacle were not so different from what he and other Indian allies expected in their dealings with government agents and army officers: compliance brought income and privileges but never erased the presumption of cultural difference. From Two Bears's point of view, acting in the "Echo Canyon" camping scene in *May Cody* was perhaps no less strange than following Father De Smet and his banner of the Virgin Mary into a Hunkpapa village where eighty tribesmen and a missionary smoked a peace pipe in front of an audience of five hundred tribesmen.[12]

The year after Two Bears's tour, Cody took a step toward more systematic employment of American Indian performers. For the 1878–79 season, he engaged a band of Pawnee to tour with *May Cody* and *The Knights of the Plains*. The Pawnee, who had agreed in 1859 to accept reservation status in central Nebraska and had provided scouts for the army since 1864, had such a strong reputation as scouts and fighters that the intertribal sign-language term for *scout, wolf,* and *Pawnee* was the same, two fingers held up near the head to suggest wolf ears.[13] Pawnee had helped to protect workers building the Union Pacific lines during the time that Cody had hunted buffalo for the railroad, and Cody had also served with Pawnee scouts in the Fifth Cavalry. He even obtained one of his most famous horses in a trade with a Pawnee scout under General Carr's command in 1869: Buckskin Joe, Cody's mount during military operations and celebrity hunts, briefly loaned to Grand Duke Alexis to ensure that the Russian nobleman would have experienced help in getting close to buffalo herds. Since Major Frank North, the trusted commander of the Pawnee scouts since 1864, had gone into a cattle-ranching partnership with Cody in 1877, it is likely that North helped facilitate Cody's contacts with the Pawnee in 1878. By that time the Pawnee had agreed to move away from their lands in Nebraska, and times were hard for them. Needing work, accustomed to working with whites in the army, on hunting trips, even on the baseball field, they welcomed the kind of opportunity Cody offered.

Cody had a lot to learn about dealing with the federal bureaucracy that oversaw Indian affairs, however. The theatrical season had barely begun when he learned that government officials had criticized his hiring Indians. As he paternalistically put it in his autobiography, "my Indians were to be seized by the Government and sent back to their agency." Cody contacted the Secretary of the Interior, Carl Schurz, who told him that as wards of the government Indians were not allowed off their reservations. Cody's autobiography archly invoked his experience as an Indian fighter: "I told the Commissioner [of Indian Affairs] that the Indians were frequently off of their reservations out west, as I had a distinct remembrance of meeting them upon several occasions 'on the war path.' " Then, according to his account, he set forth the argument he would continue to use throughout his career: "I thought I was benefitting the Indians as well as the government, by taking them all over the United States, and giving them a correct idea of the customs, life, etc., of the pale faces, so that when they returned to their people they could make known all they had seen."[14] The argument prevailed, and Cody was allowed to continue his tour, with the proviso that he give bonds for the Indians' safe return at the season's end. This arrangement, in which the employer had to contract with the Indian agency as well as the performers, shaped Cody's business practices when he began to organize the outdoor Wild West exhibitions.

WILD INDIANS IN THE WILD WEST: THE CASE OF SITTING BULL

When Cody presented his first Wild West season in partnership with Doc Carver, he was already experienced in hiring show Indians and had very clear ideas about who should participate in the show and under what terms. During the spring of 1883 he sent Carver instructions and urged him to meet with his ranching partner, Frank North, indicating in his exuberant—if also racially reductive and patronizing—way the significance of North's cooperation as a conduit to the Pawnee and other Indians with scouting experience:

> I hope this will find you and my old true and tried Pard North
> together and happy and that you will have heep big talk with
> him. I have written him about getting us a heap of Indians but
> I think about sixty Indians will be enough and if North will go
> after them he can get a few Cheyennes to mix in with the
> Pawnees, about thirty bucks or forty the balance women &
> children. Talk it over with North. I go a heap on North's *savva.*
> If North will go with us we can afford to give him a big salary.
> He can handle Indians better than any man living.[15]

Cody planned to rely on North to organize and discipline the performers, and he envisioned a larger group, including women and children as well as warriors, than he had yet assembled.

North did "go with" Cody, and his cooperation contributed largely to the success of the Wild West's opening season. Despite a few mishaps, the pattern for the show began to fall into place. In an early rehearsal of the Deadwood stagecoach act, disaster was narrowly avoided when the mules drawing the stagecoach bolted out of control. Then the Indians chasing it became so enthusiastic that they forgot to exit when Buffalo Bill and his men appeared. After this confusion, North was said to have advised Cody to abandon the idea of using real Pawnee in his act. "Bill, if you want to make this d——show go, you do not need me or my Indians," he is said to have commented. "You want about twenty old bucks. Fix them up with all the paint and feathers on the market. Use some old hack horses and a hack driver. To make it go you want a show of illusion not realism."[16] But Cody had worked with actors dressed as Indians, and he had also tried a less systematic way of recruiting his cast. By 1883 he knew that the Indians were essential for his show, and he had faith that, with the help of good intermediaries, he could work with the skilled riders and huntsmen he had known as army scouts.

Perhaps it was Cody's experience with Two Bears in 1877–78 that convinced him that the Wild West would be enriched by an Indian celebrity whom the public could recognize as a significant figure in his own right. Since the first Wild West season, he had been interested in recruiting the Sioux chief Sitting Bull, well known to the general public, although perhaps erroneously, as a major figure in the Battle of the Little Big Horn. In imagining Sitting Bull as a show Indian, however, Cody made a major break from his practice of hiring Indians who were already committed to cooperation and conciliation. That Cody would want Sitting Bull—and that the Sioux resistance leader would agree to work with him—signaled a watershed in the history of the Plains Indians and in the development of Wild West show business.

In February 1883, Cody wrote to Carver, "I am going to try hard to get old 'Sitting Bull' have written to Teller Secretary of the Interior if we can manage to get him, our ever lasting fortune is made."[17] But the request was premature, since Sitting Bull had only recently surrendered to army custody and was still a closely guarded prisoner. The persistent showman tried again in the spring of 1885. The Secretary of the Interior initially rejected this request, writing "Make a *very* emphatic No" on Cody's telegram. But Cody reassured the government that he had experience in "the management and care of Indians," mobilized letters of endorsement from General Sherman and Colonel Eugene A. Carr as well as his highly placed military supporters Philip Sheridan, Nelson Miles, George Crook, and Alfred Terry.[18] Eventually the Secretary assented, and Sitting Bull joined the Wild West in June 1885.

Sitting Bull was the most prominent American Indian leader to appear in Buffalo Bill's Wild West, and his tour with Cody has often been cited as an example of how performing Indians were subjected to patronization, distortion, even humiliation. In Robert Altman's film, Buffalo Bill, played by Paul Newman, treats Sitting Bull as an infuriating nuisance. In Arthur Kopit's play *Indians*, Sitting Bull responds to Cody's claim that they were friends by remarking coldly, "I never killed you . . . because I *knew it would not matter*"[19] But in fact, contact between the two men was valued by and important for both of them.

By 1885, Sitting Bull had witnessed a decade of devastating defeat for the Sioux nation. After the Battle of the Little Big Horn, the American army had poured resources and furious resolve into the Indian wars. Within a year of Custer's death, the Sioux were reeling from a powerful military attack and a damaging land grab that sent floods of miners and settlers into the Black Hills. In May 1877, the powerful resistance leader Crazy Horse gave himself up to military custody; he was killed in a scuffle within four months. Sitting Bull, hoping to avoid a similar fate, led a band of nearly a thousand people into exile in Canada, where they stayed for almost four years. But the defection of many of his followers, and the failure of the rest to support themselves by hunting the rapidly diminishing northern herd of buffalo, eventually induced Sitting Bull to return to the United States and surrender to military control. Although he continued to request the right to ride and hunt freely, after he surrendered his rifle on July 20, 1881, Sitting Bull was dramatically reminded that he was now subject to American government domination, first isolated as a prisoner of war at Fort Randall, and then placed under strict regulation at the Standing Rock Agency. At Standing Rock he had to farm an allotment of land, abandon the traditional tepee for a log cabin, submit to the discipline of agency-regulated courts and police force, and report to Indian agent James McLaughlin, who regarded him as a "nonprogressive" troublemaker.[20]

Although he had tried every method he could think of to prevent the destruction of traditional Sioux culture, Sitting Bull had not shunned contact with whites. In Canada, he had worked closely with an officer in the North-West Mounted Police, Major James M. Walsh, in a relationship of "mutual trust and respect and finally true friendship."[21] Walsh attended council meetings, mediated the Indians' disputes with American army representatives, and arranged Sitting Bull's first meetings with journalists. Walsh tried to make himself the center of the Canadian government's relations with Sitting Bull and was removed from his post, but he retained the Sioux leader's respect, and Sitting Bull traveled two hundred miles in an attempt to meet him before finally agreeing to return to the United States. Two other white men likewise established good relations with Sitting Bull in Canada. Gus Hedderich, who ran a trading post, commiserated with Sitting Bull over his people's poverty and taught him to write his name in English. And the French-Canadian Jean Louis Légaré, who spent a good deal of his own money getting provisions to Sitting Bull's starving band, helped to transport them across the border to their final, peaceful surrender to American forces.[22]

Back in the United States, even while a prisoner of the army, Sitting Bull was treated with a strange mixture of contempt and adulation. In 1881, after remaining for a few days at Fort Buford, the site of his surrender, Sitting Bull and his family were taken first to Fort Yates, at the Standing Rock Agency, and then to Fort Randall, where he would be held as a prisoner for nineteen months. But his travels resembled a celebrity tour as much as a military trans-fer. Within a month, he sat for a formal photograph. In Bismarck, less than

Sitting Bull,
photograph by
Orland Scott Goff,
August 1881

two weeks after his surrender, Sitting Bull was invited to ride in a railroad car (which he declined) and treated to a reception and dinner at a hotel; the souvenir bill of fare he was given describes a succession of courses culminating in an ice-cream dessert. It was Sitting Bull's first visit to a city as well as his first experience of many aspects of white culture. He told visiting journalists he was curious about the sights he was seeing and asked how ice cream could be made so cold in the middle of summer. Even while observers were judging and evaluating his clothing, his speech, and his attitude, he was attentively studying American habits and institutions.[23] And he was also discovering he could sell his autograph as well as his pipes and other possessions. Commercial exchange and mutual cultural tourism thus marked his post-surrender relationship with the non-Sioux world.

During his imprisonment at Fort Randall, Sitting Bull continued to develop contacts with the white world and to explore issues of representation and self-representation. A German artist and journalist, Rudolph Cronau, who visited in October 1881 to interview him and paint his portrait, recalled that Sitting Bull and his family showed great interest in his paintings. Two months later, a missionary arrived for a visit with copies of pictographs that Sitting Bull had made years before. Asked to explain their meaning, Sitting Bull showed that he was well aware of the effect of his self-representations on a white audience: he declined to explicate the pictures of battles with American soldiers. He had already learned the importance of exerting whatever control he could over his self-representation. When, in 1882, Sitting Bull prepared at least three compilations of autobiographical pictographs, now aimed at a white audience, he omitted scenes of military struggle with the U.S. Army and incorporated some of the techniques he had observed in Cronau's works.[24]

After his return to the Standing Rock Agency, Sitting Bull participated in further events where he was on display as a celebrity. In the fall of 1883, he helped lay the cornerstone of the capitol building in Bismarck, the newly designated capital of Dakota Territory. He marched in a parade, carrying a United States flag, sat on the speaker's platform, and signed autographs. In March 1884, he spent two weeks being honored in St. Paul, Minnesota, and surveying aspects of white culture there—a newspaper printing press, a wholesale-grocery house, clothing factories (including a shoe factory that produced a custom-fitted pair of shoes for him), bank, post office, and school. At the fire department, Sitting Bull pushed the button that set off an electric alarm signaling firemen to slide down the pole, fit up their hoses, and speed away. According to his biographer, Sitting Bull sought out these opportunities and "welcomed excursions to the outside world, both to relieve the tedium of the reservation and to earn money."[25]

Several months after the trip to St. Paul, Sitting Bull agreed to go on an exhibition tour organized by the proprietor of the hotel he had visited there, Alvaren Allen. Allen had enlisted McLaughlin's support; McLaughlin, though he regarded Sitting Bull as an "old fool," thought that travel was making him more tractable, and he seized on the opportunity to send his protégés and relatives on what he hoped would be a lucrative venture.[26] The Sitting Bull Combination was exhibited at a wax museum in New York, where it drew large crowds, then moved on to other Eastern cities. Luther Standing Bear, a young Lakota attending the Carlisle Indian School, saw it in Philadelphia, and remembered that the translators had shamelessly misrepresented a speech of Sitting Bull's about peace and education, claiming that he had been describing the Battle of the Little Big Horn.[27]

When John Burke went to Standing Rock in June 1885 to negotiate the terms for Sitting Bull's appearances with Buffalo Bill's Wild West, both Cody and the Sioux chief knew something about what they wanted from their partnership. Cody wanted the attention Sitting Bull's presence would attract to his show; he did not require him to act in the melodramatic chase and rescue scenes or to display any skills. Merely riding in the parade and appearing on the show grounds was enough. Sitting Bull also knew what he wanted, and negotiated a contract that specified a salary of fifty dollars a week, with two weeks' pay in advance and a bonus of $125; he would be accompanied by five men at twenty-five dollars a month and three women at fifteen dollars a month, plus his own chosen interpreter, William Halsey, who would be paid sixty dollars; transportation to and from the show was to be included in the package.[28] He would also retain the right to sell his own photographs and autographs. According to Moses, the salaries compared favorably with those paid to agency employees at Pine Ridge. Within only four months, Sitting Bull would earn nearly half the annual salary of an Indian agent and two-thirds the annual salary of an agency physician.[29] And after the disastrous experience with the treacherous translators in the Sitting Bull Combination, having an interpreter he trusted meant that he could control the tone and content of his public statements.

The summer season of 1885 appeared to fulfill the expectations of both Sitting Bull and the Wild West management. The former seemed pleased with the chance to travel, for the tour took him to many places he had not yet visited, as well as to Canada, where he hoped to make contact with Major Walsh, whom he still remembered in a friendly fashion. His Wild West contacts also helped him in his efforts to evade the supervision of McLaughlin and communicate directly with American government policymakers, for Cody arranged an interview for him with President Grover Cleveland in Washington, and Nate Salsbury helped him prepare a letter to the Commissioner of Indian Affairs listing a number of grievances and requesting a hearing.[30] In his many press interviews, speaking through Halsey, he expressed peaceful and cooperative sentiments. "I want to travel and see all I can," he was reported as saying. When asked about the Custer battle, he responded in a proud but conciliatory fashion: "That is of another day. I fought for my people. My people said I was right. I will answer for the dead of my people; let the pale faces do the same on their side." In other interviews he declined to criticize the Indian agency's policy of turning the hunting tribes to agriculture: "Being asked what the Indians would do now that the buffalo were all gone, he said they must take to farming and this, he was sure, they would do." He even endorsed the idea of sending Indian children to government schools: "When I came away I didn't want my children to go to school. But now I want them to be educated like the white children are." Yet he lost no opportunity to assert that the American government had a responsibility to live up to its obligations (and by implication, to remind white audiences that it had broken many former treaties): "All he asked for was that the government should keep its promises to his people, and that they should receive what was their just due."[31] Sitting Bull's biographer Robert M. Utley has argued that his exposure to the white press helped to change the American public's simplistic, demonized view of American Indians in general and Sitting Bull in particular. If so, the Buffalo Bill tour offered many opportunities to advance this process.

In his interviews, Sitting Bull also spoke positively about Cody—"Long Hair," as he sometimes referred to him—and his troupe, and there is some evidence that these expressions of friendship were more than simply diplomatic rhetoric. He showed special warmth toward two company members, Annie Oakley and Nate Salsbury. (Burke had reported that a photograph of Annie Oakley helped convince Sitting Bull to sign the contract in the first place.) The Sioux chief had seen Oakley in a show in St. Paul, and had exchanged gifts and photographs with her. He gave her a Sioux name, "Watanya Cecilla," or "Little Sure Shot," and said she should consider herself his adopted daughter. Oakley's husband and manager, Frank Butler, saw the publicity potential in this association, and took out an ad in the *New York Clipper* announcing that Sitting Bull had made friends with "the premier shots, Butler and Oakley."[32] Sitting Bull also "adopted" Nate Salsbury, in a

ceremony in Boston at the end of July. Although the white press, and perhaps
Salsbury and Annie Oakley themselves, were bemused and slightly condescending about these "adoptions," the language of kinship was an important
part of Sioux culture, and we can conclude that for Sitting Bull they were
gestures of affiliation.

Kinship also brought mutual responsibility, and Sitting Bull clearly welcomed the assistance of Salsbury and Cody in his dealings with government
officials. In token of mutual commitment, he exchanged gifts with Oakley,
Salsbury, and Cody. Butler's advertisement stated that Sitting Bull had given
Annie Oakley "a large feather taken from the head of a Crow chief," as well
the pair of moccasins he had worn at the Little Big Horn, though this is
unlikely, since all of Sitting Bull's band were tattered and threadbare when
they returned from Canada in 1881. The moccasins and bow and quiver he
gave Nate Salsbury can still be seen in the Western History Collection at Yale
University. When Sitting Bull returned to Standing Rock, Cody gave him a
hat and the gray horse he had ridden in the show, both of which the Sioux
leader kept until his death. Of course, Sitting Bull would never have chosen
performance with the Wild West over the traditional hunting life of the
Great Plains. But in the tragic context of the disruption of that way of life and
the constraints of his situation as a distrusted prisoner of the American government, it seems to have offered him both a degree of freedom from sur-
veillance and general recognition as a representative of his people. The work
as a show Indian was reasonably interesting and remunerative, and was certainly no stranger or more degrading than life at Standing Rock. His words,
deeds, and exchanges of goods indicate that he found Cody and his associates
worthy of some degree of alliance.

Cody needed Sitting Bull even more than the chief needed him. In the
summer of 1885, it must be remembered, the Wild West was fighting for its
survival in the embarrassing mutual lawsuits with Doc Carver. Within a
month of securing Sitting Bull's participation, Cody was spending time in
lawyers' offices giving depositions. He had to post twenty-six thousand dollars
in bonds in mid-July to keep his show from being attached in response to
Carver's suit for libel and malicious arrest.[33] The dispute ruined Carver, but
Cody was able to keep afloat because he could raise the cash and ride out the
legal proceedings. Signing Sitting Bull gave Cody an edge in the battle for
public attention, too. In at least one courtroom appearance he was accompanied by William Halsey, as if to reinforce his own claims to authenticity. In
contrast to the disastrous winter season of 1884–85, which had culminated in
the rains of New Orleans, the summer season of 1885 played to a million
viewers and earned one hundred thousand dollars.[34] Sitting Bull's presence

was clearly a factor in turning Cody's fortunes around and attracting enough customers to survive Carver's challenge.

Burke and Salsbury did their best to arouse spectator interest in Sitting Bull. They had the delicate task of presenting him as a serious warrior without frightening their audience. In their portrayal of Sitting Bull they enacted the basic promise of the Wild West: that it was a spectacle wild enough to give viewers a thrill, yet safe enough to qualify as mass entertainment. But as they moved to incorporate more "authentic" Indian performers, they began to shift the tone away from the more lurid dime-novel themes. Whereas a broadside for Cody and Carver's show in 1883 had advertised Buffalo Bill as "the terror of the red men," a similar announcement for the 1885 season quoted a milder description from General Carr, "He is King of them all," and announced the participation of "The Renowned Sioux Chief, Sitting Bull, and Staff."[35] Although the 1885 program still had a full-page illustration of Cody's scalping of Yellow Hand, it also included a long article on Indian religion excerpted from Richard Dodge's *Our Wild Indians* of 1882, a sort of proto-ethnography, trying to explicate the religious beliefs of "the Indian," and concluding, "a Homer might find many an Indian hero as worthy of immortal fame as Achilles." The booklet also featured a piece on John Nelson, a guide and trapper who had married an Oglala woman. Nelson had first appeared as the interpreter for Two Bears in 1877–78, and in 1885 he was cited as an example of the lure of the Plains Indian way of life: "It is hard to realize that hundreds of our own race and blood, very often intelligent and even accomplished men, gladly exchange all the comforts and advantages of our mode of life for the privations and danger, relieved by the freedom and fascinations of the nomads of the Plains." Nelson, his Indian wife, and their six children were all part of the Wild West exhibition in 1885, yet another point of contact between white and Indian cultures, helping audiences to feel comfortable with the Sioux chief and his entourage.[36]

In 1885, Cody and his managers found new ways to stir public interest in their American Indian performers. In Boston, they staged a Western-style banquet for a dozen newspapermen, who duly reported the event in long, enthusiastic articles. An ox was roasted "in true frontier fashion" over a fire, and visitors sat on the ground, eating with a sharpened stick and a tin plate. After the meal, Sitting Bull answered questions. The barbecue was a success, and similar events were scheduled in other cities. Reporters took all this as proof of the authenticity of the Wild West experience and, flattered by their access to Cody and Sitting Bull, wrote enthusiastic stories designed to arouse public interest in the show.[37]

The tour of 1885 was a remarkable juxtaposition of two self-described antagonists who benefited from their association. Sitting Bull's participation in Buffalo Bill's Wild West offered a complex web of meanings for white spectators, ratifying their sense of superiority and triumph in the wars against the Plains Indians, but at the same time transmuting that life-and-death struggle into the realm of harmless entertainment and transforming old enemies into providers of pleasure and excitement. A remarkable series of photographs taken during the tour in Montreal by the photographer William Notman shows these meanings, and the images were deeply significant for both Sitting Bull and Cody in following years.

Eight different pictures show Cody and Sitting Bull standing before a painted backdrop in Notman's studio. Both are elaborately dressed, Cody in thigh-high boots, a wide-buckled belt, an embroidered shirt, and a broad-brimmed hat, all of which he wore in other souvenir photographs produced around this time. Cody the consummate showman was clearly experienced at this. Sitting Bull's elaborate clothing also seems to be a costume he is wearing for the occasion. We know from the accounts of reporters who interviewed him that his ordinary dress was more hybrid and Europeanized. "Over a figured calico shirt he wears a waistcoat of plush brocade," wrote one Montreal reporter, "and his trousers are of blue broadcloth, with a wide welt standing out from the outer seams, bordered with fancy braid and dotted with brass buttons. His feet are remarkably small and well formed thrust in moccasins with india rubber soles." Another reporter commented that "he usually dresses in a print shirt, black pants and beaded slippers. He wears a red or loud necktie, massive rings and sleeve links."[38] In the Notman photograph, rings are visible on his hands and his trousers hang like broadcloth, but the fringed jacket, floor-length headdress, and beaded bag slung on a band across his chest are his stage clothing. He is an actor every bit as much as Cody.

In the photographs, the renowned Sioux leader and the struggling showman seem to meet as well-matched equals. The two figures divide the picture plane, separated by the vertical line of a rifle, barrel pointed upward, between them. In one pose, the two men look directly at each other across the gun; in another, they shake hands; and in a third pose Buffalo Bill stands slightly behind Sitting Bull, gazing with him off to the right.[39] But the most widely distributed one, sometimes captioned "Enemies in '76, Friends in '85," places them in a pose that speaks volumes. Here the balance of power seems to tip toward Cody. Sitting Bull stands in three-quarters profile, his face impassive and his eyes in shadow as he looks off to the right, with one hand hidden in the fringes of his jacket and the other grasping the rifle

Buffalo Bill and Sitting Bull, photograph by W. Notman, 1885

lightly on the barrel. Cody stands more frontally, one hand resting at the top of the rifle barrel hovering a finger's-breadth above Sitting Bull's, the other pointing toward the right of the picture as if directing the Sioux chief's gaze. Cody's face, below the broad-brimmed hat, is flooded with light, and his eyes are wide open, his gaze attentive and firm. While the photograph shows both

Sitting Bull, photograph
by W. Notman, 1885

Sitting Bull, oil painting
by Catherine Weldon, 1890

men in a dignified light, Cody seems active and masterful, pointing the way
to the acquiescent warrior. "Enemies in '76" reminds viewers that Sitting
Bull was widely regarded as a dangerous and powerful opponent. "Friends in
'85" suggests that Wild West viewers need have no fear of him. But the
"friendship" offered in this photograph—and in Wild West performances—
honored American Indian dignity only at the expense of surrender to white
dominance and control.

Notman also produced several individual portraits of Sitting Bull. One,
depicting the Sioux chief in the same costume in front of the same backdrop,
shows him grasping the now-upraised rifle in both hands. Although his
expression is still impassive, perhaps detached and resistant, its solemnity
may have represented an assertion of dignity and power for Sitting Bull, who
deeply resented the lack of respect with which he was treated by government
and military leaders and Indian agents. While it is hard to know whether he
could control the poses he assumed in the Notman portraits, he did later put
the photograph to uses of his own. In 1890, Sitting Bull became friendly with
a Brooklyn widow and educator named Catherine Weldon, who moved into
his home with her young son and supported him financially. She served as
his secretary, taught classes for the women of his household, and painted his

portrait in oil. The painting, which was found in his cabin after his death (and was damaged in the struggle in which he was killed), was said to be a favorite possession, "the pride of his vanity," according to the soldier who snatched it from the house.[40] Clearly, Weldon's painting was based on the Notman photograph, suggesting both that Sitting Bull kept a copy of the photograph and that he valued it. An image of an image, the painting suggests Sitting Bull's struggle for dignity and control in the years after his surrender.

Both Cody and Sitting Bull had reason to be pleased with the results of the 1885 season, and both wanted to repeat the experience the following year. However, Agent McLaughlin, perhaps aware that Cody had helped Sitting Bull make independent contact with government officials, had hardened in his attitude. He resented the Sioux chief's generosity on the reservation, and feared that the money he had earned on his tour was enhancing his power in the tribe. In McLaughlin's view, Sitting Bull was "a consummate liar and too vain and obstinate to be benefited by what he sees."[41]

In some ways, Sitting Bull's successful tour with Buffalo Bill became a liability. His ability to assert some control over the fruits of his celebrity (distributing his earnings according to the Sioux custom of gift-giving) and his efforts to establish independent channels of communication with government officials provoked McLaughlin to see him as a symbol of continuing, incorrigible resistance. In fact, it could be argued that Sitting Bull's fame, enhanced by his appearances with Buffalo Bill, contributed to his death five years later.

In the years after his tour with Cody, Sitting Bull continued to live at Standing Rock. He was vocal in his opposition to the land settlement of 1888, by which nine million acres were removed from the Sioux reservation and sold to settlers, and he opposed assimilation and "Americanization" for his people. "The farther my people keep away from the whites, the better I shall be satisfied," he told a missionary, Mary Collins. "I want you to teach my people to read and write but they must not become white people in their ways; it is too bad a life, I could not let them do it."[42] McLaughlin continued to consider him dishonest and treacherous, a leader of Sioux malcontents, particularly after his attempt to organize resistance to the signing of another land cession agreement in 1889. Then, when a religious craze swept into Sioux territory from Nevada in 1890, Sitting Bull alarmed McLaughlin by showing interest in learning more about its claims.

The new faith, centered around a Paiute holy man named Wovoka, represented a blend of Christian and Indian beliefs and announced that followers of the new Messiah could restore the land, the buffalo, and the Lakota way of life by observing certain rituals, including a Ghost Dance and the wearing of special clothing that would make them invulnerable to the white man's weapons. Indian agents, missionaries, and military officials all believed this was a new form of Indian resistance that presaged a return to warfare. Their determination to exterminate the Ghost Dance movement led to the bloody massacre of Sioux men, women, and children at Wounded Knee on December 29, 1890. But two weeks earlier, as part of the government's increasingly nervous response, the army sent a troop of Indian police to arrest Sitting Bull, who continued to insist that he wanted to travel to other reservations to investigate the new religious belief. In the tension of a pre-dawn raid on his cabin, pushing and shoving led to gunfire, and Sitting Bull was shot and killed, together with his son and five of his followers, as well as six Indian policemen.

Sitting Bull's association with Buffalo Bill marked him, as much as his speeches and appearances at council meetings, as a continuing focus for the white culture's understanding of Sioux resistance. Furthermore, Cody himself figured in the frenzy that had led to the order to have Sitting Bull arrested. In the winter of 1890, Cody left his show in Europe and came back to the United States to defend the treatment of the American Indians in his show against charges lodged by reformers. At this critical moment, he was eager to prove he was not just a showman who exploited his performers but a continuing player in American Indian affairs. His old friend General Nelson Miles, who was dealing with the Ghost Dance tensions from his headquarters in Chicago, sent a telegram asking Cody to meet with him. Anticipating the possibility of fighting in the Great Plains, Miles probably wanted the old scout to supply information about the terrain he knew so well. For Cody, the chance to play on the military stage came at a propitious moment, since his authority and authenticity were under attack. He may have convinced Miles he could draw on his special relationship with Sitting Bull. At any rate, the result of their conference was an order by Miles authorizing Cody "to secure the person of Sitting Bull" and directing officers in the field to give transportation and protection to his party. McLaughlin was horrified at the possible interference of someone he considered a meddler. He thought Cody was a "threat," and telegraphed the Commissioner of Indian Affairs to try to stop Cody's mission. Soldiers at Fort Yates worked to delay Cody by trying to get him drunk (working in relay shifts, they kept him drinking into the night but could not prevent him from leaving at eleven o'clock the next morning). However, McLaughlin's protests led to an order from the President of the United States rescinding Cody's instructions, and the flurry over Cody's mission probably led to the hasty deployment of the Indian police force and the fatal arrest attempt.[43]

Cody always maintained that he could have persuaded Sitting Bull to come peacefully to the agency. He had set out on his mission unarmed and with a wagon full of gifts, suggesting that he viewed the encounter not as a military event, as the trigger-happy Indian police certainly did, but as a diplomatic encounter. And there is some evidence that he might have succeeded. Even while continuing his bitter opposition to American government policies, Sitting Bull had continued to work with whites whom he trusted, including Catherine Weldon. And when the Indian police first arrived, Sitting Bull agreed to go with them. The trouble started after nervous policemen shoved and bullied him, which Cody never would have done.

There was even a surrogate representative of Buffalo Bill present at Sitting Bull's death, the gray horse Cody had given him as gift, which Sitting Bull had been insisting he must ride instead of the wagon the policemen had brought with them. Legends arose that the horse, hearing the gunfire, began to perform the tricks it had learned in the Wild West. It is unlikely that these stories are true, but their existence reinforces the close association between Cody and Sitting Bull. Cody bought the horse back, and it continued to appear in the Wild West, ridden by the standard-bearer in a parade at the White City in 1893 and later by the actor playing Custer in the dramatization of the Battle of the Little Big Horn.[44] The horse, present at Sitting Bull's death, added to the illusion that the spectators were present at Custer's death. Thus, even into the 1890s, the Wild West retained a complex connection to the life-and-death events transforming the world it portrayed.

AMERICAN INDIANS IN SHOW BUSINESS

Creating roles for "authentic" American Indians on stage and in the Wild West, Cody and his performers were improvising, experimenting, testing the waters. In the early years, in the hybrid world of entertainment spectacles, both the border scout and the Plains Indians attracted attention because of *who they were*. The content of their performance was secondary to their very presence on the stage or in the arena. But as Wild West shows proliferated during the 1880s, and as the situation on the plains changed rapidly at the same time, frontier show business became more clearly understood as fictionalized entertainment rather than news from the front lines. By the last two decades of the century, neither Cody nor the Indian performers could think of the stage performances as reflecting life on the plains. Just as Cody had traded military work for show business as his main occupation, Indian performers began to identify themselves as showmen and -women. And they found that touring as performers with the Wild West was an occupation at least as rewarding as the agency-enforced life in subsistence agriculture.

By the late 1880s, new approaches to Indian affairs had come to dominate both U.S. government agencies and increasingly vocal reform groups who wanted to improve Native Americans' material and moral conditions. Groups such as the Women's National Indian Association and the Indian Rights Association campaigned for better living standards and greater access to education and religious instruction for native peoples, with an eye to their ultimate cultural transformation and assimilation into mainstream society. Starting in 1883, these associations participated in an annual Lake Mohonk Conference of the Friends of the Indian, in New York State, their stated goals, as one historian has summarized them, being deep-seated changes in American Indian life:

> They placed their faith in the transformation of Indians from savages to citizens by three means: first, to break up tribal relations and the reservations that sustained them; . . . second, to make Indians citizens and therefore subject to and beneficiaries of the laws of the states, the territories, and the nation in which they lived; and third, to make available a government educational system designed to create self-reliance and self-sufficiency. Education would be provided for adults, if they were willing to submit, and their children regardless of either's wishes.[45]

In 1889, a new commissioner of Indian Affairs, Thomas Jefferson Morgan, an educator and Baptist minister, declared his commitment to these goals: "Indians must conform to 'the white man's ways,' peaceably if they will, forcibly if they must. . . . This civilization may not be the best possible, but it is the best the Indians can get. They cannot escape it, and must either conform to it or be crushed by it."[46]

Given this shared commitment to assimilation, both reformers and government officials viewed the Wild West with alarm and made a concerted effort to discredit Cody and other employers and to restrict American Indian participation. In the late 1880s, the Bureau of Indian Affairs engaged in a series of investigations of the entertainment enterprises that employed American Indians. Although the Secretary of the Interior, John Noble, refused to support a ban on Indian employment in Wild West shows, the Commissioner of Indian Affairs threatened retaliation for reservation dwellers who ignored his disapproval and joined the shows. The show Indians "must not look to this Office for favor or assistance," he declared.[47] In 1890, charges were leveled against Cody, stemming in part from the deaths of five Indian performers traveling abroad with the Wild West (two died from smallpox, two from heart attacks, and one from influenza). When Cody sent five more ill performers home and one died in a hospital in New York, the case was publicized by James O'Beirne, assistant superintendent of immigration in New York, who criticized the Wild West's treatment of Indian performers in newspaper interviews. John Burke, sensing trouble, sent a telegram to the Indian interpreter who had translated the complaints of the returned performers, urging him to meet another returning Indian, Chief No-Neck, and to contact a reporter at the *Illustrated News* for press coverage. The resulting stories were more favorable to Buffalo Bill.[48] But when the summer season ended, Cody, Burke, and Salsbury decided to leave the show in winter quarters in Europe and return to the United States to defend their employment practices.

On November 14, 1890, the day after their ship docked in Philadelphia, Cody, Salsbury, and Burke, together with some of their American Indian performers, arrived at the Indian Bureau in Washington to testify about working conditions in the Wild West. The commissioner, who interviewed the Indians without the employers present, found them loyal and supportive. To questions as to whether they had been starved, Rocky Bear stroked his cheek and asserted that they "eat everything; that is the reason I am getting so fat. When I come back to the reservation I am getting poor." Black Heart addressed the charges that they were coerced and mistreated. "If Indian wants to work at any place and earn money, he wants to do so; white man got privilege to do the same—any kind of work that he wants."[49] Despite intimations that the Indians had been coached and bribed, the testimony, and the publicity Burke generated, went a long way toward restoring Buffalo Bill's reputation and ensuring that he could continue to hire Indian performers for the next season.

In this battle between assimilationists and entrepreneurs, it is difficult to ascertain the point of view of the Indian performers themselves. Some complained about their treatment to reporters and government officials, while others supported their employers. But one must pay attention to the *terms* on which they discussed their relationship to the Wild West. Rocky Bear's assertion that he was well fed may be seen as playing into the stereotype of Indians as childlike wards of the nation, but Black Heart's insistence that he and his colleagues had a right to seek work of their own choosing was more militant, and he described life with the Wild West in ways that confirmed the assimilationists' fears that working as showmen helped Indians to maintain a "savage" way of life instead of embracing more "civilized" occupations. "We were raised on horseback; that is the way we had to work. These men furnished us the same work we were raised for; that is the reason we want to work for these kind of men."[50] Black Heart posed for a photograph wearing a shirt decorated with the stars and stripes of the American flag together with a war bonnet and bone hairpipe breastplate, which suggests an awareness of costume, a willingness to perform and a claim to his own form of cultural synthesis.

In a similar vein, news accounts of a meeting between the Commissioner of Indian Affairs and a group of show Indians in February 1891 quoted the latter as defending their choice to travel with the Wild West rather than staying at home and living on government rations. "Why do they object to our men seeking money, clothes and food by doing work with Buffalo Bill that we can do without an effort?" one chief was reported as saying. "Ugh! This

Black-Heart

makes me smile. Buffalo Bill does not take school-children, farmers or students for the ministry. He takes men who know how to ride and shoot, and when they come back they know much about the world, and they tell us about it."[51] The speaker makes clear his preference for being one of the "men who know how to ride and shoot," rather than one of the "school-children, farmers or students for the ministry." American Indians may have been viewed by both the Wild West management and the assimilationist reformers and government officials as the *object* of policy choices, but the resulting publicity allowed them to speak in ways that suggest how the issues appeared to them as *subjects* of their own stories.

Another way to assess the Indians' attitudes toward their work as showmen is to examine the experiences of particular performers. On the Wild West's first European tour, the Sioux Ogila-sa, or Red Shirt, became the focus of press attention. He was one of the Indians chosen to be presented to Queen Victoria, and he told her he had crossed the water to see her and "felt glad"; his words were widely quoted and the queen recorded the encounter in her diary.[52] Like other Wild West cast members, Red Shirt agreed to sit for souvenir photographs in London, posing for a formal studio portrait as well as standing with bow and arrow in front of an outdoor backdrop, a tepee erected at the head of a flight of stairs at the Wild West's camp. Like Sitting Bull before him, Red Shirt seems to have acquiesced in the presentation of a professional persona and was engaged, no less than Cody, in show business.

American Indian performers' views of their work in the Wild West can also be found in the memoirs that were published in English by Wild West veterans. Of course, since the writers were addressing English-speaking readers, they knew they were speaking to an audience outside the American Indian community. Like their predecessors who bridged cultures for military and political purposes, these writers had their own reasons for communicating with a broader American society.

Luther Standing Bear's memoir *My People the Sioux* was published in 1928, when its author was sixty years old. Born on the plains, and given the name Ota K'te, or Plenty Kill, he was the eldest son of a Lakota Chief, Standing Bear. As the Plains Indians struggled with the destruction of their hunting culture and the regimentation of reservation life, the young Ota K'te traveled to William Henry Pratt's new school in Carlisle, Pennsylvania. Returning to the plains, he became a mediator between white and Sioux cultures, serving as an influential tribal spokesman and working as a teacher, rancher, clerk, assistant minister, performer in Buffalo Bill's Wild West, and eventually actor in Hollywood films.

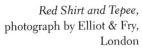

Red Shirt and Tepee,
photograph by Elliot & Fry,
London

Luther Standing Bear wrote four volumes of memoirs, joining other American Indian writers such as Charles Eastman (Ohiyesa) and Gertrude Simmons Bonnin (Zitkala-Ša) to portray native folklore and customs in a positive light for non-native audiences. The preface to *My People the Sioux* makes Standing Bear's purpose explicit: the book, he wrote, "is just a message to the white race; to bring my people before their eyes in a true and authentic manner." Criticizing both the tradition of dime novels and stage melodramas, and also the reformers' assimiliationist dogma, he added, "white men who have tried to write stories about the Indian have either foisted on the public some blood-curdling, impossible 'thriller'; or, if they have been in sympathy with the Indian, have written from knowledge which was not accurate and reliable." His book aimed to help "all people know the truth about the first Americans and their relations with the United States Government."[53]

Yet Luther Standing Bear regarded his own career as a performer with pride. He decided to travel to England with the Wild West in 1902 after new Indian Bureau policies made it impossible for him to support his family as a cattle rancher. He worked as an interpreter and a manager for the show Indians, enforcing Cody's rules (including his no-alcohol policy) but also speaking up when he felt his people were being mistreated. He helped them manage their money (and assisted them in buying new fur coats in Chicago on their way home). Luther Standing Bear played the role of Indian performer with gusto, apparently finding it morally acceptable and financially remunerative. He and his wife agreed to have their newborn child exhibited on the show grounds, and they named her after the Queen of England, a city on their itinerary, and his employer: Alexandra Birmingham Cody Standing Bear. "It was a great drawing card for the show," wrote Standing Bear, pleased that the exhibition benefited both the Wild West and his family, since visitors dropped off gifts and money for the baby. "The work was very light for my wife, and as for the baby, before she was twenty-four hours old she was making more money than my wife and I together."[54]

Standing Bear described Cody as a fair employer, who intervened to stop abusive practices by his staff who sometimes gave inferior food or more difficult horses to the Indian performers. Buffalo Bill "fixed things to our satisfaction" with "a twinkle in his eye," and also invited him into his tent to discuss Indian affairs, Standing Bear reported.[55] This advocate for Indian dignity wrote with relish about his work with the Wild West, the fine outfits and spirited horses, and the visits to interesting places. His memoir presents the work as a show Indian as an honorable and even enjoyable occupation.

Other American Indians who worked for Buffalo Bill left records of their motivations and attitudes toward their performances. Black Elk, who narrated accounts of his life to John Neihardt in 1930, was already known as a visionary and healer when he decided to go to England with Buffalo Bill in 1887. "I might learn some secret of the Wasichu [white man] that would help my people somehow," he explained. He was curious about the cities and people he visited, but the trip disappointed him. "I could see that the Wasichus did not care for each other the way our people did," he commented. "They had forgotten that the earth was their mother." He felt solidarity with the other American Indian performers, and took pride in the aspects of the show that reflected Indian life: "I liked the part of the show we made," he observed, "but not the part the Wasichus made." He too met with Queen Victoria: "She shook hands with all of us. Her hand was very little and soft," he commented. "That was a very happy time." Later, Black Elk became separated from the troupe in Manchester and spent some time with another showman named Mexican Joe. In Paris he was befriended by a French family, and then reunited with Buffalo Bill. "He was glad to see me. He had all his people give me three cheers. Then he asked me if I wanted to be in the show or if I wanted to go home." Black Elk chose to return to Pine

Ridge, and Cody gave him a ticket and ninety dollars. "Then he gave me a big dinner. Pahuska [Buffalo Bill] had a strong heart."[56]

But Black Elk's experiences as a show Indian could not help him to avert the tragedy that was about to strike the Sioux. Returning to Pine Ridge in 1889, he found his people starving and weakened, "shut up in pens" on the reservation and forbidden to hunt buffalo. Despite hopeful visions he experienced during the Ghost Dance ceremonies, he was a heartsick witness to the slaughter at Wounded Knee, marching into the storm of bullets holding only his sacred bow. He recalled the scene to John Neihardt in 1930:

> When I look back now from this high hill of my old age, I can still see the butchered women and children lying heaped and scattered all along the crooked gulch as plain as when I saw them with eyes still young. And I can see that something else died there in the bloody mud, and was buried in the blizzard. A people's dream died there. . . . You see me now a pitiful old man who has done nothing, for the nation's hoop is broken and scattered.

The story Neihardt asked him to tell, "not only the story of your life, but the story of the life of your people," ended for him after the destruction at Wounded Knee. Yet among the memories of hunting, warfare, and spirituality the aging Lakota recounted, the tale of his travels with Buffalo Bill stands out as an attempt to make a connection with the white world. "It seemed that there was a little hope," he wrote of his decision to travel with the Wild West.[57] And perhaps he felt the same way more than forty years later when Neihardt asked to interview him. His cordial memories of Buffalo Bill may have helped make possible his cooperation with the writer who made him famous.

Black Elk also expressed positive opinions about work as a show Indian to others who shared his spiritual vision and cultural concerns. Frank Fools Crow, nephew of Black Elk and a Teton Sioux spiritual leader, reported that his uncle had told him that traveling as a performer would enhance his reputation as a medicine man and could help him to perpetuate the remnants of traditional culture. "Black Elk went on to say that, as I traveled to competitions and toured with Wild West shows, word of my healing and prophetic power would spread. Then people who were doubters would ask me to prove what I could do by telling my visions and performing my ceremonies for them." Black Elk advised Fools Crow to retain some control over his own performances, keeping showmanship separate from worship, and he seems to have done so. "In our Wild West shows we Indians rode, sang, and danced. The dances were social performances, though, and never sacred ones."[58] Fools Crow later acted in and helped to promote Western films and, like his uncle, appears to have believed that show business was an honorable and enjoyable profession that offered at least some means to shape self-presentation and perpetuate aspects of traditional culture.

Performance in the Wild West doubtless had levels of meaning for many American Indian performers that spectators and white co-workers could only guess at. When the 1892 show closed its final performance in Glasgow, one performer, Kicking Bear, lingered in the arena. The interpreter reported that he was recounting in Lakota his deeds of valor.[59] Adapting the script to his own purposes, Kicking Bear seized the opportunity to perform his own version of his history.

AFTER WOUNDED KNEE

After the massacre at Wounded Knee, the history of the Plains Indians entered a new phase, and so did the enterprise of Indian showmanship. For Cody's Indian performers, much had been lost; for Cody himself, much had been gained. He had won the right to continue to use Indians in his show and had re-established his position as an active participant in Indian affairs. In January 1891, he toured the Wounded Knee battlefield with General Nelson Miles, where he posed for pictures. A colorful poster of Cody on his characteristic white horse shows him riding at the head of a group of soldiers toward an Indian village for a peace meeting. When thirty Sioux "troublemakers" associated with the Ghost Dance movement were removed from Pine Ridge and taken to Fort Sheridan in Chicago, Cody won the blessing of General Miles to recruit as many of them as he could. Cody's argument about the educational mission of his show had won the day, and he solved a difficult problem for military authorities at the same time. Twenty-three Ghost Dance prisoners were among the nearly one hundred Sioux who went to Europe with Cody during the 1891–92 season. Cody's service to the government in this saved his career as an entertainer by restoring his credibility as a participant in the "real" life of the American West and reaffirming his right to employ Indian performers.

The dramatic re-emergence of violence in Indian affairs brought a change in the Wild West's publicity strategy. John Burke saw a continuing

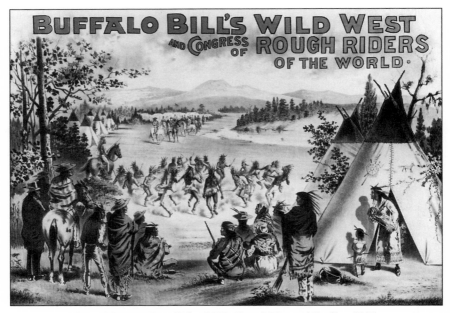

Peace Meeting, Pine Ridge 1891, Gen. Miles and Staff, c. 1895,
color lithograph, poster by A. Hoen & Co.

opportunity to present the Indian performers as privileged informants who
could bring spectators closer to real-life events. At the same time, he was
careful to build a reputation for good relations with them so that the Wild
West would never again be accused of neglect or mistreatment. Reporters
were given more access to Indian performers, and the resulting articles—by
turns respectful, humorous, and bemused—emphasized the juxtaposition of
"native" and "civilized" cultures. Photographs like ones showing the Indians
in a Venetian gondola or at the foot of Mount Vesuvius, engravings depicting
them visiting St. Paul's Cathedral or the Vatican, and interviews that
recorded their reactions to the sights they were seeing, became an important
part of the Wild West portfolio.

American Indian performers in Buffalo Bill's Wild West played their
parts, in and out of the arena, with apparent equanimity. At the Columbian
Exposition in 1893, they joined the opening ceremonies, appearing on a
parapet just as the band struck up "My Country 'Tis of Thee." On Italian
Day at the fair, they enacted a tableau about the landing of Christopher
Columbus: "When the curtain parted twelve Sioux Indians stood revealed.
Before them stood Columbus, the banner with the green cross in his hand. A

stalwart brave filled the center of the scene. His arm was thrown out, as if to welcome the navigator. . . . The Indians posed with rare grace, and it was for them that 2,000 people shouted and cried 'Bravo!,' 'Encore,' and 'Again.' 'Do it again.' "[60] Incongruously dressed in their Plains Indian costumes and feathered headdresses as they impersonated Caribbean natives, Buffalo Bill's show Indian may have found this task no more strange than anything else they were asked to do. Enacting the white man's script was all in a day's work, as long as the performers could follow Black Elk's path and keep its inner meaning to themselves.

As Wounded Knee receded into the past, newspaper articles about the Indians in Buffalo Bill's Wild West took on the rosy glow of human-interest stories. During the show's residence in Brooklyn in May 1894, two cast members were married in a ceremony that received enough press coverage to gratify even John Burke. "Col. Cody Gave the Blushing Bride Away," one headline read. "Mrs. High Bear in a few days will be the executive head of a tepee which is now being completed in the Indian camp connected with the Buffalo Bill Wild West show at Ambrose Park," reported the *Brooklyn Eagle*. "It was only this morning that she became Mrs. High Bear, being known heretofore as Tasina Wakan, or Holy Blanket, that is, blanket which is holy. The marriage was the only event of its kind which has ever taken place in the East." The ceremony was performed by the pastor of the Twelfth Street Reformed Church, and Rocky Bear, a senior performer who often spoke for the group, recommended that future marriages be conducted within the Christian church. "If you publish this marriage . . . it will show our people in the West that we are following the example of the white man and that we are adopting his religion. In future we will endeavor to have all our marriages performed by Christian ministers. We believe it will put us high in the estimation of the Great Spirit." Close readers of the press learned that Holy Blanket was a widow whose first husband had been killed at Wounded Knee, but most of the coverage stressed the colorful costumes of the participants and what one reporter called the "strange blending of paganism and barbarity with civilization."[61] Resolutely turning away from the tragic narrative of the plains as well as the heroic narrative of the Wild West performance, the press began to portray the American Indian performers as colorful exotics who no longer threatened the march of "civilization."

Human-interest stories about American Indian performers became a staple of Wild West publicity. In 1896, a newspaper reported the visit of a group of Wild West Indians to a penitentiary in Ohio, where they cheered an elderly Choctaw prisoner by singing Sioux songs and listening to her speak her

(*above left*) *Plenty Shawls on Bicycle*, from the tan scrapbook, 1897

(*above right*) *Motoring Illustrated*, January 24, 1903, from W. F. Cody scrapbook, 1902–3

(*left*) *Every Window Was Crowded to the Sills*, from W. F. Cody scrapbook, 1907

native language. "When the Indians had finished their strange music they gravely bade 'Aunt Elsie' adieu, shook her hand and left her happier than she had been for many a day." A feature article in 1897 reported on the encounters of two Wild West performers with everyday American culture: Black Fox, the chief of police in Buffalo Bill's Wild West, visited a Turkish bath, and Plenty Shawls, a horseback rider and participant in the show's re-enactment of the Ghost Dance ritual, learned to ride a bicycle. The next year a feature article reported, in a humorous way, that one of Buffalo Bill's performers was in love with a woman who had waved her handkerchief at him in Madison Square Garden. In later years, yet more articles told of Indians riding in motor cars and visiting sick children in a hospital.[62]

John Burke was a key influence in this change of tone. In a rare article focusing on the press agent himself, a journalist interviewed Burke, who was known to style himself "Arizona John," in his log cabin at Ambrose Park. "John Burke was a 'character' and a 'hail fellow well met' in theatrical circles many years before 'Buffalo Bill' ever thought of becoming a theatrical star," wrote the journalist. He described Burke's "delicious drawl and voice of vocal velvet" and recounted two lengthy stories of his, one about Sitting Bull and the other about Wounded Knee. "It is pleasant to know, however," he concluded, "that the Indians who have traveled with Buffalo Bill are firmly convinced of the white man's power and of the hopelessness of the Indian's trying to cope with it. They have done more in the interests of preserving peace than all the school educated Indians in the country."[63] Leaning back and smoking a cigar, Burke spun stories of the West in which American Indians were colorful and interesting but safe—very much the terms on which the Wild West would continue to be viewed into the twentieth century.

IMAGE-MAKING

The visual images produced in conjunction with Buffalo Bill's Wild West were especially effective in shaping ideas about American Indians for non-Indian audiences. Important as the words were, the images were among the most enduring and widely disseminated representations of American Indians at the time, before, or since. Visually, the Wild West drew on familiar conventions from dime novel and book illustrations, but its posters, programs, and staged spectacles were far more gripping because they were so large and colorful. It is no surprise that many of the Wild West images moved directly into the repertory of early film and continue to this day in movies and televi-sions. Millions of people saw Buffalo Bill's Wild West during its heyday, but many millions more saw the posters plastered over every surface when the show came to town, and souvenir books, programs, and photographs became part of the spectators' imaginative life. Like the texts, the images often showed Indians as the *objects* of their own story, but sometimes, thanks to col-laboration or alternative image making, the images offered insights into their own view of their status as *subjects* as well.

In many of the posters, American Indians were shown as villains, advertis-ing the melodramatic portions of the show such as the attack on the settler's cabin, the ambush of the Deadwood stagecoach, and the re-enactments of battles from the Indian wars. *On the Stage Coach*, a poster from around 1893, shows an image dating back to Cody's 1879 autobiography and the early program engravings: the Deadwood stagecoach, drawn by mules gal-loping at full speed, surrounded by fierce, attacking Indians, with brave defenders inside, and Buffalo Bill and a party of scouts and soldiers riding to the rescue. The Indians, arrayed across the width of the foreground, are the largest and most colorful figures; they are depicted riding bareback, dressed in fringed buckskin pants and moccasins, naked from the waist up, with feath-ers in their hair. Three of them are shown in the act of shooting arrows; one is falling, wounded, with his horse; and the leader is reining in his rearing horse as if preparing to flee from the rescue party. They are mostly pictured from the back or in profile; they are exotic and threatening, but not individualized.

More sinister and detailed Indian figures can be seen in another poster from around the same time, *Buffalo Bill to the Rescue*. Here, Buffalo Bill rides into the center of an Indian village, guns blazing, just in time to rescue two white captives being burned at the stake by dark and demonic Indians. The Indians' wide-open eyes indicate cowardice; although one holds a gun threateningly, another falls, wounded, so we know that Buffalo Bill will save the day. The weeping white woman on the left is balanced by an Indian woman on the right who runs away with her baby in a cradleboard and a dark-skinned young child. But hints of Indian domesticity only slightly soften the image of a clear-cut struggle between good and evil.

Even as late as 1907, a poster like *The Death of Chief Tall Bull* made the dying Indian a celebratory image. A rearing horse is the focus of the poster image; the small figure of Buffalo Bill (face hidden behind his rifle) is almost negligible. The Indian's legs still straddle the horse's back, while his head hangs back grotesquely and his arm reaches out in a dying gesture, parallel to the rifle that flies through the air with the force of the blast. His round shield looks like a bull's-eye, suggesting that the Indian is a natural target for the sharpshooting scout. The "hostile redskin," as the poster text identifies him, is solely the object of the white man's marksmanship, a fantasy enemy about to bite the dust.

Other Wild West posters presented Indians with more individuality and dignity. *An American,* a version of a poster image Cody had used since 1885,

On the Stage Coach, c. 1887, color lithograph, poster

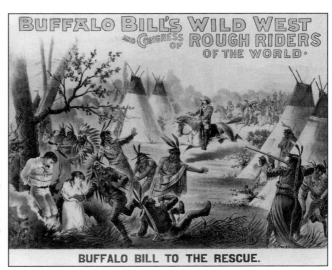

Buffalo Bill to the Rescue, c. 1887, color lithograph, poster by A. Hoen & Co.

The Death of Chief Tall Bull, c. 1907, color lithograph, poster

shows an Indian on horseback on top of a grassy knoll. He peers out into the distance, one hand raised to shade his eyes; he wears buckskin pants and jacket, has a feather in his hair, and carries a rifle in a pack on his back. Whether he is a hostile Indian or a friendly scout, like the Pawnee who were Cody's first Indian performers, he is an object of contemplation rather than a frightening danger. By 1893, when the caption "An American" was added to this poster, the Wild West used this image in conjunction with other posters showing other national types—cossacks, Mexicans, Arabs—to advertise the Congress of Rough Riders of the World; the Indian is seen in the context of the show's pomp and display rather than its melodrama, and is honored as a representative American. By the early twentieth century, the Wild West's Indians were being promoted as virtual trademarks for the show. *Chief Iron Tail with Buffalo Bill's Wild West* depicts the Indian as a recognized celebrity. Especially after he was credited with being one of the models for the Indian Head nickel, first issued in 1913, Iron Tail was seen as a star in his own right, an individual separate from the role he played in the show. Unlike Sitting Bull, whose celebrity came from his historical and military accomplishments, Iron Tail attracted favorable attention because he was a symbolic figure of "Indianness," safely enshrined in the nation's own pantheon and in a form every American could carry in his or her pocket—its money.

In the souvenir programs, images of Indians functioned in very much the same way as on the posters. The earliest programs showed them in military engagements like the scalping of Yellow Hand. The back cover of the 1883 program for Cody and Carver's Wild West depicted a fierce Indian battle with Cody stabbing an Indian in horseback combat, but by the early twentieth century the programs suggested that the Indians, like other actors, were playing roles. A 1907 booklet was shaped like an Indian's head, with a portrait of Cody nestled in its cutout silhouette. Inside, an article stressed the person-

An American,
color lithograph, poster

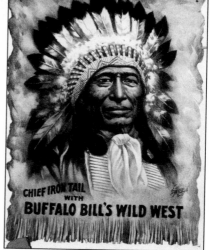

Chief Iron Tail with Buffalo Bill's Wild West,
poster, Circus World Museum,
Baraboo, Wisconsin

able professionalism of Iron Tail, "a dignified but genial soul—a magnificent specimen of the old Sioux warrior. When I stood beside him to be snap-shotted he removed his eagle-feathered war bonnet, and with friendly humor placed it on my head."[64] As the Indian wars faded into the past, the Wild West's publicity materials increasingly treated the Indian performers as enter-tainers rather than as embodiments of the parts they enacted.

(*above*) *The Wild West—Buffalo Bill and Dr. Carver*, 1883 program, back cover

(*left*) Indian-Head Courier, 1907

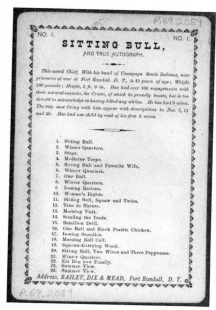

Sitting Bull, cabinet photograph
by Bailey, Dix and Mead, Fort Randall,
Dakota Territory

*John Nelson and Family, Scout,
Interpreter and Guide,*
photograph by Elliot & Fry, London

Souvenir photographs had also helped to shape public perceptions of American Indians. Sometimes, like Sitting Bull, the performers benefited directly from their sale; in other cases, it is not clear whether they were given fees for each photograph sold, paid a single fee for posing, or not compensated at all. Photographic sets were made like the one advertised on the back of a portrait of Sitting Bull by Bailey, Dix & Mead of Fort Randall, Dakota Territory: customers could choose from twenty-four different related images. Elliott & Fry of Baker Street, London, produced portraits of Wild West performers including both individuals like Little Chief (or Macaci-Kaola, as he was identified in the souvenir booklet for the London exhibition) and family groups like that of John Nelson with his Indian wife and children. Assuming a conventional pose against a painted backdrop, but wearing the colorful clothing of the Western plains, Nelson and his family suggest safety but also exoticism. Like other portraits of famous people (Mathew Brady's Civil War series, for example), the formal photographs satisfied public curiosity and acknowledged the celebrity of those portrayed.

Other photographs depicted Wild West personnel in performance or in visits to the campgrounds before or after the show. In these photographs, the

Wild West stereograph

object of scrutiny is not the "real" person who plays a role, but the role itself. In photographs of the show's vignettes performed at Earl's Court, London, men, women, and children pose with their horses in front of the stage tepee and painted backdrop: it is a moment of stage practice, not a "real" scene of Indian life. A stereographic print shows an Indian family outside a tepee in a wooded clearing, commemorating the visits that tourists could pay to the camp of the Wild West before or after shows. Stereographs, which seem magically to spring to life when seen through the viewing apparatus that gives them the impression of three-dimensionality, offered viewers a particularly vivid image to reinforce their memories of the Wild West.

It is difficult to say whether American Indians posing for souvenir photographs had any control over their costumes or poses. Clearly they could arrange their faces in expressions that satisfied them, so we can imagine that the solemn, straightforward appearance in many of the photographs represents the sitter's choice. Some evidence suggests that Wild West members could refuse to have their photographs taken if they wanted. According to one observer, a group of Wild West Indians under the leadership of Iron Tail refused to pose with a statue of Christopher Columbus in Genoa. " 'Indians no like Columbus. Columbus no good! No want photograph.' And no photograph was taken, for the Indians marched off."[65] Thus we can assume that the very dramatic photographs showing American Indians on tour through Europe—posing in a Venetian gondola or at the Colosseum in Rome—represented at least a partial collaboration and that the Indian subjects were willing to be portrayed. Just as the Wild West management wished to suggest its "conquest" of Europe, the Indian performers may have seen these photographs as representations of their own success abroad.

A different sort of representational collaboration resulted in a remarkable set of photographs taken around the turn of the century by Gertrude Käsebier, a Photo-Secessionist whom Alfred Stieglitz called the leading portrait photographer of her day.[66] Käsebier wrote to Cody asking for permission to photograph Indians from his show after watching the parade that opened the Wild West's 1898 season in New York from her studio near Madison Square Garden. Having grown up in Colorado, she evidently responded to the American Indians themselves rather than to the roles they played in the show. When a delegation of show Indians came to her studio the next day, she fed them tea, bread, and frankfurters, and took the first of several groups of portraits she would produce during the next few years. Although she took an interest in their careers with the Wild West, Käsebier appears to have appreciated her Indian subjects as individuals rather than simply as performers, and continued to exchange letters, gifts, visits, and pictures with them. Her granddaughter remembered being taken to the Wild West as a child, but her most vivid memory was not of the show itself but the exhilarating and terrifying moment afterward when one of her grandmother's Indian friends stepped outside his role as performer, lifted her on a horse, and rode with her around the deserted ring. Another grandchild recalled meeting Sioux visitors at the Käsebiers' summer house on Long Island.[67]

Käsebier's Indian portraits create a bridge between the conventional poses of the souvenir photographs and a more interior, psychological portrait style. Her portrait of Lone Bear, posed in profile, wearing a full headdress, beaded vest, arm- and wristbands, and holding a bow and arrow, evoked souvenir portraits like those of Notman or Elliott & Fry. Perhaps Lone Bear, an older performer, had already posed for such photographs and was prepared to adopt a stylized position and arrange his face in a solemn and dignified expression. A portrait of his son, Samuel Lone Bear, on the other hand, breaks with the conventions of souvenir photographs. Posed in a diagonal posture, leaning on one arm, full face, with eyes turned to one side as if in thought and with a pensive expression, the younger man seems more personally accessible to the viewer. Although his clothing identifies him as Indian—braided hair, armband, a decorated vest, feathers—he does not fit the show-Indian stereotype. Even more surprising is the portrait of Joe Black Fox, holding a cigarette and looking directly at the camera with a trace of a smile. The two younger men, identified by English first names as well as

(*left*) Gertrude Käsebier, *Samuel Lone Bear*

(*below*) Gertrude Käsebier, *Samuel Lone Bear, Jr.*

Anglicized Indian surnames, represented a generation of American Indians like Luther Standing Bear, who were educated in Indian schools but who nonetheless chose to tour with the Wild West. Their cooperation with Käsebier suggests that they could put on or take off the show-Indian persona. The photographer's desire to connect with her subjects as individuals rather than as showmen seems to have been met by gestures of friendship on the part of the men and women she photographed. Samuel Lone Bear corresponded with Käsebier for several years, offering to send her beaded moccasins made by his mother, asking for a pink handkerchief, and writing expressions of affection: "I send love to you / I am my close letter now / I hope you are well / That is all now / I will shake hand with me / I am your friend."[68]

Käsebier's encounter with the well-known Iron Tail suggests that members of the Wild West had decided views about how they looked in photographs. In a magazine article about her Indian portraits, Käsebier recalled requesting that Iron Tail pose without the decorative clothing he had worn to the sitting. "I want a real *raw* Indian for a change," Käsebier recalled thinking, "the kind I used to see when I was a child." The photograph, with the

Gertrude Käsebier,
Joseph Black Fox

Gertrude Käsebier, *Iron Tail*

subject in a relaxed pose, full face, eyes looking to the side, and lips partially open, is startlingly direct. This was the image Käsebier wanted, but it did not please the sitter. "When the portrait was handed to him some days later, he tore it in two and flung it from him. Luckily, however, an explanation and a second sitting in full regalia entirely restored his peace of mind."[69] The second photograph more nearly matches the conventional souvenir pose, with the subject seen in profile and his full eagle-feather headdress strongly lit. In fact, the headdress is the most prominent feature, suggesting the reasons for Iron Tail's destruction of the first, bare-headed photograph. He far preferred the image that stressed the symbol of his history and status. Like Kicking Bear reciting his proudest deeds in Lakota before leaving the arena, Iron Tail had strong ideas about his own representation.

Käsebier's Indian subjects also created images of their own. The magazine account of Käsebier's Indian portraits reproduces a number of drawings done by Samuel Lone Bear, Joseph Black Fox, and others, and Käsebier also photographed her subjects as they drew. Like Sitting Bull, the Cheyenne warrior Howling Wolf, and other Plains Indian artists who adapted the Native American tradition of the pictograph in their contacts with Western visual

Gertrude Käsebier, *Profile of Iron Tail with Headdress*

Gertrude Käsebier,
Indians Drawing

Joseph Black Fox, *Deer*   Wm. H. Frog, *Vaquero, Horse, Steer*

"This is American Bison"

culture, they used simple forms to represent subjects that interested them: a horse, a tepee, a dancer. Joseph Black Fox drew an elk with branched antlers, legs curved in a pose that resembles equestrian statues he might have seen in his travels in American cities and towns, and he signed his name at the bottom of the page. As if to reclaim the very animal that served as a symbol for Cody's show, one artist filled the paper with a detailed depiction of a buffalo, head turned toward the viewer, and labeled "This is American Bison." Other drawings showed scenes from the Wild West performance: a Mexican vaquero with lasso, a steer, an Indian dancer.

In what was perhaps a playful set of images, different Indian sitters drew versions of a scene outside a tepee featuring a smiling woman and one or more figures with blankets over their heads. One drawing, entitled *Catch Girls*, is signed at the bottom by "Sam Lone Bear Jr." During the period of his friendship with Käsebier, Samuel Lone Bear became something of a favorite with reporters covering the Wild West because of his sense of humor and his willingness to talk to them. He was the subject of a humorous article alleging that he had fallen in love with a visitor to the Wild West. Another article focused on his decorative vest, claiming that he sold the ornamental elk's teeth on the garment whenever he needed to raise money.[70] *Catch Girls* may be a humorous reflection of a running joke between Samuel Lone Bear and Käsebier; one of his letters from Pine Ridge reported, "Plenty girls over

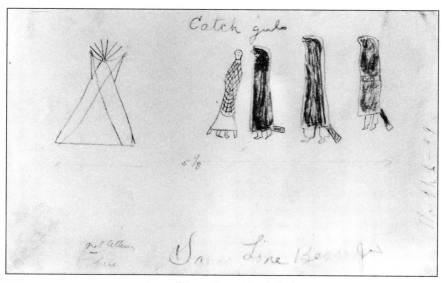

Samuel Lone Bear, *Catch Girls*

(*right*) Gertrude Käsebier,
Red Man

(*below*) Gertrude Käsebier,
Blanket-Draped Figure

hear."[71] In the drawings and letters, Samuel Lone Bear and his associates asserted a representational initiative in offering the photographer words and images. And it is at least possible that the blanket-draped figures in these drawings gave Käsebier an idea for her most famous and successful photograph in the American Indian series, the mysteriously shrouded *Red Man*. As Käsebier later remembered the circumstances, the photograph arose from a spontaneous gesture on the part of one of her subjects: "I never could get what I wanted. Finally, one of them, petulant, raised his blanket about his shoulders and stood before the camera. I snapped and had it."[72] This account makes the photograph appear to be the result of a onetime event, but in fact it is only one of several images of the blanket-draped figure. Whatever it meant to Käsebier, draping a blanket over the head was a meaningful gesture to the American Indian sitters. Makers of images and experienced in public self-presentation, the Indians who posed for Käsebier participated in their own depiction in ways known, ultimately, only to themselves.

FINDING MEANING IN INDIAN PERFORMANCES

The Wild West show would never have developed into such a powerful entertainment form without its American Indian performers, and, as we have seen, it had complex and changing meanings for the American Indians who joined it. Asked to collaborate in staging representations of their own history and culture, they were presumed by outside observers to guarantee the "authenticity" of the Wild West's version of frontier life. But they well understood the difference between what they did in the arena and Plains Indian life as it had been before Little Big Horn. American Indians had complex motives for choosing to work for Buffalo Bill, including the desire to travel and earn money, the pleasures of riding and racing, the choice of a lesser evil as compared to the grim life of the reservation or, in the case of the Wounded Knee prisoners, jail. With the disappearance of the buffalo and the end of their free life on the plains, they compared working for the Wild West with other available occupations such as farming, carpentry, domestic service, or any of the trades for which the Indian schools were trying to prepare them. For many, work as a show Indian was a reasonably good alternative. Also, performing for the Wild West may have satisfied other purposes obscure to white observers: preserving their culture, securing leadership and status, even perpetuating spiritual traditions.

American Indian *spectators* had various responses to the Wild West as well. Sometimes students at Indian schools went to the show to see their relatives perform. In 1897, the elderly leaders Red Cloud and American Horse, traveling east to meet with government officials, saw the Wild West performance from a box in Madison Square Garden and met with Cody and the performers afterward. And in California, Ishi, the last surviving Yahi Indian, was taken by his friend and physician, Saxton Pope, to Buffalo Bill's Wild West.[73] It is difficult to know how the show appeared to these Indian spectators. For Ishi, the depiction of Plains Indian culture would have been as exotic as it was for the professors who accompanied him, but they reported that he appeared to enjoy himself. For Plains Indian spectators, the performances may have been bittersweet. The press account of Red Cloud's visit to the Wild West struck a tone of pathos: "So Red Cloud, greatest of the war chiefs of the Sioux, sat under a roof with thousands of palefaces and above the mimicry of that which had been wrested from his people[,] their mastery of the broad American plains." But it is possible that Indian spectators had some of the detachment expressed by Eya Matao, or Rocky Bear, in an interview evaluating an English-language play he had seen in Philadelphia:

> Me no understand everything, but understand plenty to make laugh. Sioux have plenty fun, too. He dance Omaha dance when he feel like fun; white man no understand and say it war dance; no war dance, but dance for fun. . . . White man no understand all of Indian fun; Indian no understand all of white man fun, but understand enough to laugh and see good time.[74]

Like Luther Standing Bear finding bitter amusement in the mistranslation of Sitting Bull's remarks during a performance in the 1880s, Indian spectators attending the Wild West could enjoy a joke when Sioux performed Omaha dances, or understand a subversive monologue when Kicking Bear recited his deeds in Lakota. Additionally, if the response of students from Lincoln Institute Indian School is any guide, they may have joined non-Indian audience members in simply having a good time. Like other spectators, Indians at the Wild West might have responded to the performance's energy and color and, in Rocky Bear's terms, had fun.

For non-Indian audiences, multiple meanings were also possible. Press stories stressed the adventure, exoticism, and sometimes pathos of the American Indian performers. They elicited excitement almost always and admiration often. In 1894, one newspaper caption read "The Red Men Still the Favorites," and went on to explain: "The Indians are of all the interesting people the greatest attraction. This may be due to the fact that the real flesh-and-blood Indian seen here is so entirely different from the cold, stoical, crafty and revengeful red man told of in leaded small pica."[75] Sometimes newspaper accounts portrayed Indians as sly, as in a report of Red Cloud muttering about scalps when he was greeted effusively by Buffalo Bill, or in the story about Samuel Lone Bear selling his elk's teeth to pay his gambling and drinking debts. But rarely were Indians seen as objects of humor. In this sense "the Indian" was quite different from other racial stereotypes in contemporary dramatic presentations. Although male Indian performers were commonly referred to in racialized animalistic language as "bucks," they were rarely the object of cruel jokes, as were African-Americans or the Irish. The "stage Indian" might be a figure of terror but was rarely one of humor.

In its avoidance of racialized humor, the Wild West was quite different from other forms of nineteenth-century entertainment, especially the minstrel show. And yet there were important relationships between the Wild West and the minstrel show. Ever since the 1820s, white performers had put on blackface to present exaggerated versions of African-American cultural forms as humorous entertainment for white audiences. Minstrel shows used song, dance, and dialogue in vignettes purporting to depict black character and glimpses of plantation life in the old South. White actors and audiences invested many meanings in this racial masquerade, including class and ethnic self-definitions.[76]

By the time the Wild West emerged in the 1880s, dozens of *black* troupes also performed minstrel shows, with African-American actors wearing coal-black makeup and performing stylized song, dance, and joke routines in a multilayered carnival of satire. The cakewalk, developed on the plantation as a parodic imitation of the dress and manners of white society, became part of the minstrel show's exotic vision of black culture. When African-American minstrels performed it, they were parodying a parody of a parody.[77] For black entertainers, minstrelsy could lead to success and recognition in the theater, but it left performers in an ambiguous relationship with the material they enacted. Black audiences flocked to hear black stars such as Jim Bland, composer of "Carry Me Back to Old Virginny" and "Oh, Dem Golden Slippers," appearing with groups like Sprague's Georgia Minstrels. Although the sheet music depicted stereotyped black figures and the lyrics followed the Stephen Foster conventions of celebrating antebellum plantation life, African-American audiences enjoyed the shows, and black performers found in minstrelsy an attractive alternative to sharecropping and other manual labor. Tom Fletcher, who began his career in Uncle Tom shows and minstrel performances in the 1880s, recalled the meaning of show business for his colleagues in terms very much like those that might describe the attitude of Wild West performers to their work:

> It was a big break when show business started, because singing and dancing was the way in which [former slaves] had amused themselves for years. . . . Salaries were not large, but they still amounted to much more than they were getting, and there was the added advantage of the opportunity to travel with the company taking care of them . . . All of us who were recruited to enter show business went into it with our eyes wide open. The objectives were, first, to make money to help educate our younger ones, and second, to try to break down the ill feeling that existed toward the colored people.[78]

Although black entertainers could use the minstrel stage for their own ends, as he eloquently states, they were locked into an entertainment form that required them to present themselves as objects of humor. Like Wild West performers, they were following a script not of their own making, and could evade or subvert its implications only through indirection.

Cody and Salsbury had a complicated relationship to the blackface minstrel tradition. Salsbury's Troubadours had included minstrel acts, and on the ship carrying the Wild West to England in 1887, three veterans of that troupe now working for Cody presented an evening's entertainment that included minstrel numbers complete with dueling banjos, illustrated by a program that sported a caricature of Salsbury in blackface. The Wild West employed various black entertainers, including at different times musicians and a clownlike figure who posed in a dunking machine.[79] In 1895, Salsbury had the idea for an all-black musical and created an entertainment patterned on the Wild West called "Black America." With about 620 African-American entertainers under the leadership of the black minstrel star Billy McClain, the show featured well-regarded performers such as Madam Flowers, Fred Piper, Charley Johnson, May Bohee, Madam Cordelia McClain, Jube Johnson, Ed Harris, Billy Farrell, and Doc Sayles, together with one hundred dancers, seventy-five athletes, fifty male vocal quartets, and a squadron from the Ninth Cavalry to execute army maneuvers. Black America, which opened at Ambrose Park, in Brooklyn, claimed the same "educational" aims

*Wild West Program,
On Board of the
Good Ship State
of Nebraska,
April 11, 1887*

as the Wild West: "For the first time in the history of this country the Negro as he really is, will be placed in the AMUSEMENT world as AN EDUCATOR with natural surroundings." Advertisements featuring portraits of antislavery figures like Harriet Beecher Stowe, Abraham Lincoln, Frederick Douglass, and John Brown emphasized the show's historicity and authenticity. Visitors could tour the performers' living quarters (real cabins, with poultry and transplanted cotton bushes); cast members operated a cotton gin in the "perfect reproduction of a cotton plantation," then performed minstrel standards such as "Old Black Joe" and a cakewalk.[80] Although the African-American star Tom Fletcher recalled Black America as "a milestone in the development of show business," the production drew lukewarm reviews and folded after a few months.

The fact that both Salsbury and Cody presumed they could apply their experience with the Wild West to the production of a minstrel-like entertainment is instructive for a number of reasons. It confirms that the theatrical impresarios themselves recognized a parallel between the self-representation

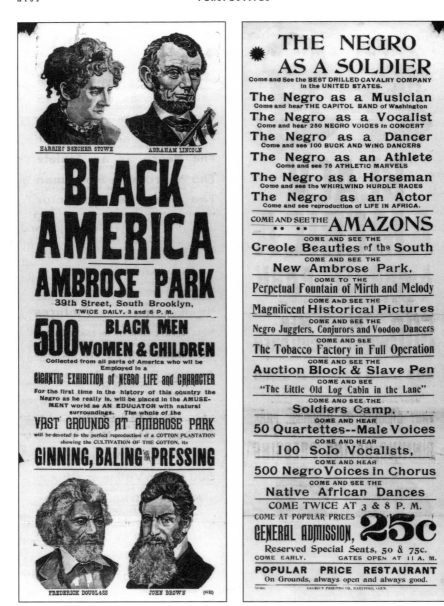

Black America, posters

of American Indians in the Wild West and the position of African-American blackface minstrels. Yet the very qualities that made Black America different from an ordinary minstrel show highlight the ways in which they differed. Black America was not primarily a humorous show. It made claims to historical authenticity and highlighted real achievements of its subjects. And, if Fletcher is correct, its entertainers could shape their own performances. It did not rely on mockery to give spectators a sense of solidarity through difference.

Neither Black America nor the Wild West fit neatly into the minstrel show's conventions of racial hierarchy, but both were in a broader sense implicated in late nineteenth- and early twentieth-century ethnographic conceptions of racial difference. In New Orleans, London, Paris, and Chicago, the Wild West had performed in conjunction with world's fairs and benefited from the enthusiasm for the exotic that characterized them. In the years before World War I, both European and American fairs promulgated an imperialist worldview that celebrated Western bourgeois culture by displaying its industrial and consumer products and contrasting it with "simpler," more "primitive," and less commercially advanced cultures. Marx and Engels described these fairs as occasions for the bourgeoisie to exhibit "with self-congratulatory pride the gods it has created for itself," and later Walter Benjamin characterized them as "pilgrimage sites of commodity fetishism."[81] As has been discussed earlier, its audiences understood the Wild West in the context of the long tradition of entrepreneurial exhibition of non-European peoples dating back to Columbus and including the display of live humans in zoos, theaters, and museums.[82] Although the Wild West was a separate enterprise at fairs such as the World's Columbian Exposition, its display of American Indians could be seen by spectators as continuous with the ethnographic presentations inside the White City.

The Wild West's White City season is the most vivid point of intersection with prevailing ethnographic concepts. Ethnology formed an important underpinning for the Exposition's claim to represent four hundred years of human progress, the replacement of "savage" with "civilized" societies throughout the New World. According to Frederick Ward Putnam, director of the Columbian Exposition's Department of Ethnology and Archaeology, exhibitions of pre-Columbian cultures taught an "object lesson" to fairgoers:

> What, then, is more appropriate, more essential, than to show in their natural conditions of life the different types of peoples who were here when Columbus was crossing the Atlantic Ocean and leading the way for the great wave of humanity that

was soon spread over the continent and forced those unsus-
pecting peoples to give way before a mighty power, to resign
their inherited rights, and take their chances for existence
under the laws governing a strange people?[83]

Ethnological exhibitions had an implied historical and political moral: the
superiority of European civilization and the inevitability of its dominance.
This assumption governed the ethnological exhibits produced under Department M of the Columbian Exposition, including the Smithsonian Institution display in the Government Building, the exhibition of artifacts in the
Anthropological Building, the living ethnographical exhibit along the banks
of the South Pond, and the eighty cases representing "Woman's Work in Savagery" lent by the Smithsonian to the Woman's Building.[84] As many commentators have pointed out, the display of exotic peoples on the Midway
reinforced the concept of racial hierarchy. One guidebook commented that
the Midway was "filled with things calculated to draw a visitor's last nickel,
and to leave his pocket-book looking as if one of Chicago's twenty-story
buildings had fallen upon it."[85]

Yet the celebratory flavor of these displays threatened to undermine cultural hierarchies and overthrow the very power relations they asserted.
Museum directors and anthropologists were disappointed that the Midway
was more popular than the Anthropological Building. According to a writer
in a Chicago newspaper, "The Anthropological Building is the most serious
place on the face of the earth. The man who enters there leaves fun
behind."[86] And Richard Henry Pratt, founder of the Carlisle Indian School,
understood that even the serious and ideologically inflected presentation of
indigenous culture in the anthropology exhibits opened the door to subversive possibilities for pleasure and enjoyment. He refused to contribute to the
fair's ethnological exhibits because he feared that the colorful display of
American Indian traditional artifacts would "keep the nation's attention and
the Indian's energies fixed upon his valueless past, through the spectacular
aboriginal housing, dressing, and curio employments it instituted."[87] Like
the Midway, the Wild West was perceived as "fun," and its ethnological
dimensions were blurred by the vividness of its melodrama and by the unambiguous pleasure spectators were encouraged to take in its colorful display.

Nothing in the Wild West contradicted the imperialistic, hierarchical
assumptions woven so deeply into contemporaneous ethnographic displays.
The heyday of the Wild West also saw the establishment of natural-history
museums in major American cities where spectators could see glass cases

containing artifacts and representations of living people that comfortably assumed white middle-class cultural superiority. The audiences for Wild West shows could also see minstrel shows and vaudeville acts representing African-Americans and other ethnic groups as objects of low comedy. And yet, as newspaper stories continued to assert, the Indians were special favorites with audiences, and human-interest stories about Indians touring in gondolas, riding bicycles, ascending elevators, and visiting children in hospitals complicated the racial stereotypes and hierarchies. In all its complexity, the audience's encounter with the American Indian performers continued to be one of the Wild West's defining features.

CHAPTER SIX

MEMORY AND MODERNITY

Although Cody's publicity team produced a barrage of interpretative images and texts that maintained the Wild West had a transparent, straightforward meaning, spectators saw the show in differing, even contradictory, ways. Newspapers explained the show from the women's viewpoint, the children's viewpoint, the Eastern viewpoint, the Western viewpoint. John Burke trumpeted a heroic tune, while Cody's rivals and competitors interpreted Buffalo Bill's career cynically. These paradoxes were, in fact, a crucial sign of the Wild West's modernity. Audiences understood that its spectacle was fiction but approved its claims to authenticity. They realized it represented an exaggerated and idealized view of frontier life but thought they were seeing "the real thing."

And always Buffalo Bill's entertainment spectacle raised the question: what *was* "the Wild West" this show purported to display? When and where was it located? At the beginning of Cody's acting career, his managers and publicists made a convincing case for the proposition that Buffalo Bill's frontier was contemporaneous but spatially distant; it existed *right now* on the Great Plains, and Buffalo Bill had just arrived to tell his audience all about it. Performing *The Red Right Hand* just months after the Battle of the Little Big Horn and including poetry and news releases about it in the program, Cody and his managers traded on the audience's belief that they were transmitting news from the front, representing events actually unfolding on the plains even as spectators sat watching in Boston, New York, or Omaha. But by the time Cody and his troupe had returned from their first European tour, after the Battle of Wounded Knee had put an end to the Indian wars and the railroad had opened the West for tourism and trade, it was hard to argue that the "Wild West" still existed in anything like the form it took in Cody's entertainment. In the early days, the claim to "realism" rested on physical remoteness, but after 1890, the Wild West made its best case for authenticity by invoking a temporal remoteness from the events it purported to represent. By the last decade of the nineteenth and into the twentieth century, this was its most prominent note. The multiple meanings of the Wild West could continue to be convincing because it claimed them for the past, not the present. And because it came to be associated with nostalgia and retrospection, Buffalo Bill's Wild West took its place as part of America's national memory.

According to the French historian Pierre Nora, memory took on a new significance in the modern era, with its alienation from traditional sources of communal identity. What Nora calls *lieux de mémoire*, sites of memory or memory-places, are repositories for shared meanings in the modern world: "*Lieux de mémoire* are fundamentally vestiges, the ultimate embodiments of a commemorative consciousness that survives in a history which, having renounced memory, cries out for it." Buffalo Bill's Wild West appeared in just such a cultural moment, as the United States was emerging into modernism, urbanization, and participation in world politics and military operations, in the midst of a culture "fundamentally absorbed by its own transformation and renewal."[1] Understanding the Wild West as a site of memory helps to explain its powerful attraction for a variety of spectators and its long-lasting survival as a cultural myth. We should not ask whether audiences believed the Wild West's claims to truth and authenticity, but rather, to what did the Wild West appear to them to correspond? Surely its most important, and most contradictory and complex, meanings were in the realm of memory.

MEMORIES OF NATURE

Buffalo Bill's Wild West was, to begin with, a place. In the years after the Civil War, that place had become even more vivid in the minds of American audiences as visual images of it proliferated. Panoramas, oil paintings, photographs, stereographs, magazine illustrations, and chromolithographs made the splendid landscapes of the Rocky Mountains familiar to armchair travelers in the United States and around the world. If these images represented places that existed nowhere but in the imagination, as critics have suggested, it is nonetheless true that the Wild West performed for audiences whose scenic vocabulary and associations had been shaped by a visual culture that included these landscapes. The imaginary West already so familiar to Buffalo Bill's audiences was a place they could plan to visit, one that in the post–Civil War era was being rapidly opened to settlement and tourism by the very Indian wars the Wild West celebrated. But when they got there, nineteenth-century travelers were already predisposed to see inscribed in its natural wonders a history of triumphant conquest. As a number of art historians have argued, nineteenth-century Americans increasingly located the burden of their history, of European dominance of the North American continent, in the landscape of the West. The West was seen *as* America, a place whose natural features invoked culturally understood memories of America's "invented pasts."[2]

The dynamic of nature and culture, past and future in the American understanding of Western landscape is well expressed in an icon of postbellum popular culture, Currier & Ives's lithograph *Across the Continent: "Westward the Course of Empire Takes Its Way,"* based on a drawing by the artist Fanny Palmer and published by the lithography firm in 1868 to celebrate the anticipated completion of the transcontinental railroad. In this attractive, hand-colored lithograph, a passenger train dashes diagonally across a green prairie on a gleaming track that stretches toward the distant horizon. Its prominence focuses the viewer's thoughts on the bright technological future, but the image also pays homage to the past. The straight, steady track lined with telegraph poles runs beside a narrow, twisting wagon trail along which now-obsolete covered wagons lumber westward. On the right side of the tracks, mountains, rivers, and grassy plains stretch invitingly, populated only by tiny figures: men in boats, minuscule horsemen chasing a herd of buffalo on the distant horizon, and two Indians who rein in their horses warily as the locomotive smoke engulfs them. This breathtaking landscape represents a memory of the West as it was before the arrival of the train and the settlements. Inside the train cars, marked "Through Line, New York–San Francisco," passengers in city clothes can view both the unspoiled scenery of the past and the frontier village that indicates the future. On the left, vignettes depict the changes the railroad will bring: men are chopping down trees, children enter a public school, a woman holding a baby stands in the door-

Currier & Ives, *Across the Continent*, color lithograph

way of a log house, and railroad workers build another set of tracks. Even as the viewer looks at the print, the viewers within the print observe the spectacle of Western settlement, and their vista harmonizes with the one presented by Buffalo Bill: from a position of safety they contemplate wildness as entertainment, reassured that civilization will bring progress and pleasure.

Across the Continent holds in balance its celebration of a technological future and its remembrance of the undisturbed landscape of the past. Although it portrays the future (the passage of a railroad that had not yet been completed when the print was issued), it also evokes the mellow satisfactions of retrospection. The title itself is a memory, a citation from a well-known poem by the eighteenth-century writer Bishop George Berkeley, which had once supplied the Hudson River painter Thomas Cole with the title for a series of paintings about the rise and fall of an imaginary civilization and then later the theme for Emanuel Leutze's monumental mural for the U.S. Capitol building in Washington, *Westward the Course of Empire Takes Its Way*. Cole had sounded a note of alarm in his 1836 series, *The Course of Empire*, imagining a mighty nation that arose from a wilderness inhabited by bow-and-arrow-wielding hunters only to fall victim to its own luxury and corruption; but Leutze saw promise for the hardy band of frontiersmen who blazed the way for pioneer families traveling toward a Western paradise they could just glimpse from the summit of snow-capped mountains.

Emanuel Leutze, *Westward the Course of Empire Takes Its Way*, mural in the United States House of Representatives

Westward the Course of Empire, poster, Circus World Museum, Baraboo, Wisconsin

Paintings like Leutze's, displayed in the most prominent of public spaces, became a reservoir of images and associations to which audiences could connect the Wild West's spectacle. John Burke's first "Salutatory" message almost seemed to describe Leutze's painting when it asserted that Buffalo Bill's Wild West aimed to evoke the period of frontier settlement by dramatizing the contributions of "the little vanguard of pioneers, trappers, and scouts, who, moving always in front, have paved the way—frequently with their own bodies—for the safe approach of the masses behind."[3] One of

Cody's posters from 1898 inserted Buffalo Bill into this already familiar image of frontier settlement, echoing Leutze's *Westward the Course of Empire* with Buffalo Bill standing guard for an advancing band of settlers. The horsemen, now clothed in fringed buckskin and colorful capes like Wild West performers, gesture approvingly to a vignette where woodsmen tame the wilderness by chopping logs like the cheerful settlers in *Across the Continent*. Each wagon in the Wild West poster holds admiring women and children watching the spectacle of the West from a safe seat, like the riders on the Currier & Ives train and like Cody's audiences. This image, like the program text, associated Buffalo Bill with the process of settling the West, even while it proudly displayed a wildness available for audience viewing. The poster itself was a landscape spectacle, made up of twenty-eight sheets and measuring twenty-four feet long, and any building, board, or wall on which it was posted was transformed, however briefly, into a representation of Western landscape scenery.

The scenic backdrops used in the Wild West's performances enhanced its suggestions that viewers were experiencing the Western landscape. When Matt Morgan designed elaborate sets for the 1886 Madison Square Garden season, his special effects included a prairie fire and a tornado. The Wild West carried scenery to England in 1887, a description of which says that a canvas backdrop surrounded the arena of the American Exhibition "to a great height, shutting out the neighboring houses. It is merged at the bottom into rocks, trees, and shrubbery, giving a realistic representation of a rocky pass in the mountains through which the scouts and Indians defile upon the plains represented by the arena."[4] Even when performing outdoors, the Wild West used whatever theatrical resources it could muster to evoke its imaginary Western frontier.

As early as 1884, the Wild West's program used color lithographs on its covers to picture the already memorialized landscape to which Buffalo Bill invited his spectators in their imaginations. The brilliant green front of the 1884 program shows Buffalo Bill on horseback, standing guard over a wagon train heading for a range of beautiful snow-capped mountains. As the settlers thread their way toward their destination, Buffalo Bill lingers behind in the tall prairie grass, a part of the pioneer past that enables the development of the future. This image also uses the trompe l'oeil technique of several other early cover designs: on closer inspection, this vivid Western landscape is a kind of billboard or book cover, its edges decoratively beveled, its right side shaded, and the tree branches on the left reaching in front of it, challenging the viewer's initial attempt to read it as a "real" representation of a landscape scene. It suggests a landscape that viewers are already prepared to understand and interpret, and it invites them to enjoy the illusion-making process. The back cover shows three other landscapes: scenes of buffalo grazing and of soldiers chasing Indians, and, most arrestingly, a stunning vertical image of Buffalo Bill as a lone horseman overlooking a deep mountain gorge. The spectator is gazing over Buffalo Bill's shoulder, entering with him into a moment of awed appreciation. This image enacts a deep American desire in the encounter with nature: to stand alone, as Emerson put it, in an "original relationship with the universe."[5] Just as a horseman on a billboard might be seen as really riding the plains, an experience shared with thousands of other spectators in a grandstand might re-create a moment of sublime solitude in the wilderness. In the program art, Buffalo Bill has traveled to the edge of the frontier. Horse and rider may look longingly toward the distant mountains, but the path they are riding on has come to an end. The solitary encounter with nature is only a memory, but spectators can try to recapture it.

Of course, in Buffalo Bill's Wild West as in American culture generally, the admiration for unspoiled nature and the celebration of forms of progress that necessarily transformed it created an unresolved tension. As the cultural

Buffalo Bill's Wild West, 1884 program, cover

historian Leo Marx suggested, the interrupted pastoral is a continuing theme in American art and literature.[6] A poem in the Wild West's 1885 program describes the Western landscape as a Garden of Eden, a "mount-inclosed valley, close sprinkled with fair flowers," a "wild Western Paradise." The poem is about what the historian Henry Nash Smith termed the "Virgin Land" of the frontier, yet also about the disruptions that settlement will bring. According to the poet, the idyllic scene is destroyed by "savage" Indians who turn the valley into a "vale of death," but the defeat of the Indians in the poem's conventional outcome does not restore pastoral simplicity. Buffalo Bill and his victorious soldiers inherit the legacy of a landscape that battle has transformed into a wasteland, where "slowly rises the smoke from heaps of slain."[7] Even while romanticizing the Indian battles, the poem, like the Wild West show itself, suggests that settlement has its costs. Visitors to the Columbian Exposition in 1893, with its vision of world conquest fresh in their minds, could still read this troubling poem in the program for Buffalo Bill's Wild West.

Nature's promise lures the settlers to the West, but the process of settlement forever changes the face of nature: this is the dilemma Americans began to sense in the late nineteenth and early twentieth centuries. Buffalo Bill's Wild West tried to deny the contradiction between nature and progress by locating both in the realm of memory, by offering viewers a chance to celebrate both the green prairie and solitary mountain peak and the forces that would transform them. It never relinquished its celebration of the forces of "progress": the stagecoach, the settler's cabin, the pony express, and the cattle ranch.

By the end of the nineteenth century, it was clear to many commentators that the landscape in Buffalo Bill's Wild West existed only in memory. "The wastes over which he guided troops to the camps and lurking places of hostile savages are now traversed by railways," wrote one reporter in 1896. "Towns have sprung up where the Indian lay in wait for the pioneer; Indian wars and massacres have become a memory."[8] For a reporter from the *Kansas City World*, the Western landscape had become thoroughly domesticated:

> Hay fields grow brown in the sun where the wandering tribes of Indians pitched their tepees and the dolorous squawk of the promising papoose has been succeeded by the rhythmic lullaby of the unoiled corn-sheller. Only Buffalo Bill remains. Standing as the connecting link between the past and the present, he draws back the curtain of retrospection and reveals the

picturesque figures who played dramatic parts in the border
life of American history. Buffalo Bill's Wild West show is a living picture of other days.[9]

Progress has already transformed the landscape of Buffalo Bill's Wild West,
but theatrical experience (drawing back the curtain) remains an important
way to recapture memory.

By the early twentieth century, program material for Buffalo Bill's Wild
West frankly promoted Cody's development schemes, the Wyoming city
named for him, the hotel he named for his daughter Irma, and "Pahaska
Tepee," the hunting lodge he ran as a tourist attraction. In 1896, Cody told
one reporter he was planning to retire from show business to devote himself
to development projects; the same year, he bragged about his work in domes-
ticating the Wyoming landscape. Irrigation, he asserted, "makes farming a
pleasure and crops a sure thing. With an irrigating canal you can water your
crops whenever they need it, as you would water a house plant."[10] But Cody
continued to celebrate Western wildness as well. A two-page spread on
Wyoming tourism in the show's 1907 courier was built around a text that
described Cody's interest in making Yellowstone National Park accessible for
more tourists who wanted to admire its "transcendently beautiful and awe-
inspiring scenery."[11]

Memories of wild nature were imperfectly evoked by the Wild West's
painted scenery and its program and poster art; but Buffalo Bill's Wild West
brought audiences into more direct contact with living embodiments of the
wilderness in the form of the animals that were always among its stellar
attractions. Live animals brought energy and excitement to Wild West performances; Nate Salsbury had been drawn to his partnership with Cody
because of his sense that displays of horsemanship would win audiences all
over the world. When Cody and Salsbury took their troupe to England in
1887, they carried across the ocean 176 horses, twelve mules, nine elk, two
deer, eight wild Texas steers, two oxen, and sixteen buffalo.[12] The wild animals, especially, seemed to reinforce the show's promise to bring spectators
into contact with the unspoiled nature of the West. But they were important
precisely because they continually re-enacted the loss of their wildness.
Bucking broncos were mastered by cowboy riders, steers were roped and
felled for branding, buffalo were hunted, ostensibly for their meat and skins.
The subduing of wild animals during the show was, of course, a fiction—the
broncos would buck again, the steers would flee the lariat, the buffalo would
race away from their pursuers again at the next show, and all of them could

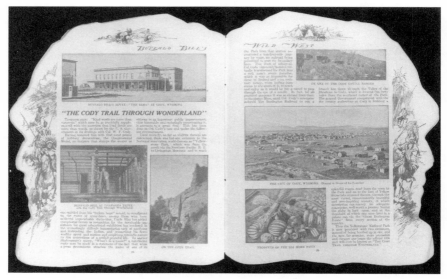

Wyoming tourism in Indian-Head Courier, 1907

be seen on the show grounds between performances. But an essential element of the Wild West was the impression of an encounter with the wild at the moment when it came under human domination.

The Wild West also brought to its audiences the illusion of an intimate, life-and-death encounter with the wild nature of the frontier. As a plains showman, Cody had been particularly successful as a guide for hunting parties, and his exploits as a hunter figured largely in his autobiography and the program text for the Wild West. Scholars today have commented on the connection between imperialism and the sport of hunting, but the Wild West's presentation of hunting differed from an imperial tiger shoot, for example, in its insistence on democratic rather than aristocratic values in the sport and its willingness to "go native," to extol and imitate American Indian hunting techniques.

In 1894, an article published under Cody's name in *The Cosmopolitan* magazine detailed some of his experiences as a hunting guide decades earlier on the Western plains. Although he focused on three aristocratic British hunters, Sir George Gore, Sir John Watts Garland, and Lord Adair, he emphasized the cooperative qualities rather than the imperial dominance of each of them. Sir George "adapted himself to his surroundings" with "ready good fellowship," being "a most unassuming man in dress and appearance." Sir John discarded English saddles and adopted the frontier practice of drink-

A Camp on the Plains, William F. Cody, "Famous Hunting Parties of the Plains, by 'Buffalo Bill,' " *Cosmopolitan*, 1894

Sir John Watts Garland's Camp in the Big Horn Mountains, William F. Cody, "Famous Hunting Parties of the Plains, by 'Buffalo Bill,' " *Cosmopolitan*, 1894

ing spirits before breakfast: "His democratic ways made him very popular
with the plainsmen. When he went out with a party, he roughed it like the
rest of us, slept in the open on his blanket, took his turn at camp duty and
rode his own horse in the races which we often got up for our amusement." A
number of photographs accompanying the article purported to represent
hunters' camps. A *Camp on the Plains* shows a simple tent and several men
standing near horses saddled for action, reiterating the theme of democratic
simplicity. Other illustrations suggested that hunting was the ultimate form
of landscape tourism. *Sir John Watts Garland's Camp in the Big Horn Mountains* is a scene that could come from a Bierstadt painting, a mountain
meadow surrounded by towering mountains, with a small tent right at its
heart. Masculine, imperial, and warlike, but also, in Buffalo Bill's version,
cooperative and democratic, the sport of hunting is connected in such
images with the aesthetic appreciation of nature, an appreciation made more
poignant because this privileged access to nature is understood to be a thing
of the past. "In these days, when the elk and buffalo are traditions, it is difficult, perhaps, for sportsmen to realize the wild exhilaration attending their
pursuit on horseback," the article states. On a more recent hunt, "It was sadly
evident that there was no more big game to be had. The buffalo, elk, and
antelope had long since disappeared." The very premise is retrospective:
titled "Famous Hunting Parties of the Plains," the article presented a memory of the past. Buffalo Bill's Wild West was a place where hunters still plied
their trade, where wild nature was still abundant. Its portrayal of animals in
the process of losing their wildness was another way of showing the transformation of the frontier itself. "The destruction of the big game in the West,
about which so much has been written, and which has been ascribed to so
many causes, is simply a natural consequence of the advance of civilization.
There is no longer any frontier."[13]

By far the most thrilling hunting tales, in text and performance, centered
around Buffalo Bill's namesake, the American bison. The bison was the
largest living indigenous life-form in the Americas, and it gave Plains Indians
and white settlers both food and trade commodities. Recent scholars have
tried to understand the mystery of the catastrophic collapse of this animal's
successful adaptation to the environment of the Great Plains. An ecology
that had lasted for ten thousand years and produced populations as large as
twenty to thirty million animals in the early nineteenth century was drasti-
cally altered within less than two decades of the end of the Civil War.[14] By
the time the Wild West began its performances, the buffalo were already in
serious decline, due partly to climate change, to disruptions in American

Indian society, and to the land use and hunting practices of the white pioneers. The southern herd, of which 3.7 million buffalo were killed by hide hunters in three years, ceased to exist by 1875, and the northern herd was too sparse to hunt by 1882.[15] When the program for the Wild West's 1885 season advertised "Lassoing and capturing Wild Buffalo, to be brought over 2,000 miles from their native pastures to assist in adding realism to the great 'Wild West,' " spectators could expect an encounter with a rare and exotic beast that was indeed "fast disappearing."[16] In 1887, Cody told a newspaper that "there are not so many buffaloes on the whole American continent as there are in the exhibition."[17] This was not literally true, of course, but that very same year the Smithsonian Institution recognized the dramatic diminution of the buffalo herds and began efforts to save the species from extinction. Cody's programs later reprinted an 1887 letter from General W. T. Sherman commenting on the Wild West's portrayal of "the history of civilization on this Continent during the past century," with an emphasis on the transformation of the wilderness. "As near as I can estimate there were *in 1865 about nine and a half of millions of buffaloes* on the plains between the Missouri River and the Rocky Mountains; all are now gone—killed for their meat, their skin and bones." To charges that this slaughter represented "desecration, cruelty, and murder," Sherman countered that the buffalo had been "replaced by twice as many *neat* cattle."[18] The 1885 program announced that "Messrs. Cody & Co. have a herd of healthy specimens of this hardy bovine in connection with their instructive exhibition, 'The Wild West.' " And the 1893 program added to the last sentence the phrase "rendered interesting as the last of their kind."[19] By 1907, the program advised viewers, "Remember the Buffaloes," and commented that "out of the many million buffalo that thirty years ago roamed over the great Western prairies scarcely five hundred head are now living."[20]

Newspaper accounts of the Wild West could joke about Cody's identification with the buffalo, as in one cartoon that showed him sitting in a restaurant receiving a bill from a buffalo with an apron, over the caption "Which is the Buffalo Bill?" or a sketch of a natty-looking Cody drawing on his gloves with a buffalo head on his shoulders.[21] French newspapers called him *Guillaume Bison* and printed humorous dialogues about the Wild West, including one in which a speaker pretends to think he is going to see *"les buffles à l'eau."*[22] But the significance of Cody's nickname should not be underestimated. He enjoyed telling and retelling the story of its origin in his buffalo-hunting days with the Union Pacific Railroad; when another old frontiersman came forward in 1911 to claim he was entitled to call himself the "real" Buf-

(*above*) *Buffalo-Shooting at the Earl's Court Exhibition*, from an 1892 scrapbook

(*left*) *Fancy Portrait of Colonel W. F. Cody, ("Buffalo Bill"),* from an 1892 scrapbook

I Am Coming, chromo-lithographic poster by Courier Lithography Co., 1900

falo Bill because he had used that name even before Cody, the showman sent an emissary to buy him off.[23] In 1907, the Wild West courier was assuring readers that Cody "never killed a buffalo unless the carcass was utilized to a good purpose; he never shot buffaloes for the mere sport of shooting."[24] By identifying himself with the buffalo, Cody attached himself to the mystique of the Great Plains and its natural environment. But this symbol of power and wildness was, from the early days of Cody's performance career, also a symbol for the rapid transformation of the Great Plains.

A turn-of-the-century lithographic poster shows the power of Cody's identification with the buffalo and suggests some of the ways in which the Wild West offered its audiences memories of American nature that could be balanced against the claims of progress. In front of a pale-green background with no visible horizon, an enormous brown bison fills the entire frame, all four feet off the ground in a running position, head turned to the viewer, white eyes and horns gleaming, its shape echoed by other dimly seen buffalo in the background. Set against the bison, like a circular target where its heart should be, is a head-and-shoulders portrait of a dignified "Col. W. F. Cody" in a decorated shirt, fringe-collared jacket, and gray Stetson hat, with white beard and long hair. Large letters proclaim "I AM COMING." On a simple level, this is a clever promotional poster of the type regularly placed in towns and cities by the Wild West's advance-publicity crew. (Another version was produced for the Wild West's tour of France, proclaiming "Je Viens," and after the troupe's return from Europe, the running buffalo was captioned "Here We Are! Home Again from Foreign Lands."[25]) It is striking that no explanatory text was needed. By 1900, the image makers could expect that viewers would immediately understand that the buffalo symbolized "Buffalo Bill's Wild West." *I AM COMING* suggests an almost messianic promise, an epiphany or revelation. But who is the "I" and where is he coming from? Buffalo Bill, a white-haired relic of older days, and the ever-youthful buffalo, running among the now-vanished herds in a dreamlike landscape, are vestiges of the past, heralds of memory. Buffalo Bill's Wild West represented itself as a place, a landscape of memory and imagination, in which spectators could temporarily suspend their awareness of the contradiction between progress and the preservation of unspoiled nature.

HIDDEN MEMORIES OF WAR

Buffalo Bill's Wild West traded overtly on certain kinds of memory and covertly on others. Just as a tension between progress and preservation underlay its evocation of the Western landscape, its narrative of frontier settlement was premised on the romance and terror of warfare. Audience awareness of the Indian wars created the interest in Buffalo Bill in the first place, and military conflict was the context for his celebrity until the day he died. Buffalo Bill's Wild West evoked memories of war—but what kind of memories, and what kind of war?

Cody began his stage career less than eight years after the close of the Civil War, the bloodiest conflict in American history, whose effects were still being reckoned, and which produced suffering unimagined by hawks on either side a dozen years earlier. More than a tenth of the male population had been killed in the war, the South struggled to rebuild its ruined cities and farms, the North recoiled from the assassination of Lincoln, and communities throughout the nation sought ways to understand and commemorate the sacrifice and disruption the war had wrought. Even as the effort of reconstruction and reconciliation continued, Cody was swept to celebrity on the strength of an enormous public appetite for fiction and drama that depicted scenes of war in the physically and imaginatively remote reaches of the far West. Frontier war stories, always a staple of American popular culture, took on a new significance, and Buffalo Bill became a symbol of this postbellum refiguring of military conflict.

The United States Army, heroically portrayed in Buffalo Bill dime novels, stage shows, and the Wild West, had been dramatically transformed during the Civil War years. In both North and South, the Southern secession brought a huge and rapid growth of military forces that contradicted the traditional American aversion to standing armies. In 1860, the United States Army was limited to fewer than thirteen thousand men, but millions of soldiers would be recruited during the conflict, officers trained, and budgets expanded. Even after the war's end, military forces retained a prominent place in American life: in 1870 there were still more than thirty-five thousand troops in uniform and almost three million veterans of military service, North and South.[26]

The transformations that began during the Civil War continued to have an important effect on military practice. The Indian wars of the 1870s were directed by some of the same generals who had risen to fame in the Union army. From the end of the Civil War until the abolition of the position in 1903, the post of Commanding General of the Army was held by a succession of Union army generals: Ulysses S. Grant, William T. Sherman, Philip H. Sheridan, John M. Schofield, and Nelson A. Miles. Sheridan, Cody's most consistent patron and supporter, commanded the Division of the Missouri, comprising much of the West, from 1869 to 1883. Civil War experiences influenced these generals' approach to the Indian wars. Both Sheridan and Sherman favored applying to the Great Plains the methods of total war they had used to break the back of the Confederacy. Yet the army and its leaders had powerful political enemies during these years, and many of their activities were controversial, such as using the army to suppress strikes and urban disorders.[27] The Civil War had created a modernized army and with it new questions about the military's role in American society.

The postbellum army also loomed large in the imagination of millions of veterans. The memory of Civil War service was kept alive in the North with the founding of the Grand Army of the Republic (GAR) in 1866, which gave former soldiers a continuing sense of connection to the United States Army through meetings, parades, and public events. The war had to recede by more than two decades before a parallel Confederate organization, the United Confederate Veterans, was launched in 1889, but throughout the South, Ladies' Memorial Associations (in which men often played important roles) promoted cemetery projects, so Southern white communities had ways to recognize the Confederate dead and their survivors.[28] By the time Buffalo

Bill began his stage career, the Civil War was being memorialized with parades, reunions, banquets, and civic monuments on both sides of the Mason-Dixon line.[29]

Fresh and painful Civil War memories were still being explored in literature and the visual arts in those same years. Walt Whitman's *Drum Taps* (1865) and Herman Melville's *Battle Pieces* (1866) registered the anguish of war. Mathew Brady, Alexander Gardner, and George Barnard published albums of sobering photographs of dead and wounded soldiers and ravaged landscapes. By contrast, dime-novel literature, stage melodrama, minstrel shows, and circuses all provided escapist relief from tragedies that touched almost all Americans directly or indirectly. It is worth inquiring into the relationship between memories of war and popular entertainment forms — including Cody's melodramas and frontier exhibitions — that glorified adventure and conflict.

During this period of controversy about American military identity, dime-novel, melodrama, and Wild West representations of the Indian wars offered a chance to reimagine the legacy of the Civil War. By returning to earlier conventions of individual heroism, by figuring the army scout as an intrepid individual rather than part of a sophisticated war machine, and by portraying battle as an unproblematic campaign against a known enemy (Indians) rather than a deadly struggle between two groups who shared language, culture, and history (the Civil War), Buffalo Bill's performances could disentangle the complexities of the post–Civil War era. No wonder General Sheridan supported him so enthusiastically: Buffalo Bill's Wild West made the army look good at a time when its social and political purpose was highly contested.

Yet structurally and thematically, the Wild West nonetheless evoked memories of the Civil War. The American flag was prominent in its spectacle. For many seasons, the flag-bearer was a public figure named Sergeant Bates, a Civil War veteran who had traveled around the country with a flag, giving patriotic lectures. Publicity about the Wild West's English season emphasized the fact that Queen Victoria had risen to salute the Stars and Stripes when Bates carried it into the ring. Performances by the cowboy band often included "The Star-Spangled Banner," not yet the country's national anthem but made ever more familiar through GAR programs and the Wild West.

Both Cody and Salsbury were Civil War veterans, and both were members of the GAR. Salsbury had joined the Fifteenth Illinois Volunteer Infantry at the age of fifteen and saw action for five years. He was always proud of his military service and liked to tell of a belated recognition that he received in 1888 at a dinner for the dramatist Dion Boucicault, when General Sherman, another guest, described an incident he had witnessed in Georgia: despite grueling conditions, a young Union soldier had showed his spunk and courage by climbing on a stump to entertain his friends, singing minstrel songs, reciting a speech from Hamlet, and dancing a jig; singing a verse from the song the general was recalling, Salsbury proved that he had been the soldier. "The General reached his hand across the table, grasped my hand and said 'That was the class of men that made the best soldier.' "[30]

Cody was active in the GAR and appeared at many Civil War memorial occasions. During a Memorial Day march down Fifth Avenue in New York in 1894, he rode as an aide to the GAR grand marshal; following a group of schoolgirls wearing caps made of American flags, a group of veterans carried a wreath in the shape of a cross surrounded by a circle, inscribed "Not Forgotten."[31] In England in 1892, the Wild West featured "Captain Jack Burtz, A Veteran of the Army of the American Republic," along with heroes of the frontier wars.[32] Cody's close association with the GAR shaped his politics in the 1890s: although he described himself as a lifelong Democrat and gave interviews praising William Jennings Bryan, by September 1896 he was traveling with a group of generals supporting McKinley. "For fifteen years I followed and obeyed some of the generals of the United States Army," he told the crowds. "You, who followed them before, will you hesitate now? You young men, think who they are. Think how your fathers obeyed them."[33] After thirty years, Cody was still using the rhetoric of Civil War memory. In 1897, he included in his program an engraving showing himself surrounded by portraits of military leaders under the title "Some of the Famous Generals of the U.S. Army Under Whom Buffalo Bill Has Served."

Yet, despite the close ties between the Wild West and the former Union army, Cody's shows were well received in the South. Although the 1884 New Orleans engagement was plagued by bad weather, it was enthusiastically reviewed by the local press. A reporter for the *Daily Picayune* compared it favorably to the circus and the dime novel, and concluded, "the entertainment is refined as well as instructive, and the best people of society attend it in Northern cities."[34] At the state fair in Richmond, Virginia, in 1888, Cody apparently attended the dedication of a monument to Confederate General George Pickett, and the Wild West traveled extensively in the South in 1895 and again in 1896, including stops in Richmond and Norfolk, Virginia; Wilmington, Goldsboro, Raleigh, Greensboro, Salisbury, Asheville, and Charlotte, North Carolina; Columbia and Charleston, South Carolina;

Some of the Famous Generals of the U.S. Army Under Whom Buffalo Bill Has Served,
Buffalo Bill's Wild West, 1894 program, page 4

Savannah, Augusta, Macon, Columbus, and Atlanta, Georgia; Montgomery, Birmingham, and New Decatur, Alabama; and Nashville and Chattanooga, Tennessee.[35]

Thematically, the Wild West resonated with Southern preoccupations. Hard riding, marksmanship, individual heroism, the battle between "civilization" and "savagery" were all familiar themes in the South. Some of the most popular Buffalo Bill novels and stage plays were written by Prentiss Ingraham, a Mississippian who had fought in the Confederate army.[36] *The Knight of the Plains,* one of Ingraham's scripts for Cody, deploys the chivalric metaphor with which the South understood its own cause. Furthermore, this Southern writer may have been responsible for the persistent presentation of the fight with Yellow Hand as if it were a duel of honor, in which the Indian chief insolently challenges the noble scout to single combat. The dime novel on which Cody's Yellow Hand stage play was based, *The Red Right Hand; Or, Buffalo Bill's First Scalp for Custer,* was later said to have been written by Ingraham.[37] Buffalo Bill's productions on stage and in the arena always stressed the heroic rescue of women and children from ruthless foes and the bravery of the handsome and gentlemanly scout, thematically resembling plantation literature of the postbellum period.

Furthermore, the Western dramas evoked racial attitudes familiar to the white South. Although the show brought "others"—Mexicans and Arabs and Cubans and American Indians—into the limelight in demonstrations of riding and roping, and although there were at least a few African-American per-

Judge Lynch, from an 1892 scrapbook

formers in some Wild West seasons, the melodramatic narratives returned again and again to stories of white settlers battling threatening Indian "savages." During the troubled years of Reconstruction, and when racial tensions increased with the imposition of Jim Crow laws throughout the South, the Wild West's emphasis on pageantry, patriotism, and (implied) white supremacy could not have been unwelcome to white Southerners. In 1892, the Wild West even included an enactment of a lynching, set in a Western context as the punishment for a horse thief but performed with uncritical gusto. Engravings of the lynching sequence show a dangling corpse that looks suspiciously like an African-American Union soldier. The Wild West performance of this sequence took it dangerously close to a celebration of racial violence at a time when lynching in the South was becoming a national scandal.

During the 1880s and 1890s, when Cody's popularity was at its height, Civil War memories re-emerged in a national attempt at memorialization and reconciliation that helped frame Cody's performances of heroism. From 1884 to 1887, *The Century* magazine ran a series called "Battles and Leaders of the Civil War," reviving the memory of the war for a new generation, but stressing personal valor rather than political or ideological differences. In the interests of balance, each issue included one article by a Confederate and one by a Union soldier. Battlefield commemorations also began to bring former Confederates and Union soldiers together, and so-called Blue-Gray reunions had become common. In 1888, a banquet in honor of Ulysses S. Grant's birthday was attended by a member of Robert E. Lee's wartime staff, who was received courteously.

The last quarter of the nineteenth century also witnessed the memorialization of Robert E. Lee as a national symbol of heroism and honor. When Lee died in 1870, he was mourned throughout the South, but a dozen years later, he was being celebrated as a hero to Americans of all camps when a series of monuments to him were erected. Eight thousand spectators gathered in 1883 to witness the unveiling of a recumbent statue of the general placed over his grave at Washington and Lee College in Lexington, Virginia. The sculpture's detailed portrayal of the general, sleeping but ready for active duty, suggested a wistful melancholy. Far more heroic was the equestrian statue of Lee unveiled with great ceremony in Richmond in 1890. Nine thousand people helped drag the statue to its site, then the rope with which it was hauled was cut into small souvenir pieces, like the relics of a saint. As many as one hundred thousand people participated in the dedication, in which Lee was compared to a Roman general; he was said by one spectator to have passed "forever from the gaze of time—into history."[38] By the centennial of Lee's birth, in 1907, a ceremony at Washington and Lee College included the New England historian Charles Francis Adams, Jr., who declared Lee "a great man—great in defeat, a noble, moral character."[39] In the early twentieth century, the dead Lee and the living Cody were being represented in remarkably similar ways, as exemplars of a vanished age of individual heroism that was admired by North and South alike.

The subterranean memories of the Civil War that underlay Wild West performances can help to explain its persistent themes of requiem and regret, from the very earliest performances. The elegiac tone of the Wild West's program, with its salute to a host of departed figures—old-time scouts and frontiersmen, vanishing buffalo and Indians—is characteristic of the memorializing impulse of the post–Civil War years. The Wild West celebrates, but it also mourns—a familiar duality in Civil War remembrances North and South.

Furthermore, the Wild West told a curiously inflected story of military conflict. Its enactments portrayed war as glorious, but returned again and again to incidents where heroic individuals fought, not to conquer land or wealth, but to repulse the savage attacks of a dangerous enemy. As the historian Richard White has pointed out, this narrative of white victimization inverts the history of white-Indian contact on the Great Plains. "[Buffalo Bill's] spectacles presented an account of Indian aggression and white defense; of Indian killers and white victims; of, in effect, badly abused conquerors."[40] But the Wild West's focus on defensive struggle meshes perfectly with postbellum remembrances of the Civil War. As the issues of the war faded and the desire for a shared history grew, war memorials came to celebrate individual acts of sacrifice (as represented, for example, by the anonymous young soldiers perched atop monuments in town squares, North and South, identically cast by the same foundries) and to interpret the war as an act of self-defense on both sides: protection of the Union in the North, and defense of hearth and home against heartless invaders in the South. In the attack on the settler's cabin or the Deadwood stagecoach, audiences could revisit their memories of the Civil War, now figured as a gallant struggle against a ruthless aggressor.

Historians have suggested that the Spanish-American War of 1898 finally ended the breach that had been opened by the Civil War, uniting the country behind its military forces and allowing the white South to vindicate its honor and emotionally rejoin the Union.[41] Buffalo Bill's Wild West was the precursor for that move, giving audiences in North and South a common experience of patriotism and uniting former enemies against a symbolic common enemy. In Buffalo Bill's Wild West, Civil War memories were evoked and transformed in the service of an emerging nationalism.

MEMORIES OF THE INDIAN WARS

From the time of his earliest stage plays, Buffalo Bill of course staked his claims to historical authenticity on the conflict that made him famous, the Indian wars. The relationship between this ostensible subject and the silently invoked Civil War was clearest in a figure prominent in both conflicts: General George Armstrong Custer. A flamboyant Civil War soldier known for his theatrical flirtations with danger, Custer had become a martyred symbol of postbellum military ardor after the Battle of the Little Big Horn in 1876. One meaning of his death was that it offered Americans a chance to revisit the theme of loss and sacrifice. Victor and victim, Custer represented both the modern military machine of the Union and the lost cause of the Confederacy.

Cody had dramatized his association with Custer in *The Red Right Hand* only months after the Battle of the Little Big Horn, and drew on his association with the general in many ways, from the battlefield press dispatches to the display of Yellow Hair's scalp to the engravings in his autobiography and program booklets. An enactment of Custer's Last Stand entered the Wild West repertory as early as 1887, and it was reintroduced to the program halfway through the 1893 season at the Columbian Exposition. Reviews in Chicago and in subsequent seasons told audiences that viewing this re-enactment could make them feel they had witnessed the historical events themselves. "The reproduction of the 'Battle of the Little Big Horn' was wonderfully realistic," wrote a reviewer in 1894. "One sitting in the grand stand need no great stretch of the imagination to bring himself to feel that he was on the plains within eyeshot of the spot where Gen. Custer made his last charge. . . . It was a scene long to be remembered, so vividly were the minutest details portrayed of the slaughter of those brave men who were with Custer in his last charge."[42] By remembering the performance, the reviewer implies, the spectator could have the illusion of remembering the event itself and sharing the emotions it provoked.

Furthermore, the Wild West's presentation of the battle gave audiences an opportunity to recast defeat as victory. Although the dramatic enactment portrayed the death of Custer and his men, Buffalo Bill rode onto the stage at

Wild West enactment of Custer's Last Stand, 1894

the incident's conclusion, counter-factually suggesting a triumphant happy ending. Indeed, the Wild West's version of Custer's Last Stand could be seen as an act of revenge for the Battle of the Little Big Horn. Again and again, reviewers stressed that Indian performers in the Wild West had been, or were believed to have been, actual participants in the battle. Not only did the claim bolster the Wild West's pretensions to authenticity, but it also suggested that the tables were now turned: Indians who had mastered Custer were now under the control of Buffalo Bill. After Wounded Knee, a three-way dynamic emerged. In 1894, a reviewer noted that ten of the Indians in the show "took an active part in the massacre of Gen. Custer and his command," while the cavalrymen who performed beside them, including the "personator" of Custer, had served in the battle of Wounded Knee, where, presumably, the slaughter of Sioux avenged the death of Custer and his men.[43] By alluding to the best-known battle of the Indian wars, which also aroused deep emotions associated with the Civil War, the Wild West encouraged audiences to imagine their own participation in historical memory and, indeed, to rewrite history.

Cody was not alone in evoking the memory of the Battle of the Little Big Horn, of course. Custer's legend penetrated American culture on many fronts, from politics to poetry to biography to popular culture.[44] But it may have been the popularity of Buffalo Bill's enactments of the Battle of the Little Big Horn in the 1890s that helped to inspire the brewer Adolphus Busch to commission a print of Custer's Last Stand to help promote his beer, Budweiser, as a national brand. Busch had already acquired a massive painting of the subject by Cassilly Adams. He gave that work to Custer's own military unit, the Seventh Cavalry, and arranged to have F. Otto Becker do a lithograph of it, issued in a first-run edition of fifteen thousand in 1896.

The Becker lithograph, which soon hung in saloons all across America and was reissued many times, was seen by millions of people and functioned, like the Wild West's re-enactments, to rewrite popular historical memory. Although no white participants were known to have survived the Battle of the Little Big Horn, in later days numerous purported eyewitnesses emerged, often basing their stories on the image in the lithograph. One old-timer was said to have pointed out the place where, he said, he lay for two days after the battle: "I was right there," he announced, striking the picture with his cane, "right there under that hoss."[45] Becker's lithograph showed the battle scene as smoky and crowded with figures, not unlike the arena representations of Custer's Last Stand, and it also featured a central vignette of Custer in hand-to-hand battle with a single Indian. Of course, Cody's claim to have struggled in single combat with Yellow Hand was by now well known, from the stage plays to the autobiographical writings: "I know you, Pa-he-haska; if you want

F. Otto Becker, *Custer's Last Fight*, lithograph

Custer's Last Rally, c. 1893, color lithograph, poster by A. Hoen & Co.

Death of Custer, photograph by Siegel Cooper & Co., Chicago

to fight, come ahead and fight me."[46] At about the same time the Becker print became widely known, the Wild West used an image of Custer's Last Stand on a poster, and it, too, showed Custer in heroic individual combat. Did a memory of Cody's performance become the basis for a representation of Custer that then became the foundation for the Wild West's version of the same event? A photograph entitled "Death of Custer" shows five performers from Buffalo Bill's Wild West posed against a painted backdrop. As three dead Indians lie at his feet, Custer struggles with a single antagonist, who stabs him. His upraised sword in one hand and pistol in the other, the figure of Custer echoes the echo of Buffalo Bill.

The Wild West offered several other scenes in addition to the Battle of the Little Big Horn that were to be understood as representations of "real" incidents of the Indian wars, including the Battle of Summit Springs, in which Cody helped to rescue a white captive and killed Tall Bull. Still other generic episodes also claimed to be truthful to the facts of border warfare. The attack on the settler's cabin and the rescue of the Deadwood stagecoach shared the scenario of Custer's Last Stand and its emotional power. Exciting battles with Indians appeared to be morally and emotionally authorized because they were understood as white retaliation against Indian aggression. As many commentators have noted, the Wild West's war narratives glorify American conquest and invite spectators to unite in their enmity toward a demonized "other" in the form of the American Indians.[47] Although the final result of the Indian wars was still at issue before Wounded Knee, Buffalo Bill's Wild West always presumed the outcome: the "triumph" of "civilization" over "savagery."

And yet, the participation of American Indians themselves in the enactment of their defeat enabled the Wild West to bathe its war stories in a mellower light. Encouraging audiences to hate "the savages" but love the Indian performers, it suggested an attitude the nation could take—triumphant in war but magnanimous to its former enemy—that suited Americans as memories of the Civil War faded into the distant past. By presenting the Indian wars—indeed, the Indians themselves—as spectacles of memory, the Wild West lent the immediacy and conviction of live performance to the proposition so often advanced in popular fiction and patriotic oratory, that war was a noble undertaking and that heroism and even sacrifice were justified by a righteous cause. As memories of Civil War losses receded and veterans North and South reaffirmed their allegiance to the kind of romantic patriotism that had brought it about, Buffalo Bill's Wild West helped to make war imaginatively appealing once again.

By the end of the century, the Indian wars themselves retreated into the past, and Cody's performances interpreted other military events as memories of the Indian wars. America's war with Spain in 1898 seemed to invite America's most visible symbol of military heroism to cross the border once again from showmanship to military duty. When conflict with Spain loomed on the horizon, Cody tried to make a dramatic intervention, which would have advanced in a new and more powerful way the claim of military leadership he had been making for twenty years. In early April 1898, the *New York World* published a proposal by Cody to raise a troop of American Indians to fight the Spanish in Cuba. Under the headline "How I Could Drive Spaniards from Cuba with 30,000 Indian Braves," Cody sketched a scenario in which the Indian warriors of the past would ride again, this time fighting on the side of the United States Army. Drawing on the very image of the fierce redskin that animated the Wild West performances, Cody proposed to turn those qualities to the advantage of American patriotism. "I wish to say first that every Indian would be loyal to the American flag," he asserted, then proposed that American Indians could be effectively mobilized against Spain. "The American Indian has by no means forgotten how to fight. He is a natural-born fighter, and is just as anxious to go to war now as he ever was, and he would rather fight Spaniards than any other people on earth. Why? Because Spain sent the first white man to America." After naming a number of American Indians he considered great war leaders, from Chief American Horse to Chief Joseph to Geronimo, Cody envisioned an attack on Havana by "shouting Indian braves on horseback, resplendent in brilliant war paint, the eagle feathers on their war bonnets fluttering in the wind."[48] Cody projected the capture of Havana as if it were already an act in Buffalo Bill's Wild West; he imagined war imitating the re-enactment of war and, in particular, modern war replaying the Indian wars. The article was excellent publicity for the Wild West, of course, for however slim were the chances of American Indians being sent to Cuba, that season every reader could go to Ambrose Park and see the scene Cody described being performed twice a day. And the article also sums up the struggle between Cody and the pro-assimilation Indian reformers, who must have been horrified to read Buffalo Bill's claim that Indians were naturally warlike, had not forgotten the old ways, and were eager to resume them. Audiences were apparently happy to participate in Cody's latest military fantasy. A few weeks later, another New York newspaper printed a photograph of a group of Wild West Indian performers listening to one of their leaders, with the caption, "Red Horn Bull Telling Sioux that Uncle Sam May Need Them."[49]

Buffalo Bill, "How I Could Drive Spaniards from Cuba with 30,000 Indian Braves," from an 1898 scrapbook

Red Horn Bull Telling Sioux That Uncle Sam May Need Them, from an 1898 scrapbook

But in 1898, Cody was not able to cross the line between performance and military action as readily as he could in 1890, when he was asked by General Miles to play a part in the aftermath of Wounded Knee. Although Cody told Miles he was willing to go to the battlefield and sent his horses ahead to be ready for him, he was never active in the Spanish-American War. He told reporters in March and April that he was "eager to go" and "ready to start immediately," but the call never came. A newspaper interview in July reported that Cody sat in his tent sporting his decorations — jeweled buffalo heads from Grand Duke Alexis and a watch charm from the Prince of Wales—while wishing he were in Cuba with the American troops: "Buffalo Bill sat a typical American, longing more than anything else for an opportunity to get down to the front with the troops of scouts and rough riders which some time ago he tendered to the government."[50] By the time Miles himself arrived on the scene, the war was almost over; Spanish forces in Cuba surrendered on July 17, just ten days after his arrival.[51] In fact, Cody had been superseded as a national symbol by Lieutenant Colonel Theodore Roosevelt, whose charge on San Juan Hill became a new symbol for American military heroism. But Roosevelt reaped his fame by echoing the vision of war Buffalo Bill had made so familiar: his First Regiment of United States Volunteer Cavalry took on the title of the "Rough Riders," a phrase that had entered the national vocabulary through the Wild West.

Although Buffalo Bill did not go to Cuba, Cody and his managers did bring Cuba to the Wild West, where performances about the Spanish-American War appeared to mesh seamlessly with those of the Indian wars. Cuban war veterans performed in the show as early as March 1898. Newspapers reported that "Battle-Scarred Cuban Soldiers [were] the Feature of the Wild West Show," and described the crowds as "Wild for Old Glory and the Single Star [the Cuban independence flag]." In June, a performance was disrupted when the audience caught sight of two little girls waving United States and Cuba Libre flags. The "storm of cheering and applause" caused Cody to interrupt the act in the arena, ride toward the grandstand, and order the cowboy band to play "Yankee Doodle," bringing "the enthusiasm of the audience to its highest possible pitch."[52] Gallant as was Cody's response, he could not have been pleased to be upstaged. His advertising took on a more overtly military theme. In August 1898, a flier called the Wild West "the Show that Means Something" and promised "Now Bigger and Better Than Ever, Military Display, Unique, It Stands Alone. Up to the Spirit of the Times, Many New Features Added." The three acts promoted in largest letters were the Rough Riders, Custer's Last Battle, and "Cuban Heroes."[53]

In 1899, the Wild West added to its program an enactment of the Battle of San Juan Hill, complete with "detachments from Roosevelt's Rough Riders." Although Buffalo Bill could no longer present himself as a participant in the war he represented, the program text waxed even more eloquent in its claims to historical accuracy. Nate Salsbury's introductory statement reached new heights of rhetoric, proclaiming that "the historian on horseback has Truth for his amanuensis," and describing the Wild West as

the grandest and most cosmopolitan Object Teacher ever projected by the exceptional experience and executive genius of
man, scrupulously truthful in every respect, with every feature
herein or elsewhere announced forthcoming, every historical
and personal reference authentic, and every narrative,
endorsement and criticism correct in spirit, context and appli-
cation, as regards incident, person, time and location. It presents, with a colossal perfection and verisimilitude utterly
impossible under any other management, living spectacles of
heroic deeds of patriotic devotion and savage resistance; the
pomp and circumstances of royal and republican martial array
and wildly picturesque and fearsome panoply; the rush, the
rally, the splendid force and action of embattled mounted
hosts; artillery in skilled and stirring evolutions.

The program cover took a dramatic turn, portraying a much older-looking
Buffalo Bill, as if to quell any possible questions about his absence on the bat-
tlefields of 1898. And the text made a strong case for the proposition that the

Buffalo Bill's Wild West and
Congress of Rough Riders,
1899 program, cover

Rough Riders at San Juan Hill were, in a sense, an extension of Buffalo Bill himself: "The powerful, practical, patriotic influence of Buffalo Bill's Wild West and Congress of Rough Riders of the World as a mighty and masterly National Object Teacher was strikingly manifested in the suggestion, formation, and even the popular naming of the most fearless and famous single military organization in all martial annals—Teddy Roosevelt's Regiment of Rough Riders."[54]

Now that the scope of the Wild West included other, more modern wars, further new acts were added. Some of these reflected the United States' dramatically altered world stance after the territorial acquisitions of the Spanish-American War. The 1899 printed program included a section on "Strange People from our New Possessions. Families of Porto Ricans, Sandwich Islanders and Filipinos." The Wild West expanded its international interest beyond the display of horsemanship from around the world to take on a quasi-ethnological mission:

> We have delayed the publication of this historical narrative until the last possible moment, in hopes—which as we go to press we are gratified to be able to announce have been fully realized—that our special agent sent to Porto Rico and the Sandwich and the Philippine Islands would be able to secure the finest representatives of the strange and interesting aboriginals of the West Indies and the intermediate and remote

Strange People from Our New Possessions, Buffalo Bill's Wild West and Congress of Rough Riders, 1899 program, page 63

International performers,
*Buffalo Bill's Wild West
and Congress of Rough
Riders,* 1899 program,
page 29

Pacific isles, now grouped by the fate of war, the hand of progress and the conquering march of civilization under Old Glory's protecting folds.

A photograph of Filipino natives showed the same kind of condescending curiosity about the world's peoples that had led to earlier articles like "An Indian's Religion" and "The Bow and Arrow." An illustration from the same program showing various acts from around the world, including acrobats and jugglers, no doubt reflected this turn toward imperialist thinking as well as the increased influence of James Bailey and his pull toward circus acts. By 1900, Filipino performers were appearing in acts like the relay races, and in 1901, two new international conflicts were represented on the program: the Boer War was recognized through the presence of wounded veterans in the Grand Processional—a commando group of Transvaal Boers, a delegation from the Canadian Strathcona Horse (Mounted Police), and a band of Baden-Powell's Defenders of Mafeking—and the Boxer Rebellion in China was enacted in "Battle of Tien-Tsin," in which Allied forces replaced "the Royal Standard of Paganism" with "the Banners of Civilization."[55] But, although the new internationalism appeared to be a turn away from the Wild West's traditional focus on the story of the American frontier, the multiple meanings embodied in its presentation of American Indian performers could be found in its new international perspective as well. Presented as curiosities, valued for their differentness, but safely encased in the presumption of remoteness, the international peoples of the Wild West were also viewed, like the buffalo and the American Indians, as memorials of an imaginative world distant in time and space. But no matter how many new narratives were added, the Wild West continued to present every struggle as a memory of the Indian wars and perhaps, covertly, of the Civil War as well.

MEMORY AND FILM

Cody's efforts to create and disseminate memories of war took one final, surprising turn toward the end of his life. In 1913, he produced an ambitious film, *Indian War Pictures*, that re-enacted battles from three campaigns of the Indian wars on the original sites and with the participation of many survivors. This enterprise carried the impulse of Buffalo Bill's Wild West into the age of cinema; it recorded for motion-picture cameras the same memorializing spirit that made the arena show so compelling to its viewers, simultaneously claiming authenticity and deploying techniques of fiction. In this film, Cody himself took the Wild West to the threshold of its next phase, the film Western that would carry the incidents, images, and concerns of his productions into the late twentieth century.

Cody had experimented with new technologies throughout the history of his show. He had begun to use electricity to light the arena as early as 1893, and for the 1894 season in Brooklyn, he and Salsbury had contracted with the Edison Illuminating Company to install a powerhouse for the show grounds.[56] Perhaps on the strength of this connection, groups of Wild West performers visited Edison's laboratory that summer and fall to be filmed with his new kinetoscope technology. Edison's Wild West films featured individual performers, such as Mexicans demonstrating lasso throwing and Annie Oakley shooting at targets, but they also included several short pieces focused on the Indian war narratives: *Buffalo Bill, Sioux Ghost Dance, Buffalo Dance,* and *Indian War Council* were among the kinetoscope productions Edison advertised.[57]

During the next few years, several filmings recorded the Wild West's show-business spectacle. Cameramen photographed the Wild West parade through the streets of New York and in a smaller city, and the American Mutascope and Biography Company shot footage of the Wild West's arena performance, including Buffalo Bill's trademark sweep of his hat and announcement of the Rough Riders of the World. In 1910, the Buffalo Bill and Pawnee Bill Film Company produced three reels of film showing acts from the Wild West.[58]

Although these early efforts focused on documenting the acts themselves, recording with the camera's eye what the spectator might see in the arena, it was soon apparent to Cody and others that cinema could also attempt to tell the story of the Indian wars directly, replicating in a new medium the powerful blend of documentation and fictionality the Wild West deployed so successfully. In 1912, the Buffalo Bill and Pawnee Bill Film Company produced a one-reel *Life of Buffalo Bill* that juxtaposed an appearance by Cody with an actor's representation of adventures from his earlier career. The film begins as the "real" Buffalo Bill, Cody himself, rides along a trail. He demonstrates his tracking skills, dismounts, unsaddles his horse, and lies down to sleep. Intertitles announce "A dream of the days of his youth," and an actor playing his younger self stars in vignettes drawn directly from the arena show. Indians attack a wagon train, Buffalo Bill saves a stagecoach and captures a gang of bandits, and the "Famous Duel Between Chief Yellow Hand and Buffalo Bill" produces "The First Scalp for Custer." The everyday life of the Indian camp and the wagon train is depicted, and soldiers and Indians ride furiously across the landscape. The film ends when the present-day Buffalo Bill awakes from his dream, saddles his horse, and rides off.[59]

By the time Cody appeared in *The Life of Buffalo Bill*, Western themes were already a staple of the new film medium. In 1910, more than 20 percent of the films made in America were Westerns.[60] The year after American Mutascope and Biograph filmed Buffalo Bill's Wild West parade, cameramen for that company began to shoot a film released in 1904 as *The Pioneers*, which contained episodes closely related to the Wild West's famous "Attack on a Settler's Cabin": "Settler's Home Life," "Firing the Cabin," "Discovery of Bodies," and "Rescue of Child from Indians."[61] By 1912, Biograph had already produced more than seventy film Westerns, and D. W. Griffith had directed at least fifteen of them, including a version of Helen Hunt Jackson's *Ramona*, starring Mary Pickford, in 1910.[62] From its very birth, the film Western drew on a set of audience expectations formed by dime novels and story magazines, but, of course, also by the Wild West performances that so many millions had seen and were still seeing.

The Life of Buffalo Bill was Cody's first effort in film, and it drew on the two most powerful techniques he had developed as a showman: the evocation of Western events and landscapes as memory, and the claim to authenticity derived from the participation of "actual" Western figures, in this case

himself and the Indians from his company. As in the Wild West performances, the "historic" figure of Buffalo Bill opened and closed it, giving a
stamp of historicity to the dramatic scenes. The new film medium gave a
sense of "real life" to highly dramatic scenes; in holding these claims in balance and creating a convincing impression of shared memory, it was
indebted to the Wild West forerunner.

Indian War Pictures carried the idea behind *The Life of Buffalo Bill* a
step further. Cody had the idea of creating a "historically correct" motion
picture about the Indian wars with the cooperation of some old army
friends—including Lieutenant General Nelson Miles, Major General Jesse
M. Lee, Major General Charles King, Brigadier General Marion Maus,
and Brigadier General Frank Baldwin. Unlike *The Life of Buffalo Bill*, all
of the parts would be played not by actors but by actual participants. Since
this would mean that a sixty-seven-year-old Cody would re-enact deeds he
had done at the age of thirty, it crossed a crucial line, abandoning cine-
matic believability in the interests of historical accuracy. When the elderly
Buffalo Bill held up the scalp of Yellow Hand in the film, audiences would
realize they were watching a re-enactment, substituting the pleasure of
thinking "that is the real man" for the satisfaction of imagining "that is
what it must have looked like." And perhaps that preference for history over
drama was at least one of the reasons that the film was not popular and disappeared from view.

The task of re-creating the Indian wars for film was daunting, but the
problems were similar to those Cody had handled for years in arranging for
his traveling companies. He had to seek permission from the Secretary of the
Interior, the Commissioner of Indian Affairs, the Secretaries of War and the
Army; he had to arrange for horses, equipment, and support staff, enlist participants, and publicize his operations. He also had to find the money for his
operations, and it is important to realize that the film project came into being
just when his financial situation was at its darkest: the Two Bills show had
been forced into bankruptcy, his property was mortgaged, and he was about
to begin touring with the Sells-Floto Circus. Cody was desperate for a plan to
recoup his finances as well as his self-respect. The film project incorporated
all the aspects of the Wild West he would have to leave behind in the circus
ring: the enactment of battle scenes, the claim to authenticity, the association
with army generals and Indian chiefs. It would also allow him to pay American Indian performers who had been dismissed without salary when the Two
Bills show was closed down. Cody turned for financial support to Harry Tammen, although the latter had been responsible for forcing him into bank-

Filming *The Indian Wars*

Scene from *The Indian Wars*: First Scalp for Custer

ruptcy. Tammen, willing to realize ever more profit from his association with Buffalo Bill, helped to underwrite the production, sent a reporter from the *Denver Post* to cover the filming, and secured the expertise of the Essanay Film Company of Chicago, in which he had an interest.

Essanay was a partnership between two movie producers, with S standing for George K. Spoor, a longtime associate of Tammen's, and A for Gilbert M. Anderson, who had played the role of a passenger in *The Great Train Robbery* in 1903, and had already starred in more than 150 films as the movie cowboy Bronco Billy. Of course, the Wild West had been key in creating the cowboy mystique so effectively evoked in these early films, and even Anderson's assumed name suggested the bronco-busting displays of Buffalo Bill. Essanay's participation in the Indian-war film completed a circle: the Wild West established a popular understanding of and hunger for dramatic representations of the frontier, which the emerging film industry could tap; now a film company gave a new look to the putatively historical features of the Wild West.

Indian War Pictures was a breathtaking enterprise. The enactment of the battles of Summit Springs ("Killing of Tall Bull," 1869) and War Bonnet Creek ("First Scalp for Custer," 1876) had been staples of the Wild West

Indian Man on Hilltop with Arms Outstretched Facing Group of Indians, probably taken during the filming of *The Indian Wars*, 1913

program for years, so the contours of their presentation were already familiar to Cody and his audiences. Transferring them to film added little thematically; it mainly meant solving technical challenges, choreographing movements through the landscape and adding scenes to take advantage of outdoor locations. But the Battle of Wounded Knee (1890) was a different matter. Although the program had referred to this event for years, Cody had never staged it in the arena. And because the episode was far more recent and involved not a battlefield encounter between warriors but religious ceremonies and the slaughter of Sioux women and children by the United States Army, memories of the event were still poignant and contested for many participants. Bringing Indian survivors to the scene of the massacre, representing Ghost Dance ceremonies, re-enacting their terror-stricken flight into a ravine, simulating the firing of the deadly Hotchkiss gun that killed so many—Cody found all this unleashed more passion than he had anticipated. According to one account, Indian women chanted death songs and wept when they returned to the scene of the slaughter, and it was reported that some of the young men vowed to use live ammunition in the battle scene to avenge their fathers.[63] Opting for the greater realism made possible by the film medium, Cody had disrupted the delicate balance between role-playing and memory that his show had managed to maintain for thirty years.

Oddly enough, this also produced a schism between Cody and his old military friends. General Miles insisted that the film should show all eleven thousand troops that had come to Pine Ridge for the surrender of the Sioux, and spent several hours marching a much smaller contingent of troops in circles around the camera so there would appear to be more of them. He quarreled with Cody over his insistence that the company had to be transported to the Badlands for authenticity in shooting the scenes that occurred there. Although this was finally done, the friendship between the two men suffered.[64]

The shoot—between September 26 and November 1, 1913, under the direction of Theodore Wharton—produced over thirty thousand feet of negatives. After a screening for the Secretary of the Interior and other government officials, an edited version of the film was released to the public. Judging from surviving advertisements and promotional materials, there were at least three versions, one of eight reels, one of six, and another of five. The eight-reel version, like a Wild West performance, started and ended with references to present time: introductory glimpses of Buffalo Bill and his advisors, and concluding vignettes of then-present-day reservation life. This framing structure was like the opening and closing processionals of the Wild West performance, and also recalled the visit to the Indian encampment that was always part of the audience experience of the Wild West. The film then devoted one reel each to the battles of Summit Springs and War Bonnet Creek, but Wounded Knee (described as the Rebellion of 1890–91) was treated in much more detail, spanning five reels. As if to acknowledge the complexity of this event, the film proceeded from one vignette to another, including the rise of the Ghost Dance religion, the escalation of tensions, Buffalo Bill's failed mission to Sitting Bull, the death of Sitting Bull, the flight and capture of Big Foot's band, the outbreak of violence at Wounded Knee Creek, and the surrender at Pine Ridge. The final reel depicts life at Pine Ridge, scenes from an Indian school, and "the TRANSITION OF THE RED MAN, from the WARPATH TO PEACE PURSUITS, under the American Flag—'The Star Spangled Banner.' "[65]

Many signs indicate that, unlike Buffalo Bill's Wild West, Cody's film project never found its ruling principles of coherence. It was apparently edited and re-edited, released in the different versions at different lengths. It never seemed to acquire a single, defining title. Announcements of screenings called it, variously, *Last Indian Battles, Indian Wars, Buffalo Bill's War Pictures, Indian War Pictures,* and *Indian Wars Refought by United States Army.* It was shown under varying conditions, from theaters to clubs, in Washington, New York, and Denver.[66] But although it received much press coverage, it was never widely exhibited. By November 1914, advertisements in *The Moving Picture World* were cajoling exhibitors to show it, promising "Fifteen Different Styles of Posters, Heralds, Slides, and Lobby Displays," praising its "beautiful Photography and Realistic Scenes," and asserting that "Nothing more picturesque, more thrillingly entertaining was ever staged. Nothing to equal it will, perhaps, ever be done again. No boy, girl or grown-up should be allowed to miss this picture."[67] With so many short, dramatic, fictional film Westerns to choose from, theaters and audiences were not persuaded by the production's claims to historical authenticity.

Cody's supporters did their best to promote the film. Tammen's *Denver Post* ran special reports from the filming site in 1913, and anticipated the Denver screenings with an article "from the facile and brilliant pen of Lieutentant General Nelson A. Miles" in March 1914. Reviews stressed the film's "terrible realism" and reported that viewers were "spell-bound." "Bill, I didn't think it could be done," a veteran of the Custer campaign was said to have remarked after the Washington performance. "I didn't think until I saw these pictures that it would be possible to reproduce what we went through out there." "Nothing like this has ever been done before," a Denver review read. "Nothing to equal it will perhaps ever be done again. It is not a 'photo play.' It is not a series of 'staged spectacles.' It is War itself; grim, unpitying and terrible." In Denver, a surprise appearance at the movie theater by Cody himself enhanced the film's claims to realism. After the segments that featured his exploits, Buffalo Bill appeared onstage, riding his horse Isham. Sweeping off his hat as if he were introducing the Wild West, he patted his horse and delivered his lines: "Gee, old pard, that was a hot one; we are going swift; two victories of forty-five and thirty-eight years ago in forty minutes, and another campaign to move on for." John Burke gave press interviews touting "the sudden rise in [Cody's] fortune by the Historic Picture company's sensation in the moving film world."[68] But despite the ballyhoo, the film fizzled. Tammen tried to revive it in the surge of nostalgia after Buffalo Bill's death in 1917, and Essanay re-edited some of the scenes for a film released that same year, *The Adventures of Buffalo Bill*. Neither effort gained national attention. Although Cody had announced that he was depositing the original footage with the government, it is now lost. Copies of *Indian Wars Pictures* owned by the Buffalo Bill Museum in Cody, Wyoming, deteriorated long ago due to exposure to heat and cold. Some fragments have been found, and the film is also known from a remarkable series of stills, but there is little left of the enterprise on which Cody staked the recovery of his fortunes and the translation of his historical claims into the new medium.[69]

The experience of re-enacting scenes from the Indian wars on the original location with survivors of the event had shaken the alliance Cody had achieved with his military colleagues and his Indian performers. It also troubled his relationship with his audience. Buffalo Bill's Wild West had promised spectators that they could experience vicarious thrills without danger or discomfort, imagine war without reckoning its costs, experience the hatred of an enemy but feel reassured about their own magnanimity. The show had claimed realism and educational value, but it had shown spectators a glamorous, scripted, patriotic performance spectacle. In 1914, Cody was forced to separate the fictive from the educational aspects of his performance, playing the part of the picturesque old-timer for the circus while bringing to the screen a two-and-a-half-hour representation of war that disturbed even those who helped to enact it. Loyal John Burke, traveling in advance of Cody's Sells-Floto appearances to whip up enthusiasm, tried to put a good face on the split. In the circus, Buffalo Bill would "bring the subject of the western story in closer touch and more pleasant conditions to the little ones," while "in the moving pictures, he is an active factor as in days of old, in lifelike and life-sized scenes."[70] By dissolving the doubleness that gave the Wild West its animating tension, Cody's last ventures into the realm of memory lost their magic. *Indian War Pictures* showed spectacles too painful to be popular: the numbing brutality of war, the panic of war's victims, and the pretensions of an old man trying to recapture his youth.

CONCLUSION
PERFORMING NATIONAL IDENTITY

Buffalo Bill's Wild West helped to shape both the substance of an American national identity and the tools for its cultural dissemination. Before Frederick Jackson Turner wrote a word about the frontier, and before Theodore Roosevelt established that the virtues of the strenuous life should be the basis for national pride and political success, Buffalo Bill had brilliantly propounded the thesis that American identity was founded on the Western experience: triumphant conquest of wildness through virtue, skill, and firepower. At the same time, and equally important, the Wild West sanitized this narrative. In its fictionalized historical representation, Americans could savor the thrill of danger without risking its consequences, could believe that struggle and conflict inflicted no lasting wounds, and could see for themselves that the enemy "other" would rise from the dust, wave to the crowd, and sell souvenir photographs at the end of the day.

Buffalo Bill's frontier thesis was never an explicit, coherent theory about what America was. Rather, its power came from being a spectacle so gripping, so encompassing, so sensuous that it became part of its spectators' own experience. Buffalo Bill's showmanship *created* American memory through the medium of popular entertainment. In doing so, it heralded the opening of a new age in mass communications in which both political and economic authority would accrue to those who could most effectively spin a message, sell a product, and shape popular perceptions. Not only did Buffalo Bill's Wild West promulgate a particular interpretation of American identity, but it also demonstrated the power of mass media to formulate values.

The substance of Buffalo Bill's frontier thesis infused American thinking for most of the twentieth century. From patriotic parades to football cheers, from tourist promotions to cigarette advertising, the image of the virile Western hero never lost its allure as a symbol of the American spirit. A recent book featuring beautiful photographs of artifacts from the largest private collection of Buffalo Bill memorabilia makes plain its authors' nostalgia for the Wild West's notion of American life. The authors acknowledge their love for the "romance and ethos of the Old West." That ethos seems to them still operative: "Not only is American culture the richer and more fascinating because of [Buffalo Bill's] unique legacy, but so is the rest of the world's." At the same time, these admiring collectors specifically associate the legacy of the Old West with a set of values threatened by late-twentieth-century transformations, those of their own childhood, when nation and family seemed to follow the script so carefully crafted by Cody and his associates: "an age of heroes, when there was still widespread respect for parental authority."[1] As the authors tacitly acknowledge, the considerable cynicism in public life in the late twentieth century worked against the tradition of uncritical hero worship. A chorus of voices raised questions about the values that underlay the romance of the Old West—from Stanley Kubrick, whose *Dr. Strangelove* envisioned the doomsday nuclear bomb falling with a hat-waving cowboy riding it like a bucking bronco, to critics of the Vietnam War who associated American military arrogance with the Wild West Texas drawl of President Lyndon Johnson.[2] Yet Ronald Reagan, the most popular of American presidents after the Vietnam War, took office on the strength of a cowboy image and a promise to make America ride "tall in the saddle" once again.

Buffalo Bill's fingerprints are still found all over our culture. Every year, the Boy Scouts of America encourages millions of boys to use outdoor skills and a code of personal honor as a bridge to citizenship and national identity. The image of the *scout* as a model has its roots in the worldwide success of Buffalo Bill's Wild West. International scouting, founded in 1908 by Sir Robert Baden-Powell, expressed the anxieties of imperial Britain on the eve of a world war, but it took its immediate inspiration from the American frontier and its values. Baden-Powell had seen Cody's exhibition in London in 1887, and he immediately applied its methods to the organization of a military tournament in Liverpool. Buffalo Bill was still on his mind when he served in Africa with the British imperial army, and he conceptualized his own experiences in Wild West terms. Traveling through the African frontier, he wrote in his dairy that the coach in which he had been riding was "a regular Buffalo-Bill-Wild-West-Deadwood affair."[3] In his foundational manual, *Scouting for Boys*, Baden-Powell made explicit the link he proposed to forge between character education and the "work and attributes of backwoodsmen, explorers, and frontiersmen." His scout figure could have been adapted from any program for Buffalo Bill's Wild West: scouts are "real *men* in every sense of the word, . . . they can find their way anywhere, are able to read meaning from the smallest signs and foot-tracks. . . . They are accustomed to take their lives in their hands, and to fling them down without hesitation if they can help their country by doing so."[4] The American Boy Scouts, founded in 1910, married Baden-Powell's protomilitary organization with Ernest Thompson Seton's nature-oriented youth organization, the Woodcraft Indians, and Dan Beard's patriotic Sons of Daniel Boone.[5] Each of these drew upon the glamour and appeal of Buffalo Bill, remembered by then as "the last of the great scouts."[6] The Girl Scouts of America similarly promote a blend of character education and outdoor skills, and children's books continue to use the cowboys-and-Indians themes that can be traced back to Buffalo Bill, from child's-eye-view stories of the overland trail to the popular book series by the British writer Lynn Reid Banks, *The Indian in the Cupboard*.

The romance of the West has also been memorably transmitted to the present through twentieth-century America's most influential medium: motion pictures. More than seven thousand Western films and thousands more television Westerns have been produced, viewed, and re-viewed around the world.[7] Not only did Cody participate in the making of early Westerns himself, but the plot, characters, incidents, and personnel of the Wild West made an almost seamless leap from the arena to the early film studio. Edwin Porter's 1903 *Great Train Robbery* drew on the familiar Wild West story of the robbery of the stagecoach. Scenes from the Indian wars, narratives of captivity and rescue, Indian attack and cavalry charge, all set pieces from Buffalo Bill's Wild West, formed the backbone of many early film Westerns.

Similarly, Buffalo Bill's Wild West provided many of the performers for early Western films. Not coincidentally, a leading producer named his company the Bison Company when it moved its operations to California in 1909. Its paraphernalia and personnel were supplied by an entertainment organization that drew upon and competed with Cody's exhibitions, the Miller Brothers 101 Ranch Wild West Show, based in Oklahoma. Miller Brothers hired many show Indians from the same Pine Ridge and Rosebud reservations where Cody recruited.[8] Within a few years, Bison productions were also using the same stock and materials spectators had seen in Buffalo Bill's Wild West. Miller Brothers and Bison were among the major buyers of animals and equipment at the bankruptcy sale after the failure of the Two Bills show.[9]

The marks of Buffalo Bill's Wild West are everywhere on the film Western. The generalized "Indian" dressed in feather headdress, war paint, and mounted on a racing pony moved directly into film from the Wild West, where differences between tribes were minimized and all Indians took on a generalized Plains Indian identity. The Stetson hat, which Buffalo Bill popularized (and advertised), became part of the standard costume for the Western film star. As Western films took on a life of their own at the mid-century, they began to depart from the Wild West's cast of characters. The figure of the cowboy, the focus for Western films and novels, had occupied a relatively small place in Buffalo Bill's Wild West, and the gunfighter, a Western film and television staple, never appeared. But to the extent that he was heroic, the Western film protagonist presented the frontier virtues that Buffalo Bill's performances had made famous: masculinity, courage, self-possession. As the critic Lee Clark Mitchell has written, the Western film is defined by "a set of problems recurring in endless combination: the problem of progress, . . . the problem of honor, . . . the problem of law or justice, . . . the problem of violence, . . . and subsuming all, the problem of what it means to be a man."[10] Thematically, Buffalo Bill's Wild West had set the stage for all these preoccupations.

And, of course, the film medium took to a new level the impression of intimacy between audience and performer that gave Wild West performances a special magnetism. Cody's celebrity was always based on the palpable fact of his own extraordinary body. The crowds flocked to see "Buffalo Bill Himself," the actual man. As Cody's partners from Salsbury to Lillie to Tammen had all understood, the most valuable asset of the Wild West was the body of its star. His fans' adulation survived even the troubling indications of personal excess and weakness, from the serious to the ridiculous, from the scandal of his divorce trial to the evidence of intemperance and infirmity. When an aging Buffalo Bill took to wearing a wig to maintain his famous long hair, fans and the press pretended not to notice, even when a sweep of the famous Stetson dislodged the hairpiece during a performance.[11] The body of the performer, complete with costume and props, attracted a sort of reverence and gave audiences a feeling of familiarity that was an essential part of their hero worship.

In the age of cinema, the body of the Western hero became even more available for the audience's gaze. Mitchell points out the importance of the Western hero's physicality: "Not only is the Western a genre that allows us to gaze at men, this gaze forms such an essential aspect of the genre that it seems covertly about just that: looking at men."[12] Whether the intense engagement of the camera with its subject arouses erotic responses to the male hero or simply asserts his power and charisma, many critics agree with Mitchell. The twentieth-century Western actor whose personal appeal most nearly approached that of Buffalo Bill, John Wayne, has only recently attracted critical attention for his powerful physicality. The scholar and writer Garry Wills has analyzed Wayne's importance as a physical embodiment of cultural values, giving him an authority that transcends the particular roles he plays. "Wayne is among the most expressive of those who move about in the moving pictures. . . . His body spoke a highly specific language of 'manliness,' of self-reliant authority. It was a body impervious to outside force, expressing a mind narrow but focused, fixed on the task, impatient with complexity."[13] Like Buffalo Bill, Wayne convinced audiences that, whatever narrative he engaged in, he himself was the spectacle they had come to see. And like Buffalo Bill, Wayne represented himself as the embodiment of a set of values: patriotism, bravery, masculinity.

The substance of Buffalo Bill's legacy, then, lies in the dramatization of the cultural issues that have been basic to American national identity: the use of violence and conquest in the formation of the American nation, Americans' love-hate relationship with unspoiled nature and native peoples, gender and the meaning of heroism, and the role of the individual in an increasingly urban, industrial, and corporate society. But the Wild West's importance also lies in its very form: a mass medium that blurs the lines between fact and fiction, history and melodrama, truth and entertainment. Buffalo Bill's Wild West *became* the truth about America when it was *believed as* the truth by Americans and others around the world.

The organizers and promoters of Buffalo Bill's Wild West understood and deployed techniques of image creation, salesmanship, and promotion that would soon become standard for everything from breakfast cereal to political candidates. They created a thoroughly modern celebrity and made him into a brand name, instantly recognizable around the world. The sophisticated mass media of the twentieth century extended and elaborated upon the Wild West's ability to convince viewers they had seen "the real thing." By the time of Cody's death, Edward L. Bernays had embarked on his trailblazing career in "publicity direction," and the advertising boom of the 1920s transformed the ways in which products were marketed and designed. In 1961, the historian Daniel Boorstin's *The Image, or, What Happened to the American Dream?* pointed out the hopeless intertwining of "real events" and "pseudo-events" in journalism, tourism, and film. But the techniques of advertising were already at work throughout public life. The journalist Joe McGinniss wrote an exposé asserting that the election of 1968 was "sold" through advertising gimmicks, but soon such techniques were standard practice. By the 1990s, media campaigns for most major candidates used focus groups and targeted advertisements to convince voters to accept their view of the truth. In mid-century, doctored photographs were sometimes used to smear politicians by showing them in the company of controversial companions, but by the 1990s altered images appeared even on the cover of *Time* magazine, on the Internet, in fashion magazines, and in films like *Forrest Gump*, leaving viewers unable to distinguish documentation from distortion.[14]

Even more profoundly, public life in the contemporary world, from war to politics, took place more and more often in the realm of electronic information. The false intimacy made possible by the television image—what George W. S. Trow has called "pseudo-intimacy" in "the grid of two hundred million"—has created an impression of a close relationship between spectators and national figures, from sports heroes to politicians.[15] As the historian Michael Rogin asserts in his book *"Ronald Reagan," the Movie,* it took an experienced actor to play the role of President of the United States so convincingly that even he believed in his persona. The "uncanny slippage between life and film" in Reagan's career encouraged him to use lines from old movies when he most wanted to appear sincere. As Rogin points out, classic Hollywood cinema encouraged a confusion between "daydreams" and daily life, and Reagan's presidency did the same. Despite the opposition of the filmmaker George Lucas, Reagan harnessed the tremendous popularity of the *Star Wars* films, with their Wild West–like melodrama of good and evil, to win support for his proposal for a missile-defense system.[16] In this world of electronic persuaders, the movies could actually seem more credible than ordinary life. Garry Wills quotes the humorist Jules Feiffer as saying that Reagan would have believed in evolution if he had ever played Darwin in a movie.[17] In just this way, Buffalo Bill came to believe that the scalping of Yellow Hand he depicted so often in performance was indistinguishable from the events on the battlefield many years earlier, and that a squadron of Indian braves could repeat at the gates of Havana the performance they gave in Madison Square Garden.

It is this aspect of Buffalo Bill's legacy that makes Robert Altman's film

Buffalo Bill and the Indians (1976) such a devastatingly appropriate commentary on Cody's cultural significance. As the United States approached its bicentennial celebrations after the scandals of Watergate and the resignation of President Richard Nixon, this prolific filmmaker made a movie that looked sarcastically at the master performer of patriotic nationalism. Based loosely on Arthur Kopit's 1968 play *Indians*, Altman's film brilliantly re-creates the look and feel of Buffalo Bill's Wild West. The details of Buffalo Bill's costumes, the tunes played by the cowboy band, the cameo portrayals of figures like Ned Buntline, John Burke, and Nate Salsbury all give the impression of a roomful of Wild West posters and programs come to life. The film has the look of a lovingly accurate tribute to Cody's show, but its content is critical and somber. Paul Newman's Buffalo Bill is vain, blustering, self-satisfied, and blind to nuance. He drinks whiskey from a loving cup and keeps a warbling opera singer in his tent. Having mistaken the tall, fierce-looking Indian interpreter for the short, bland Sitting Bull, he tries to re-assert his authority by telling the chief that performing in the Wild West will give him something to fall back on in his old age and save him from being taken for an ordinary, forgettable Indian. Surprised by Sitting Bull's unexpected departure from the show grounds, he rifles through his closet looking for a "real" jacket to wear while he tracks down the escaping Indians. And the secret of Buffalo Bill's wig is at last exposed to the public. Altman's Buffalo Bill comes face-to-face with his own limitations as he struggles to justify himself to the ghost of the dead Sitting Bull, but he seems to learn nothing from the encounter. The movie ends with yet another melodramatic arena re-enactment of the scalping of Yellow Hand as Buffalo Bill, glazed eyes staring from a masklike face, performs the role from which he will never escape.

From its opening moments, Altman's film raises questions about the interrelationship of reality and illusion. It begins with what seems to be a deadly attack on a stagecoach by Indians. The camera pulls back to show that the scene is only a fiction enacted in the show arena, but when the dust has settled, stagehands run up with a stretcher because one of the actors has "really" been injured. Welcoming Sitting Bull to the show, Buffalo Bill tells him, "You'll find that it ain't all that different from real life."

This film is a bicentennial meditation on American heroism at the end of the trail, irredeemably enmeshed in showbiz posturing. If the staginess of American national identity infuses Altman's film with energy and spirit, it also rules out any unambiguous affirmation of the traditional values Buffalo Bill and his promoters always claimed to promulgate. In the contemporary world, Altman seems to argue, America's self-understanding cannot be taken any more seriously than the popular entertainments that promulgate it.

And yet, the Wild West's blend of theatricality and historical pretension had a certain self-consciousness about it that may be its final, and most important, contribution. Nate Salsbury always knew on some level that he was bluffing when he proclaimed the Wild West's exalted educational mission. Despite his claims to historical significance, Buffalo Bill finally knew that he would be remembered as a showman: "Let my show go on," he was supposed to have said on his deathbed.[18] Certainly, Cody tried until the very end to keep alive not only his mortal body but his heroic self as well. Always hoping a fortune would be just around the corner, always eager to provide a good show and to connect with the public, he played those last seasons not just to pay the bills but, perhaps more importantly, to sustain the narrative of his life. Performing in Iowa in 1915, Cody gallantly stayed in the ring to help spectators endangered by a sudden flood while four hundred workers and performers fled to higher ground.[19] If the real man had become the stage persona, the opposite was also true.

Cody's position, subsumed into his own constructed image, was remarkably modern, a fact that was recognized in a tribute by one of the most self-conscious of modernist poets, E. E. Cummings. One of Cummings's first published poems, printed in *The Dial* in January 1920, was an elegy to Buffalo Bill:

> Buffalo Bill's
> defunct
>   who used to
>   ride a watersmooth-silver
>   stallion
> and break onetwothreefourfive pigeonsjustlikethat
>   Jesus
>
>   he was a handsome man
>   and what i want to know is
>   how do you like your blueeyed boy
>   Mister Death[20]

Manuscript pages of notes show that Cummings began the poem early in 1917, probably in response to a newspaper headline announcing Buffalo Bill's death.[21] As a child, Cummings had gone to circuses and made up his own animal acts. His library included a book about Buffalo Bill, and his childhood drawings included a picture of Sitting Bull and Buffalo Bill.[22] The poem evokes the energy and glamour of the Wild West, and suggests his own childhood fascination with performance and a willingness to be swept up in the excitement. The coinage *watersmooth-silver* suggests both the color and the rippling motion of Cody's big gray horse, Isham, his favorite mount in his later years, and the run-on phrases *onetwothreefourfive* and *pigeonsjust-likethat* suggest the breathlessness of an admiring fan.

The poem, simple and straightforward as it may first appear, resonates with the complexity of Buffalo Bill's own position in American culture. Cummings opens the poem with a worldly, ironic, modern voice. The word *defunct*, with its detached, clinical sound, also seems deflationary and harsh. Cummings's notes show that he first jotted down the phrase "Buffalo Bill is Dead," which he could have read in a newspaper.[23] The poem's terse, gruff opening refuses to participate in the heroic vocabulary with which Buffalo Bill identified himself with his own myth or in the gushingly sentimental accounts of his death.

But in the final three lines the irreverent modernist creates his own mythicized fantasy, imagining Buffalo Bill entering the afterlife, still the favored, blue-eyed boy, now performing not for the cheering public but for the mysterious "Mister Death." The famous buffalo hunter and Indian fighter has always been the killer, but now he has become the prey. Yet the star is not knocked off his horse, dragged unceremoniously offstage and deprived of a red flannel scalp. In the courtly formality of the final phrase, Cummings suggests a Buffalo Bill whose heroism survives his death. Not a defunct corpse now but a handsome man who will be a blue-eyed boy forever, Cummings's hero rides offstage, radiating complexity, not unlike the living showman. Lighting out for the territory like Huck Finn, "going West" in the colloquial sense of dying, Cummings's Buffalo Bill is indeed an apt hero for the modern era, an age when images have become indistinguishable from what they purport to represent and the content of national identity seems identical to its performance.

NOTES

LIST OF ILLUSTRATIONS

INDEX

NOTES

ABBREVIATIONS

BBHC   Harold McCracken Research Library, Buffalo Bill Historical Center, Cody, Wyoming

BRTC   Billy Rose Theatre Collection, New York Public Library for the Performing Arts

DPL   Denver Public Library, Western History Collection

HTC   Harvard Theatre Collection

NSP   Nathan Salsbury Papers, Yale Collection of American Literature, Beinecke Rare Book Library

YCWA   Yale Collection of Western Americana, Beinecke Rare Book Library

INTRODUCTION

1. A solid starting point for Cody research is Don Russell, *The Lives and Legends of Buffalo Bill* (Norman: University of Oklahoma Press, 1960). Joseph G. Rosa and Robin May, *Buffalo Bill and His Wild West: A Pictorial Biography* (Lawrence: University Press of Kansas, 1989), is also informative. Nuanced and revealing discussions of Cody's significance can be found in Richard Slotkin, *Gunfighter Nation: The Myth of the Frontier in Twentieth-Century America* (New York: Atheneum; 1992); Richard White, "Frederick Jackson Turner and Buffalo Bill," in Richard White and Patricia Limerick, *The Frontier in American Culture* (Berkeley: University of California Press, 1994); and all of the essays in Brooklyn Museum, ed., *Buffalo Bill and the Wild West* (Brooklyn: The Brooklyn Museum, 1981).

2. Even a source such as General Philip Sheridan's memoirs is colored by the fact that he published them after Cody had, with his support, become a famous showman. For a debunking "memoir," see Herbert Cody Blake, *Blake's Western Stories: The Truth About Buffalo Bill, Wm. F. Cody, Wild Bill, J. B. Hickok, Dr. Carver, California Joe, Yellow Hand—Tall Bull, The Pony Express, The Old 44 Colt, Derailing of the Union Pacific Train, Reprisal on the Cheyennes Under Turkey Leg, History and Busted Romances of the Old Frontier* (Brooklyn: Herbert Cody Blake, 1929).

3. "Historical Sketches and Programme," 1902, p. 64, DPL.

4. "Buffalo Bill's Wild West Combined with Pawnee Bill's Great Far East," courier (1911?), p. 18, BBHC, MS 6, William F. Cody Collection, series VI A, box, 2.

5. *Buffalo Bill's Wild West* program, 1885, n.p., BBHC, MS 6, William F. Cody Collection, series VI A, box 1.

6. Ibid., review by Brick Pomeroy. A pamphlet reprinting this review can be found in HTC.

1. INVENTING THE WILD WEST, 1868–86

1. Biographical materials are culled from Don Russell, *The Lives and Legends of Buffalo Bill* (Norman: University of Oklahoma Press, 1960). Russell was a careful and thorough biographer who untangled the web of fact and fiction as well as could be expected.

2. Ibid., pp. 89, 96–97.

3. Russell believes this match did take place, although he admits that hard evidence is lacking (see pp. 93–94). Nellie Snyder Yost casts doubt on the whole incident in *Buffalo Bill: His Family, Friends, Fame, Failures, and Fortunes* (Chicago: Sage Books, 1979), p. 448. The only direct accounts of the incident occur in Cody's autobiography and his wife's (ghostwritten) memoir.

4. Advertisement reproduced in Louisa Frederici Cody and Courtney Ryley Cooper, *Memories of Buffalo Bill* (New York: D. Appleton and Company, 1919), p. 122.

5. From William F. Cody, *The Life of Hon. William F. Cody, Known as Buffalo Bill, the Famous Hunter, Scout, and Guide: An Autobiography* (Hartford, Conn.: Frank E. Bliss, 1879), p. 174. Cited in Russell, *Lives and Legends*, p. 94, where further details of the event are also given.

6. John M. MacKenzie, *The Empire of Nature: Hunting, Conservation, and British Imperialism* (Manchester, England: Manchester University Press, 1988).

7. See Paul Andrew Hutton, *Phil Sheridan and His Army* (Lincoln: University of Nebraska Press, 1985), pp. 151–52 and 207–16.

8. Henry E. Davies, *Ten Days on the Plains*, ed. Paul Andrew Hutton (1872; reprint, Dallas: The DeGolyer Library, Southern Methodist University Press, 1985), p. 9. Further citations from this book are to pp. 11, 27, 10, 26, and 29.

9. Buffalo Bill, "Famous Hunting Parties of the Plains," *The Cosmopolitan* (June 1894), pp. 139–40.

10. Frederick Jackson Turner, "The Significance of the Frontier in American History" (1893), in John Mack Faragher, ed., *Rereading Frederick Jackson Turner* (New York: Henry Holt, 1994), p. 32.

11. Letter to Al Goodman, Feb. 1, 1896, in Stella Foote, ed., *Letters from "Buffalo Bill"* (El Segundo, Calif.: Upton & Sons, 1990), p. 81.

12. Cody, *Autobiography*, p. 282.

13. See Hutton, *Phil Sheridan and His Army*, pp. 211–13.

14. "Alexis Among the Buffaloes," *Frank Leslie's*, Feb. 3, 1872, p. 325. The artist missed the point of Cody's role by depicting him dressed like an Indian, with feathers in his hair.

15. William W. Tucker, *His Imperial Highness the Grand Duke Alexis in the United*

States of America During the Winter of 1871–2 (1872; reprint, New York: Interland Publishing, 1972), p. 167.

16. Cody and Cooper, *Memories of Buffalo Bill*, pp. 156–57.

17. Cody's enemies claimed that Buffalo Bill was "invented" by Ned Buntline, a concept intriguingly dramatized in Arthur Kopit's play *Indians* (1969) and Robert Altman's film *Buffalo Bill and the Indians* (1976). See Herbert Cody Blake, *Blake's Western Stories*, p. 1. Russell, however, defended Cody and minimized the importance of Buntline's stories. On Hickok, see Joseph G. Rosa, *They Called Him Wild Bill: The Life and Adventures of James Butler Hickok* (Norman: University of Oklahoma Press, 1974), pp. 34–52.

18. Ned Buntline [Edward Zane Carroll Judson], *Buffalo Bill, and his Adventures in the West* (1886; reprint, ed. David Manning White, New York: Arno Press, 1974), pp. 32, 33, 198. The 1886 book was a republication of the 1869 serial, according to Russell, *Lives and Legends*, p. 501. Further quotations are from this edition.

19. Davies, *Ten Days on the Plains*, p. 25.

20. See Hutton, *Phil Sheridan and His Army*, pp. 248–54, 300.

21. Russell points out the similarity in *Lives and Legends*, p. 193.

22. Review of *Scouts of the Prairie* at Niblo's, [New York,] n.d., BRTC. "Indian Drama at the Arch," n.p., BBHC, microfilm roll #1, Stage Play Notices and Reviews, 1875–80. Also, BBHC, MS 6, William F. Cody Collection, series I D, oversize box 2, OS 3/3.

23. "The Scouts Programme!" [Chicago, 1872,] BBHC, MS 6, William F. Cody Collection, series I D, oversize box 2.

24. "Indian Drama at the Arch."

25. All from BBHC, MS 6, William F. Cody Collection, series I D, oversize box 2.

26. See Neil Harris, *Humbug: The Art of P. T. Barnum* (Boston: Little, Brown and Company, 1973), and also Philip B. Kunhardt, Jr., Philip B. Kunhardt III, and Peter W. Kunhardt, *P. T. Barnum: America's Greatest Showman* (New York: Alfred A. Knopf, 1995); on freaks, see Rosemarie Garland Thomson, ed., *Freakery: Cultural Spectacles of the Extraordinary Body* (New York: New York University Press, 1996).

27. *Montreal Herald*, n.d., BBHC, MS 6, William F. Cody Collection, series IX: Scrapbooks, etc., box 3.

28. Program, *The Red Right Hand; Or, Buffalo Bill's First Scalp for Custer*, BBHC, MS 6, William F. Cody Collection, series I C, box 3.

29. *Pittsburg Dispatch*, n.d., and *Syracuse Daily Courier*, n.d., BBHC, MS 6, William F. Cody Collection, series IX: Scrapbooks, etc., box 3.

30. Hon. Wm. F. Cody, "Prairie Prince, The Boy Outlaw, or, Trailed to his Doom," *Saturday Evening Post*, Oct. 16, 1875, p. 1; Hon. William F. Cody, "The Crimson Trail, or, On Custer's Last War-Path," *New York Weekly*, Oct. 2, 1876, p. 1.

31. Helen Cody Wetmore, *Buffalo Bill: Last of the Great Scouts: The Life Story of Col. William F. Cody ("Buffalo Bill")* (Duluth, Minn.: The Duluth Press Printing Co., 1899), p. 223.

32. Playbill, *May Cody; Or, Lost and Won*, HTC.

33. *Zanesville Times*, n.d., BBHC, microfilm roll #1, Stage Plays 1879–80.

34. *Lockport Daily Union*, n.d., ibid.

35. *New Haven Journal and Courier*, July 17, 1885, BBHC, Doc Carver microfilm roll #1, red with gold tie.

36. William F. Cody to Jack Crawford, Montreal, Aug. 11, 1885, DPL, WH 72, M, Cody L, A 121, Cody letters, ff3.

37. Michael Denning, *Mechanic Accents: Dime Novels and Working-Class Culture in America* (New York: Verso, 1987).

38. The court case is described in *New Haven Journal and Courier*, July 17, 1885. BBHC, Doc Carver microfilm roll #1, red with gold tie. The story of the rapid composition was told during the play's first season in "Ned Buntline's Gold Mine," *New York Daily Graphic*, n.d., BBHC, microfilm roll #1, Stage Plays 1879–80. Cody told of forgetting his lines in an interview in *Cleveland Herald*, n.d., BBHC, MS 6, William F. Cody Collection, series IX: Scrapbooks, etc., box 3. Both stories figure in an article from a Toledo newspaper entitled "Buffalo Bill, How the Chief of Scouts Became an Actor," [1878?,] BBHC, microfilm roll #1, Stage Notices 1879–80. His comments on acting are found in *The Players*, Sept. 23, 1892, p. 11, BBHC, microfilm roll #2, Scrapbook, England, 1892.

39. Russell, *Lives and Legends*, p. 104. P. H. Sheridan, *Personal Memoirs* (New York: Charles L. Webster & Company, 1888), vol. 2, p. 301.

40. John Burke, *"Buffalo Bill," from Prairie to Palace: An Authentic History of the Wild West* (Chicago: Rand, McNally, 1893), p. 99.

41. Ibid., p. 108.

42. See Hutton, *Phil Sheridan and His Army*, chap. 14.

43. Blake, *Blake's Western Stories*, pp. 26–30.

44. See Russell, *Lives and Legends*, chap. 17, and Paul L. Hedren, *First Scalp for Custer: The Skirmish at Warbonnet Creek, Nebraska, July 17, 1876* (Lincoln: University of Nebraska Press, 1980).

45. Cited in Russell, *Lives and Legends*, p. 230. According to Russell, the letter was published in the *Baltimore Sun* in 1936 and was then in possession of Mrs. Harry G. Schloss, daughter of Moses Kerngood. It has the misspelling and grammatical mistakes characteristic of Cody's own letters and seems authentic.

46. Playbill, *The Red Right Hand; Or, Buffalo Bill's First Scalp for Custer*, BBHC, MS 6, William F. Cody Collection, series I D, box 3.

47. Thanks to Paul Fees of the Buffalo Bill Historical Center for confirming in a telephone conversation my analysis of this photograph.

48. Hedren, *First Scalp for Custer*, pp. 66–67.

49. See Joseph G. Rosa and Robin May, *Buffalo Bill and His Wild West: A Pictorial Biography* (Lawrence: University Press of Kansas, 1989), pp. 49, 54.

50. Don Russell, "Forward," in Cody, *The Life of Hon. William F. Cody, Known as Buffalo Bill* (1879; reprint, Lincoln: University of Nebraska Press, 1978), p. vii, and Russell, *Lives and Legends*, pp. 265–84.

51. *Evening Telegram*, n.d., n.p., BBHC, Garlow Scrapbook, 1880–83, MS 6, William F. Cody Collection, series IX: Scrapbooks, etc., box 3.

52. Harris, *Humbug*, pp. 61–62, and Rosa, *They Called Him Wild Bill*, pp. 162–69.

53. Russell, *Lives and Legends*, pp. 186–87.

54. See John Culhane, *The American Circus: An Illustrated History* (New York: Henry Holt, 1990), especially pp. 92–93.

55. Lawrence W. Levine, *Highbrow/Lowbrow: The Emergence of Cultural Hierarchy in America* (Cambridge, Mass.: Harvard University Press, 1988).

56. Nate Salsbury, "The Origin of the Wild West Show," in typescript of "Reminiscences," c. 1901, NSP, box 2, folder 63.

57. See contract dated Feb. 12, 1883, establishing the partnership, YCWA, Uncat. WA MS 163 930702, Correspondence 1874–86.

58. *Wild West, Buffalo Bill and Dr. Carver, Rocky Mountain and Prairie Exhibition* [1883], BBHC, MS 6, William F. Cody Collection, series VI A, box 1.

59. Library of Congress, Rare Book Collection, GV 1821.B 8.

60. For a discussion of these lawsuits, see clippings from *New Haven Journal and Courier*, July 1885, BBHC, Doc Carver microfilm roll #1, red with gold tie.

61. For an account of a shoot-out in Hamburg, Germany, see the reminiscences of "Apache George" in a clipping at BBHC, MS 6, William F. Cody Collection, series IX: Scrapbooks, etc., box 8. Also, see clipping from *San Francisco Examiner*, Aug. 28, 1890, in BBHC, microfilm roll #1, Carver scrapbooks, green brown. For Carver's later screeds, see, e.g., Raymond Thorp, *The Spirit Gun of the West: The Story of Doc W. F. Carver* (Glendale, Calif.: Arthur H. Clark, 1957), and Blake, *Blake's Western History.*

62. See Rosa, *They Called Him Wild Bill*, pp. 242–61.

63. For a popular biography of Omohundro, see Hershel C. Logan, *Buckskin and Satin: The Life of Texas Jack and His Wife* (Harrisburg, Pa.: Stackpole, 1954).

64. For a well-researched biography, see Darlis A. Miller, *Captain Jack Crawford: Buckskin Poet, Scout, and Showman* (Albuquerque: University of New Mexico Press, 1993). Also useful is Paul T. Nolan, *John Wallace Crawford* (Boston: Twayne Publishers, 1981).

65. Miller, *Captain Jack Crawford*, pp. 83, 123.

66. In the collection of Carver papers at BBHC, a number of press clippings from 1878 are labeled "Press Agent Story" or "P.A.," including an illustrated biographical sketch from *Harper's Weekly*, July 13, 1878, that accepts the story of his childhood among Indians. Carver's "autobiography" is William F. Carver, *Life of Dr. William F. Carver, of California, Champion Rifle-Shot of the World* (Boston: Press of Rockwell and Churchill, 1878). But see Russell, *Lives and Legends*, pp. 293–94, and Rosa and May, *Buffalo Bill and His Wild West*, p. 68.

67. *New Haven Journal and Courier*, Jan. 12, 1885, BBHC, Doc Carver microfilm roll #1, red with gold tie.

68. Captain Jack Crawford to Mrs. Nate Salsbury, NSP, box 1, folder 14, Correspondence 1904–13.

69. Letter from Wm. L. Brown, Assistant Register of Copyrights, to Dr. Carver, Oct. 15, 1926, YCWA, Doc Carver Scrapbook, WA MSS S-1621, Uncat. WA MS 163 930702, Correspondence 1919–27.

70. William F. Cody to W. F. "Doc" Carver, Mar. 13, [1883,] and Feb. 11, [1883,] ibid., Correspondence 1874–86.

71. Unidentified clipping, NSP, box 1, folder 26.

72. William F. Cody to Nate Salsbury, [1884], NSP, box 1, folder 4.

73. William F. Cody to Nate Salsbury, Mar. 9, 1885, NSP, box 1, folder 4. See Russell, *Lives and Legends*, p. 303.

74. Nate Salsbury, "A Dilemma," in "Reminiscences."

75. William F. Cody to Nate Salsbury, Feb. 14, [1885,] NSP, box 1, folder 4.

76. Nate Salsbury, "Cody's Personal Representatives," in "Reminiscences."

77. *The Journalist*, Aug. 14, [1880s?,] DPL, Nate Salsbury scrapbook.

78. *The Wild West, Buffalo Bill and Dr. Carver, Rocky Mountain and Prairie Exhibition*, program,[1883], BBHC, MS 6, William F. Cody Collection, series VI A, box 1.

79. *Buffalo Bill's Wild West*, program, 1885, BBHC, MS 6, William F. Cody Collection, series VI A, box 1.

80. Sarah J. Blackstone, *Buckskins, Bullets, and Business: A History of Buffalo Bill's Wild West* (Westport, Conn.: Greenwood Press, 1986), p. 50.

81. *Buffalo Bill's Wild West*, program, 1885, BBHC, MS 6, William F. Cody Collection, series VI A, box 1.

82. *Montreal Gazette*, Aug. 15, [1885?,] DPL, Nate Salsbury scrapbook, July 1885 to Aug. 1886.

83. Ibid., *Pomeroy's Democrat*, July 3, 1886.

84. Samuel Clemens to William F. Cody, July 14, 1885, BBHC, MS 6, William F. Cody Collection, series VI G, box 1.

85. Wm. F. Cody to Nate Salsbury, Apr. 12, 1886, NSP, box 1, folder 4.

2. THE WILD WEST ABROAD, 1887–92

1. See Richard D. Altick, *The Shows of London* (Cambridge, Mass.: The Belknap Press of Harvard University Press, 1978), especially pp. 338, 320.

2. See Rosemarie Garland Thomson, ed., *Freakery: Cultural Spectacles of the Extraordinary Body* (New York: New York University Press, 1996), especially "Introduction," pp. 1–19, and Bernth Lindfors, "Ethnological Show Business: Footlighting the Dark Continent," pp. 207–18.

3. See Carolyn Thomas Foreman, *Indians Abroad, 1493–1938* (Norman: University of Oklahoma Press, 1943), especially pp. 83–84 and 121–24.

4. See Harold McCracken, *George Catlin and the Old Frontier* (New York: Bonanza Books, 1959), especially chaps. 21 and 22.

5. See Harris, *Humbug: The Art of P. T. Barnum* (Boston: Little, Brown and Company, 1973), p. 43.

6. P. T. Barnum, *Struggles and Triumphs, Or, Forty Years' Recollections*, ed. Carl Bode (1869; reprint, New York: Penguin Books, 1981), p. 152.

7. See James W. Cook, Jr. "Of Men, Missing Links, and Nondescripts: The Strange Career of P. T. Barnum's 'What is It?' Exhibition," in Thomson, ed., *Freakery*, pp. 139–57.

8. See Harris, *Humbug*, especially chap. 3.

9. Barnum, *Struggles and Triumphs*, p. 126.

10. Letter to Julia Cody Goodman, Aug. 16, 1883, in Stella Foote, ed., *Letters from "Buffalo Bill"* (El Segundo, Calif.: Upton & Sons, 1990), p. 31.

11. E. G. Cattermole, *Famous Frontiersmen, Pioneers, and Scouts* (Chicago: Donahue, 1883), quoted in Richard J. Walsh, in collaboration with Milton S. Salsbury, *The Making of Buffalo Bill: A Study in Heroics* (Indianapolis: Bobbs-Merrill, 1928), p. 218.

12. Letter from Steve Mafest (?), Aug. 6, 1886, NSP, box 1, folder 4.

13. This account according to Walsh, *Making of Buffalo Bill*, pp. 261–62.

14. Altick, *Shows of London*, p. 505.

15. See Robert W. Rydell, *All the World's a Fair: Visions of Empire at American International Expositions, 1876–1916* (Chicago: University of Chicago Press, 1984), and Timothy Mitchell, "The World as Exhibition," *Comparative Studies in Society and History* 31 (1989), pp. 217–36.

16. See Rydell, *All the World's a Fair*, pp. 23–27.

17. William F. Cody to Nate Salsbury, Feb. 14, [1885,] NSP, box 1, folder 4.

18. Rydell, *All the World's a Fair*, pp. 98–99.

19. *New York Dispatch*, July 18, 1886, DPL, Nate Salsbury scrapbook, July 1885–Aug. 1886.

20. See William Brasmer, "The Wild West Exhibition and the Drama of Civilization," in David Mayer and Kenneth Richards, eds. *Western Popular Theatre* (London: Methuen, 1977), pp. 133–56.

21. Percy MacKaye, *Epoch: The Life of Steele MacKaye, Genius of the Theatre* (New York: Boni & Liveright, 1927), vol. 2, pp. 76, 88.

22. Ibid., pp. 80, 81.

23. Ibid., pp. 80, 83.

24. Steele MacKaye to Nate Salsbury, Nov. 8, 1886, NSP, box 1, folder 4.

25. MacKaye, *Epoch*, p. 86.

26. *The (London) Times*, Nov. 1, 1887, BBHC, microfilm roll #3, red invitation scrapbook.

27. See, for example, *Buffalo Bill's Wild West and Congress of Rough Riders of the World, Historical Sketches & Programme* (Chicago: Blakely Printing, 1893), pp. 16–18.

28. Don Russell, *The Lives and Legends of Buffalo Bill* (Norman: University of Oklahoma Press, 1960), p. 326.

29. Dan Muller, who grew up in Cody's home, gives a touching account of switching from "Uncle Bill" to "Colonel" when he began traveling with the troupe. Dan Muller, *My Life With Buffalo Bill* (Chicago: Reilly & Lee, 1948), p. 142.

30. Annie Oakley scrapbook, BBHC, microfilm roll #4.

31. First clipping not clearly identified, second from *The Sporting Life*, May 10, 1887, in Annie Oakley scrapbook, BBHC, microfilm roll #4.

32. William F. Cody, *Story of the Wild West and Camp-Fire Chats* (1888; reprint, Freeport, N.Y.: Books for Libraries Press, 1970), p. 708.

33. *Globe*, Apr. 26, 1887, quoted in Russell, *Lives and Legends*, p. 328.

34. Nate Salsbury, "American Exhibition," in typescript of "Reminiscences," c. 1901, NSP, box 2, folder 64.

35. Cody, *Story of the Wild West and Camp-Fire Chats*, pp. 713–14.

36. H.C.G. Matthew, ed., *The Gladstone Diaries* (Oxford: Clarendon Press, 1994), vol. 12, p. 29.

37. Christopher Hibbert, *The Royal Victorians: King Edward VII, His Family and Friends* (Philadelphia: J. B. Lippincott, 1976), p. 32.

38. John M. MacKenzie, *The Empire of Nature: Hunting, Conservation, and British Imperialism* (Manchester, England: Manchester University Press, 1988), pp. 7, 50–51.

39. Hibbert, *The Royal Victorians*, p. 35.

40. Giles St. Aubyn, *Edward VII: Prince and King* (New York: Atheneum, 1979), p. 136.

41. Cody, *Story of the Wild West and Camp-Fire Chats*, p. 728.

42. Courtney Ryley Cooper, *Annie Oakley: Woman at Arms* (London: Hurst & Blackett, [1927]), p. 173.

43. George Earle Buckle, ed., *The Letters of Queen Victoria* (New York: Longmans, Green, 1930), vol. 1, p. 307.

44. Ibid., p. 324.

45. Cody, *Story of the Wild West and Camp-Fire Chats*, p. 737.

46. Queen Victoria's journal, May 11, 1887, quoted in Joseph G Rosa and Robin May, *Buffalo Bill and His Wild West: A Pictorial Biography* (Lawrence: University Press of Kansas, 1989), pp. 118–19.

47. Cody, *Story of the Wild West and Camp-Fire Chats*, p. 742.

48. Salsbury, "American Exhibition," in "Reminiscences."

49. Lew Parker, *Odd People I Have Met*, n.p., n.d., pp. 90–94.

50. *New York Sun*, Apr. 28–29, 1889, BBHC, microfilm roll #2, Wm. Cody France 1889, red book.

51. Ibid., French reviews quoted in an unidentified New York newspaper.

52. Ibid.

53. Ibid., story written by James Gordon Bennett, Paris, May 18, printed in the *San Francisco Chronicle*. Presumably Burke communicated with French reporters through an interpreter, since both Lew Parker and Nate Salsbury reported that his language skills were rudimentary at best. After failing to make himself understood at the Wild West grounds, Parker reported, Burke "went to camp and told the people there that I had given instructions to the Frenchmen in our employ to pretend not to understand him." Parker, *Odd People I Have Met*, p. 86.

54. See Dore Ashton and Denise Browne Hare, *Rosa Bonheur: A Life and a Legend* (New York: The Viking Press, 1981), chaps. 10–11.

55. Ibid., p. 155.

56. Helen Cody Wetmore, *Buffalo Bill: Last of the Great Scouts. The Life Story of Col. William F. Cody ("Buffalo Bill")* (Duluth, Minn.: The Duluth Press Printing Co., 1899), p. 266.

57. *New York World*, May 5, 1888, quoted by Nellie Snyder Yost, *Buffalo Bill: His Family, Friends, Fame, Failures, and Fortunes* (Chicago: Sage Books, 1979), p. 210.

58. Unidentified clipping, BBHC, microfilm roll #2, Col. W. F. Cody, Rome 1890, red book.

3. AT THE COLUMBIAN EXPOSITION, 1893

1. Richard Slotkin's provocative discussion of Buffalo Bill's Wild West describes it as expressing national mythology. I prefer to emphasize the ways in which ideology was overlaid with nostalgia, especially as the years wore on, and to view it more ambiguously. See Richard Slotkin, "The 'Wild West,' " in Brooklyn Museum, ed., *Buffalo Bill and the Wild West* (Brooklyn: The Brooklyn Museum, 1981), pp. 27–44, as well as relevant sections of Slotkin's *Gunfighter Nation: The Myth of the Frontier in Twentieth-Century America* (New York: Atheneum, 1992) and "Buffalo Bill's 'Wild West' and the Mythologization of the American Empire," in Amy Kaplan and Donald E. Pease, eds., *Cultures of United States Imperialism* (Durham, N.C.: Duke University Press, 1993), pp. 164–81.

2. Henry Adams, *The Education of Henry Adams: An Autobiography* (Boston: Houghton Mifflin, 1918), p. 342.

3. Hamlin Garland, *A Son of the Middle Border* (New York: Macmillan, 1917, 1919), pp. 458–60.

4. Horace G. Benson, quoted in Robert W. Rydell, *All the World's a Fair: Visions of Empire at American International Expositions, 1876–1916* (Chicago: University of Chicago Press, 1984), p. 40.

5. Adams, *Education of Henry Adams*, p. 343.

6. Important discussions of the White City include Reid Badger, *The Great American Fair: The World's Columbian Exposition & American Culture* (Chicago: Nelson Hall, 1979); Stanley Applebaum, *The Chicago World's Fair of 1893: A Photographic Record* (New York: Dover, 1980); Rydell, *All the World's a Fair*; Neil Harris, Wim de Wit, James Gilbert, and Robert W. Rydell, *Grand Illusions: Chicago World's Fair of 1893* (Chicago: Chicago Historical Society, 1993).

7. Alan Trachtenberg, *The Incorporation of America: Culture and Society in the Gilded Age* (New York: Hill & Wang, 1982), p. 209.

8. Warren I. Susman, "Ritual Fairs," *Chicago History* 12 (Fall 1983), pp. 4–9; Curtis M. Hinsley, "The World as Marketplace: Commodification of the Exotic at the World's Columbian Exposition, Chicago, 1893," in Ivan Karp, Christine Mullen Kreamer, and Steven D. Lavine, eds., *Exhibiting Cultures: The Poetics and Politics of Museum Display* (Washington, D.C.: Smithsonian Institution Press, 1990), pp. 344–65; Timothy Mitchell, "The World as Exhibition," *Comparative Studies in Society and History* 31 (1989), pp. 217–36.

9. John Burke, *"Buffalo Bill," from Prairie to Palace, An Authentic History of the Wild West* (Chicago: Rand, McNally, 1893), p. 196.

10. See letterhead, NSP, box 1, folder 7.

11. Don Russell, *The Lives and Legends of Buffalo Bill* (Norman: University of Oklahoma Press, 1960), pp. 374–75.

12. *Hand Book of the World's Columbian Exposition* (Chicago: Rand, McNally, 1892), p. 3.

13. *Chicago Tribune*, May 1, 1893; *Chicago Herald*, May 2, 1893, and Apr. 27, 1893; *Chicago Daily News*, May 5, 1893; advertisement, n.d.; BBHC, MS 6, William F. Cody Collection, series IX: Scrapbooks, etc, box 8, Scrapbook 1893, Chicago Season.

14. Ibid., *Chicago Record*, May 29, 1893; *Chicago Times*, June 11; n.p., July 8; *Inter-Ocean*, July 16; *Chicago Times*, Aug. 26; *Chicago Tribune*, Aug. 27; *Chicago Times*, Sept. 15; *Chicago Times*, Sept. 11.

15. Ibid., *Chicago Journal*, Sept. 16, 1893.

16. Ibid., *Inter-Ocean*, July 16, 1893; *Manitoba Free Press*, July 28; *Chicago Herald*, July 28; *Chicago Times*, July 28; *Chicago Evening Post*, July 27.

17. Ibid., *Chicago Tribune*, June 9, 1893; *Chicago Globe*, June 18; *Chicago Tribune*, June 27; *Chicago Daily News*, June 27.

18. Two different front covers for the 1893 program have the same basic design, featuring a portrait of Cody surrounded by vignettes of prairie scenes that correspond to Wild West performance segments. (In both examples I have seen, the back cover is the same.) BBHC, MS 6, William F. Cody Collection, series VI A, box 1, folder 10.

19. *Buffalo Bill's Wild West and Congress of Rough Riders of the World, Historical Sketches & Programme* (Chicago: Blakely Printing, 1893), p. 4. James Fenimore Cooper, *The Pioneers, or the Sources of the Susquehanna: A Descriptive Tale* (1823; reprint, Albany: State University of New York Press, 1980), p. 456.

20. See Ralph F. Bogardus, *Pictures and Texts: Henry James, A. L. Coburn, and New Ways of Seeing in Literary Culture* (Ann Arbor: University of Michigan Research Press, 1984), pp. 103–7.

21. *Chicago Herald*, Aug. 13, 1893; *Inter-Ocean* and *Chicago Post*, Aug. 17. BBHC, MS 6, William F. Cody Collection, series IX: Scrapbooks, etc., box 8, Scrapbook 1893, Chicago Season.

22. See especially Slotkin, *Gunfighter Nation*, chaps. 1 and 2, and Richard White, "Frederick Jackson Turner and Buffalo Bill," in Richard White and Patricia Limerick, *The Frontier in American Culture* (Berkeley: University of California Press, 1994), pp. 6–65.

23. Theodore Roosevelt, *The Winning of the West* (1889; reprint, New York: G. P. Putnam's Sons, 1896), vol. 1, pp. 1, 25, xix.

24. Ibid., pp. 30, 162.

25. Henry F. Pringle, *Theodore Roosevelt: A Biography* (1931; reprint, New York: Harcourt, Brace, 1956), p. 69.

26. Roosevelt, *The Winning of the West*, p. xvi; Theodore Roosevelt, *Ranch Life and the Hunting Trail* (1888; reprint, New York: Century, 1896), p. 24.

27. Frederick Jackson Turner, "The Significance of the Frontier in American History," in Martin Ridge, ed., *Frederick Jackson Turner: Wisconsin's Historian of the Frontier* (Madison: State Historical Society of Wisconsin, 1986), pp. 27–28.

28. Theodore Roosevelt to Frederick Jackson Turner, Feb. 10, 1894, quoted in Ray Allen Billington, *The Genesis of the Frontier Thesis: A Study in Historical Creativity* (San Marino, Calif.: Huntington Library, 1971), p. 173.

29. Turner, "Significance of the Frontier," pp. 27–28.

30. Billington, *Genesis of the Frontier Thesis*, p. 176.

31. Turner, "Significance of the Frontier," pp. 26, 47.

32. *Buffalo Bill's Wild West*, pp. 4, 64.

33. Billington, *Genesis of the Frontier Thesis*, p. 166.

34. T. J. Jackson Lears, *No Place of Grace: Antimodernism and the Transformation of American Culture, 1880–1920* (New York: Pantheon, 1981).

4. BUFFALO BILL AND MODERN CELEBRITY

1. The best account of Cody's life in North Platte is Nellie Snyder Yost, *Buffalo Bill: His Family, Friends, Fame, Failures, and Fortunes* (Chicago: Sage Books, 1979). Many of the details here come from this source.

2. "Buffalo Bill" and "A Notable Man," n.p., BBHC, microfilm roll #1, Stage Notices 1879–80.

3. Yost, *Buffalo Bill*, p. 115.

4. W. F. Cody to Jack Crawford, June 16, [1882,] DPL, WH 72, M, Cody L, A 121, Cody letters, #41. See Don Russell, *The Lives and Legends of Buffalo Bill* (Norman: University of Oklahoma Press, 1960), p. 421.

5. Yost, *Buffalo Bill*, p. 462n.

6. See Justin Kaplan, *Mr. Clemens and Mark Twain* (New York: Simon & Schuster, 1966), pp. 159–68.

7. W. F. Cody to Julia Cody Goodman, Aug. 16 and Sept. 24, 1883, in Stella Foote, ed., *Letters from "Buffalo Bill"* (El Segundo, Calif.: Upton & Sons, 1990), pp. 31, 33.

8. W. F. Cody to Jack Crawford, July 21, 1886, DPL, WH 72, M, Cody L, A 121, Cody letters, #46. W. F. Cody to Julia Cody Goodman, Feb. 14, 1886, in Foote, ed., *Letters*, p. 36.

9. Yost, *Buffalo Bill*, pp. 162, 167, 170, 178.

10. W. F. Cody to Al Goodman, July 7, 1887, in Foote, ed., *Letters*, p. 55.

11. Quoted in Yost, *Buffalo Bill*, p. 199.

12. Ibid., pp. 214–20.

13. W. F. Cody to Julia Cody Goodman, July 5, 1889, in Foote, ed., *Letters*, p. 64.

14. Yost, *Buffalo Bill*, pp. 224, 233.

15. Ibid., p. 261 and passim.

16. Interview in the *Marion (Indiana) Daily Chronicle*, July 3, 1896, BBHC, microfilm roll 1; Col. Cody, 1896, tan book.

17. Nate Salsbury, "Long Hair and a Plug Hat," typescript of "Reminiscences," c. 1901, NSP, box 2, folder 63.

18. See advertisement for "Homes in the Big Horn Basin" by Shoshone Irrigation Company, DPL, WH 72, Cody, William, another box of programs, "Greater New York, 1897." Also see brochure for development in Long Branch, N.J., NSP, box 2, folder 54.

19. Russell, *Lives and Legends*, p. 436.

20. W. F. Cody to Nate Salsbury, Jan. 29, 1895, NSP, box 1, folder 8.

21. W. F. Cody to Mike Russell, Sept. 1, 1895, YCWA, WA MSS, S-197, Cody, W. F., folder 5.

22. Nate Salsbury, "Long Hair and a Plug Hat," in "Reminiscences." Account of settlement after Nathan Salsbury's death, written by Rachel's brother S. Livingston Samuels, NSP, box 1, folder 13.

23. "Daisy Miller," "A Woman Sees Wild West," *Commercial Advertiser*, June 9, 1894, BBHC, microfilm roll #2, Scrapbook 1, Cody Brooklyn Season 1894.

24. Ibid., "Colonel Cody Talks," *New York Recorder*, May 22, 1894.

25. Louisa Frederici Cody and Courtney Ryley Cooper, *Memories of Buffalo Bill* (New York: D. Appleton and Company, 1919), pp. 1–10; William F. Cody, *The Life of Hon. William F. Cody, Known as Buffalo Bill, the Famous Hunter, Scout and Guide: An Autobiography* (Hartford, Conn.: Frank E. Bliss, 1879), p. 141.

26. See Russell, *Lives and Legends*, pp. 73–74.

27. Louisa tells this story in *Memories of Buffalo Bill*, p. 249. Russell repeats it, apparently convinced that the story rings true, in *Lives and Legends*, p. 197.

28. Russell, *Lives and Legends*, p. 77.

29. W. F. Cody to Julia and Al Goodman, Sept. 24, 1883, in Foote, ed., *Letters*, p. 33; Ed Goodman to Al Goodman, Mar. 17, 1887, in Foote, ed., *Letters*, p. 47.

30. Russell, *Lives and Letters*, pp. 257–58.

31. Yost, *Buffalo Bill*, p. 243.

32. Russell, *Lives and Legends*, p. 258.

33. *New York Press*, Oct. 30, 1898, HTC; Richard J. Walsh, in collaboration with Milton S. Salsbury, *The Making of Buffalo Bill: A Study in Heroics* (Indianapolis: Bobbs-Merrill, 1928), p. 305; Yost, *Buffalo Bill*, p. 325.

34. *New York Press*, Oct. 30, 1898, as well as undated reviews of *A Lady of Venice*, HTC.

35. Unidentified clipping, New York Public Library, Robinson Locke Collection, series 3, Cody, W. F., Scrapbook, p. 36.

36. W. F. Cody to Al Goodman, Aug. 25, 1891, in Foote, ed., *Letters*, p. 69.

37. W. F. Cody to Julia Cody Goodman, Mar. 21, 1902, ibid., pp. 89–90.

38. Yost, *Buffalo Bill*, chaps. 30–31.

39. Ibid., pp. 322, 475.

40. Ibid., p. 337.

41. Unidentified clipping, New York Public Library, Robinson Locke Collection, series 3, Cody, W. F., Scrapbook, p. 37.

42. Nate Salsbury, "Wild West at Windsor," in "Reminiscences."

43. Ibid., "Contract with Bailey,"

44. Ibid., "Nate Salsbury's 'Black America' as told by Harry Tarleton, of Taos, N.M., to Rebecca Salsbury James."

45. W. F. Cody to Nate Salsbury, Oct. 6, 1899; Nate Salsbury to W. F. Cody, Oct. 10, 1899. NSP, box 1, folder 11.

46. *Buffalo Courier*, July 21, 1895, BBHC, microfilm roll #2, Col. Cody, 1895, tan book I.

47. See Dexter W. Fellows and Andrew A. Freeman, *This Way to the Big Show: The Life of Dexter Fellows* (New York: The Viking Press, 1936), pp. 103–21.

48. See program, "Greater New York, 1895," HTC.

49. "Season of 1895," *Souvenir, Buffalo Bill's Wild West, 1896*, p. 275, BBHC.

50. Walsh, *Making of Buffalo Bill*, p. 330, and Russell, *Lives and Legends*, pp. 439–40.

51. Nate Salsbury, "Contract with Bailey," in "Reminiscences."

52. "Buffalo Bill's Wild West Company," articles of incorporation, BBHC, MS 6, William F. Cody Collection, series V, box 2, folder 2.

53. W. F. Cody to Nate Salsbury, Sept. 7, [1899,] NSP, box 1, folder 11.
54. Ibid., W. F. Cody to Nate Salsbury, Sept. 22, 1899, and Oct. 6, 1899.
55. Ibid., Nate Salsbury to W. F. Cody, Sept. 25, 1899, and Oct. 10, 1899.
56. Nate Salsbury to W. F. Cody, Oct. 9, 1902, NSP, box 1, folder 13.
57. Agreement between Cody and Salsbury, Nov. 6, 1902, BBHC, MS 6, William F. Cody Papers, series V, box 2, folder 2; Rachel Salsbury to W. F. Cody, July 24, 1903, BBHC, MS 6, William F. Cody Papers, series I C, box 1, folder 29.
58. S. Livingston Samuels, narrative in NSP, box 1, folder 13.
59. W. F. Cody to King Kendall, Dec. 31, 1902, DPL, WH 72, M, Cody, L, A 121, Cody letters, folder 10.
60. Ibid., W. F. Cody to William A. Bell, Jan. 5, 1903, and Mar. 28, 1903, folder 1.
61. Charles Eldridge Griffin, *Four Years in Europe with Buffalo Bill* (Albia, Iowa: Stage Publishing, 1908), pp. 15–16.
62. Nate Salsbury, "Contract with Bailey," in "Reminiscences."
63. Russell, *Lives and Legends*, pp. 444, 443.
64. "Indian Head" Courier, 1907, inside front cover, DPL, WH 72, box of programs.
65. See program, *Pawnee Bill's Historical Wild West, Mexican Hippodrome, Indian Museum, and Grand Fireworks Exhibition*, 1893, HTC. Also see Glenda Riley, *The Life and Legacy of Annie Oakley* (Norman: University of Oklahoma Press, 1994), pp. 45–46, and Fellows, *This Way to the Big Show*, pp. 56–57.
66. Glenn Shirley, *Pawnee Bill: A Biography of Major Gordon W. Lillie* (Albuquerque: University of New Mexico Press, 1958), chap. 12.
67. Ibid., pp. 13, 19, 102–3, 99, 177–80, 181.
68. Ibid., pp. 188–90, 194.
69. Quoted in R. L. Wilson with Greg Martin, *Buffalo Bill's Wild West: An American Legend* (New York: Random House, 1998), p. 200.
70. Shirley, *Pawnee Bill*, p. 211.
71. Ibid., pp. 205–6. For the account of Cody's relationship with Tammen, see ibid., pp. 206–11.
72. Russell, *Lives and Legends*, pp. 452–56. Lillie's sound business instincts saved Cody from worse disaster as well; since the show had been incorporated, Cody did not lose his other assets, although they were heavily mortgaged, and his mining enterprise would soon prove worthless.
73. *Story Book and Program, Sells-Floto Circus, Home of 1001 Wonders* [1914], DPL.
74. Walsh, *Making of Buffalo Bill*, pp. 355, 357.
75. Appraisal of estate, BBHC, MS 6, William F. Cody Papers, series I C, box 1, folder 1.
76. See Yost, *Buffalo Bill*, p. 403.
77. *Denver Post*, June 23, 1917.
78. Council resolution of Oglala Sioux, Pine Ridge, Jan. 12, 1917, MS 6, William F. Cody Papers, series I C, folder 2.
79. *Eulogy Delivered by Col. John W. Springer, of Denver, at the Bier of Colonel William Frederick Cody, "Buffalo Bill,"* BBHC, microfilm roll #3, Scrapbook, "Death."
80. See Russell, *Lives and Legends*, pp. 469–72.

5. AMERICAN INDIAN PERFORMERS IN THE WILD WEST

1. Chauncey Yellow Robe, "The Menace of the Wild West Show," *Quarterly Journal of the Society of American Indians* (July–Sept., 1914), pp. 224–25.

2. See Ralph E. Friar and Natasha A. Friar, *The Only Good Indian . . . The Hollywood Gospel* (New York: Drama Book Specialists, 1972), and Gretchen M. Bataille and Charles L. P. Silet, eds., *The Pretend Indians: Images of Native Americans in the Movies* (Ames: Iowa State University Press, 1980).

3. Vine Deloria, Jr., "The Indians," in Brooklyn Museum, ed., *Buffalo Bill and the Wild West* (Brooklyn: The Brooklyn Museum, 1981), pp. 45–56.

4. Chauncey Yellow Robe, "The Menace of the Wild West Show," p. 225.

5. L. C. Moses, *Wild West Shows and the Images of American Indians 1883–1933* (Albuquerque: University of New Mexico Press, 1996). See also L. C. Moses, "Wild West Shows, Reformers, and the Image of the American Indian, 1887–1914," *South Dakota History* 14 (Fall 1984), pp. 193–221. For a cautionary comment on Moses's perspective, see Alan Trachtenberg, book review, *Journal of American History* 84:2 (Sept. 1997), pp. 604–6.

6. "Alexis Among the Buffaloes," *Frank Leslie's*, Feb. 3, 1872, p. 325.

7. For a detailed discussion of Indian alliances and army policy, see Thomas Dunlay, *Wolves for the Blue Soldiers: Indian Scouts and Auxiliaries with the United States Army, 1860–90* (Lincoln: University of Nebraska Press, 1982).

8. *Chicago Evening Journal*, Dec. 12, 1872; "Scouts of the Prairie and Red Deviltry As It Is!" n.d., n.p., BBHC, MS 6, William F. Cody Collection, series I D, oversize box 2, 3/14; William F. Cody, *The Life of Hon. William F. Cody, Known As Buffalo Bill, the Famous Hunter, Scout and Guide: An Autobiography* (Hartford, Conn.: Frank E. Bliss, 1879), p. 327.

9. Don Russell, *The Lives and Legends of Buffalo Bill* (Norman: University of Oklahoma Press, 1960), p. 258.

10. Robert M. Utley, *The Lance and the Shield: The Life and Times of Sitting Bull* (New York: Henry Holt, 1993), pp. 67, 79, 252. See also James McLaughlin, *My Friend the Indian* (1910; reprint, Lincoln: University of Nebraska Press, 1989), p. 286.

11. Playbill, *May Cody; Or, Lost and Won*, HTC.

12. Utley, *The Lance and the Shield*, p. 80.

13. See Dunlay, *Wolves for the Blue Soldiers*, p. 147 and throughout chap. 9.

14. Cody, *Autobiography*, p. 305.

15. W. F. Cody to W. F. Carver, Mar. 12, [1883,] YCWA, Uncat. WA MS 163 930702, Correspondence 1874–86.

16. Quoted in Nellie Snyder Yost, *Buffalo Bill: His Family, Friends, Fame, Failures, and Fortunes* (Chicago: Sage Books, 1979), p. 133.

17. W. F. Cody to W. F. Carver, Feb. 11, [1883,] YCWA, Uncat. WA MS 163 930702, Correspondence 1874–86.

18. From records of the Commissioner of Indian Affairs, cited in Moses, *Wild West Shows*, pp. 25–27.

19. Arthur Kopit, *Indians* (New York: Hill & Wang, 1968), p. 88.

20. Utley, *The Lance and the Shield*, p. 255 and passim.

21. Ibid., p. 186.

22. Paul L. Hedren, *Sitting Bull's Surrender at Fort Buford: An Episode in American History* (Williston, N.D.: Fort Union Association, 1997), pp. 10–17.

23. Utley, *The Lance and the Shield*, pp. 236–39.

24. Ibid., pp. 242–44.

25. Ibid., p. 260. See also Robert C. Hollow and Herbert T. Hoover, *The Last Years of Sitting Bull* (Bismarck: State Historical Society of North Dakota, 1984), p. 21.

26. Ibid., p. 262.

27. Luther Standing Bear, *My People the Sioux* (1928; reprint, Lincoln: University of Nebraska Press, 1975), pp. 184–86.

28. The contract is in *Middle Border Bulletin*, vol. II, no. 2 (Autumn 1943), and cited in Russell, *Lives and Legends*, p. 316.

29. See Moses, *Wild West Shows*, pp. 8 and 284.

30. Louis Pfaller, " 'Enemies in '76, Friends in '85' — Sitting Bull and Buffalo Bill," *Prologue* (Fall 1969), pp. 23–26.

31. *Boston Daily Globe*, July 31, 1885; *Kingston (Ontario) Daily British Whig*, Aug. 20, 1885; *Montreal Times*, Aug. 10, 1885; *St. Louis Globe Democrat*, Oct. 3, 1885; *Boston Evening Traveller*, July 31, 1885; same interview reported in *Boston Journal*, July 31, 1885, DPL, William F. Cody Collection, Nate Salsbury scrapbook, July 1885–Aug. 1886.

32. Glenda Riley, *The Life and Legacy of Annie Oakley* (Norman: University of Oklahoma Press, 1994), pp. 145–46. *New York Clipper* 32:3 (Apr. 5, 1884), p. 45.

33. See clippings from *New Haven Journal and Courier*, July 1885, BBHC, microfilm roll #1, Carver scrapbooks, red with gold tie.

34. This claim was made in an ad in a St. Louis newspaper, Oct. 4, 1885, DPL, William F. Cody Collection, Nate Salsbury scrapbook, July 1885–Aug. 1886.

35. Broadside in Newbery Library, Ayer 5A, 402; advertisement in the *Kingston (Ontario) Daily British Whig*, Aug. 17, 1885. DPL, William F. Cody Collection, Nate Salsbury scrapbook, July 1885–Aug. 1886.

36. *Buffalo Bill's Wild West* program, 1885, BBHC.

37. See clippings from *Boston Evening Traveller*, *Boston Daily Advertiser*, *Boston Journal*, *Boston Post*, DPL, William F. Cody Collection, Nate Salsbury scrapbook, July 1885–Aug. 1886.

38. Ibid., *Montreal Times*, Aug. 10, 1885; *Kingston (Ontario) Daily British Whig*, Aug. 20, 1885.

39. See photographs P.6.247 and P.69.1477, BBHC.

40. Matthew Forny Steele to his mother, Feb. 15, 1891, from the files of the State Historical Society of North Dakota, North Dakota Heritage Center, Bismarck, N.D. See Utley, *The Lance and the Shield*, pp. 282–83, 304.

41. Moses, *The Wild West*, p. 31, and Utley, *The Lance and the Shield*, p. 226.

42. Utley, *The Lance and the Shield*, p. 269.

43. See Russell, *Lives and Legends*, pp. 358–64.

44. The complex story of the performing horse is unraveled in William E. Lemons, "History by Unreliable Narrators: Sitting Bull's Circus Horse," *Montana: The Magazine of Western History* 45:4 (Autumn/Winter 1995), pp. 64–74.

45. Moses, *Wild West Shows*, p. 63.

46. Ibid., p. 74, quoting the *Fifty-eight Annual Report of the Commissioner of Indian Affairs to the Secretary of the Interior*, 1889.

47. Ibid., p. 78, quoting a circular from the CIA to U.S. Indian agents, Mar. 8, 1890.

48. Telegram; letter from the reporter, John Hamilton; and clippings about Chief No-Neck in BBHC, microfilm roll #6, Crager Scrapbook.

49. "Examination of the Indians Traveling with Cody and Salsbury's Wild West Show by the Acting Commissioner of Indian Affairs," quoted in Moses, *Wild West Shows*, pp. 101–3.

50. Ibid., p. 103.

51. *New York World*, Feb. 11, 1891, BBHC, microfilm roll #6, Crager Scrapbook,

52. See Joseph G. Rosa and Robin May, *Buffalo Bill and His Wild West: A Pictorial Biography* (Lawrence: University Press of Kansas, 1989), pp. 118–19.

53. Luther Standing Bear, *My People the Sioux*, preface.

54. Ibid., p. 266.

55. Ibid., pp. 260–64.

56. John G. Neihardt, *Black Elk Speaks, Being the Life Story of a Holy Man of the Oglala Sioux* (1932; reprint, Lincoln: University of Nebraska Press, 1979), pp. 214–15, 217, 223, 228.

57. Ibid., pp. 230, 270, 278, 214.

58. Thomas E. Mails, assisted by Dallas Chief Eagle, *Fools Crow* (1979; reprint, Lincoln: University of Nebraska Press, 1990), pp. 88, 115.

59. Moses, *Wild West Shows*, p. 119.

60. *Chicago Record*, n.d., n.p., BBHC, MS 6, William F. Cody Collection, series IX: Scrapbooks, etc., box 8, Scrapbook 1893, Chicago Season.

61. *Brooklyn Eagle*, May 31, 1894; *New York Times*, June 11, 1894, BBHC, microfilm roll #2, Scrapbook 1, Cody Brooklyn Season 1894.

62. *Ohio State Journal*, July 13, 1896, Col. Cody 1896, tan book; *The World*, Sunday, May 9, 1897, Col. Cody 1897, tan book; *The World*, Sunday, Apr. 10, 1898, Col. Cody 1898, red multi-colored book, all from BBHC, microfilm roll #1. *Motoring Illustrated*, Jan. 24, 1903, *Boston Herald*, June 19, 1907, both from BBHC, microfilm roll #6, WFC Scrapbook 1909–10.

63. *Advertiser*, July 1, 1894, n.p., BBHC, microfilm roll #2, Scrapbook, Col. Cody Brooklyn Season 1894, tan book.

64. Julian Street, "With Buffalo Bill in Italy and on the Continent," in *Buffalo Bill's Wild West* (courier), 1907, p. 19.

65. Ibid., p. 22.

66. Barbara Michaels, *Gertrude Käsebier: The Photographer and Her Photographs* (New York: Harry N. Abrams, 1992), p. 11.

67. Details of the Indians' first visit to the studio are found in "Some Indian Portraits," *Everybody's Magazine* IV (Jan. 1901), pp. 2–24. See also Michaels, *Gertrude Käsebier*, pp. 29–42.

68. "Some Indian Portraits," p. 16.

69. Ibid., pp. 11–12.

70. "Big Injun Pines for New York Beauty," *The World*, Apr. 10, 1898, and "Buffalo Bill's

Entertainers Do Strange Things," *St. Louis Post-Dispatch*, May 16, [1901,] BBHC, microfilm roll #1, Col. Cody 1901, red multi-colored book.

71. "Some Indian Portraits," p. 15.

72. Michaels, *Gertrude Käsebier*, p. 30.

73. *The Sun*, May 7, 1897, BBHC, microfilm roll #1, Col. Cody 1897, tan book; Theodora Kroeber, *Ishi in Two Worlds: A Biography of the Last Wild Indian in North America* (Berkeley: University of California Press, 1961), pp. 228–29.

74. Undated clipping in DPL, Nate Salsbury scrapbook, July 1885–Aug. 1886; *The Sun*, May 7, 1897, *Philadelphia Inquirer*, Apr. 19, 1896, both BBHC, microfilm roll #1, Col. Cody 1896, tan book.

75. *New York World*, May 27, 1894, BBHC, microfilm roll #2, Col. Cody Brooklyn Season 1894, tan book.

76. See Robert C. Toll, *Blacking Up: The Minstrel Show in Nineteenth-Century America* (New York: Oxford University Press, 1974); Eric Lott, *Love and Theft: Blackface Minstrelsy and the American Working Class* (New York: Oxford University Press, 1993); and Michael Rogin, *Blackface, White Noise: Jewish Immigrants in the Hollywood Melting Pot* (Berkeley: University of California Press, 1996).

77. For interesting comments on the cakewalk, see Eric J. Sundquist, *To Wake the Nations: Race in the Making of American Literature* (Cambridge, Mass.: Harvard University Press, 1993), pp. 276–94.

78. Tom Fletcher, *100 Years of the Negro in Show Business!* (New York: Burdge, 1954), p. xvii.

79. For references to black performers with Buffalo Bill's Wild West, see "Buffalo Bill's Last Night," review of *May Cody*, BBHC, microfilm roll #1, scrapbook, Stage Notices 1879–80; "Ferris' Georgia Minstrels with the Buffalo Bill Wild West Show," *The Freeman*, 1911 (thanks to Jill Snider for finding this last reference).

80. Robert C. Toll, *Blacking Up*, p. 262.

81. Raymond Corbey, "Ethnographic Showcases, 1870–1930," in Jan Nederveen Pieterse and Bhikhu Parekh, eds., *The Decolonization of Imagination: Culture, Knowledge, and Power* (London: Zed Books, 1995), pp. 58, 60. See also John M. MacKenzie, *Propaganda and Empire: The Manipulation of British Public Opinion, 1880–1960* (Manchester, England: Manchester University Press, 1984); Tony Bennett, "The Exhibitionary Complex," *New Formations* 4 (Spring 1988), pp. 74–102; Curtis M. Hinsley, "The World As Marketplace: Commodification of the Exotic at the World's Columbian Exposition, Chicago, 1893," in Ivan Karp and Steven D. Lavine, eds., *Exhibiting Cultures: The Poetics and Politics of Museum Display* (Washington, D.C.: Smithsonian Institution Press, 1990), pp. 344–65.

82. See Barbara Kirshenblatt-Gimblett, "Objects of Ethnography," in Karp and Lavine, eds., *Exhibiting Cultures*, pp. 386–443.

83. Frederick Ward Putnam, draft of speech, Sept. 21, 1891, quoted in Hinsley, "The World As Marketplace," p. 347.

84. See Reid Badger, *The Great American Fair: The World's Columbian Exposition & American Culture* (Chicago: Nelson Hall, 1979), p. 137; *Handbook of the World's*

Columbian Exposition (Chicago: Rand, McNally, 1892), pp. 89–91; Jeanne Madeline Weimann, *The Fair Women, The Story of the Woman's Building, World's Columbian Exposition, Chicago 1893* (Chicago: Academy Chicago, 1981), pp. 393–425.

85. H. H. Bancroft, *The Book of the Fair: Columbian Exposition, 1893*, quoted in Hinsley, "The World As Marketplace," p. 346.

86. Ibid., p. 348, quoting the *Chicago Sunday Herald*, Sept. 12, 1893.

87. Richard Henry Pratt, *Battlefield and Classroom: Four Decades with the American Indian, 1867–1904*, ed. Robert M. Utley (1984; reprint, Lincoln: University of Nebraska Press, 1987), p. 303. See Badger, *The Great American Fair*, p. 105.

6. MEMORY AND MODERNITY

1. Nora, Pierre, ed., *Realms of Memory, Rethinking the French Past*, vol. 1, *Conflicts and Divisions*, trans. Arthur Goldhammer (New York: Columbia University Press, 1996), p. 6.

2. Among the most provocative recent studies of Western art are William H. Truettner, ed., *The West As America: Reinterpreting Images of the Frontier, 1820–1920* (Washington, D.C: Smithsonian Institution Press for the National Museum of American Art, 1991); Jules David Prown et al., *Discovered Lands, Invented Pasts: Transforming Visions of the American West* (New Haven: Yale University Press, 1992); Nancy Anderson and Linda Ferber, *Albert Bierstadt: Art & Enterprise* (New York: Hudson Hills for the Museum, 1991); and Richard White, "Frederick Jackson Turner and Buffalo Bill," in Richard White and Patricia Limerick, *The Frontier in American Culture: An Exhibition at the Newberry Library, August 26, 1994–January 7, 1995* (Berkeley: University of California Press, 1994). See also William H. Goetzmann and William N. Goetzmann, *The West of the Imagination* (New York: W. W. Norton, 1986).

3. John Burke, "Salutatory," *Buffalo Bill's Wild West*, program, 1885, BBHC.

4. "Buffalo Bill's 'Wild West' From the Plains of America," souvenir collection, "William F. Cody and the American Exhibition, London," BBHC, MS 6, series IX, box 27.

5. Ralph Waldo Emerson, *Nature*, in Robert E. Spiller and Alfred R. Ferguson, eds., *The Collected Works of Ralph Waldo Emerson* (Cambridge, Mass.: The Belknap Press of Harvard University Press, 1971), vol. 1, p. 7.

6. Leo Marx, *The Machine in the Garden* (New York: Oxford University Press, 1964), passim.

7. *Buffalo Bill's Wild West*, program, 1885, BBHC. Henry Nash Smith, *Virgin Land: The American West as Symbol and Myth* (Cambridge, Mass.: Harvard University Press, 1950), passim.

8. Unidentified clipping, BBHC, microfilm roll #1, scrapbook, Col. Cody 1896, tan book.

9. Ibid., *Kansas City World*, Oct. 19, 1896.

10. Ibid., *Recorder*, n.p., Apr. 12, 1896, and *Cleveland Plain Dealer*, Aug. 16, 1987.

11. "The Cody Trail Through Wonderland," *Buffalo Bill's Wild West*, Indian-head courier, 1907, pp. 28–29, BBHC.

12. "Buffalo Bill's 'Wild West' Camp," souvenir collection, "William F. Cody and the American Exhibition, London," BBHC, MS 6, series IX, box 27.

13. Buffalo Bill, "Famous Hunting Parties of the Plains," *The Cosmopolitan* XVII (June 1894), pp. 131–43.

14. See Elliott West, *The Way to the West: Essays on the Central Plains* (Albuquerque: University of New Mexico Press, 1995), pp. 51–83; and Dan Flores, "Bison Ecology and Bison Diplomacy," *Journal of American History* 78 (Sept. 1991), pp. 465–85. The scientific name of the animal is *bison*, but the name *buffalo* was used interchangeably in popular discourse.

15. See Don Russell, *The Lives and Legends of Buffalo Bill* (Norman: University of Oklahoma Press, 1960), p. 342.

16. *Buffalo Bill's Wild West*, program, 1885, BBHC.

17. Russell, *Lives and Legends*, p. 324.

18. *Buffalo Bill's Wild West and Congress of Rough Riders of the World*, program, 1893, author's collection, p. 15.

19. *Buffalo Bill's Wild West*, program, 1885, BBHC; *Buffalo Bill's Wild West and Congress of Rough Riders of the World*, program, 1893, author's collection, p. 13.

20. *Buffalo Bill's Wild West*, Indian-head courier, 1907, BBHC.

21. *Sunday Chronicle*, Apr. 19, 1903, BBHC, microfilm roll #1, Col. W. F. Cody, Wild West in England 1903, blue book with strap; *Illustrated Sporting and Dramatic News*, July 16, 1892, BBHC, microfilm roll #2, Col. Cody England 1892, red book.

22. *Le Voleur Illustré*, Aug. 8, 1889, and unidentified clipping, BBHC, microfilm roll #2, Wm. Cody France 1889, red book.

23. Russell, *Lives and Legends*, pp. 90–92.

24. *Buffalo Bill's Wild West*, Indian-head courier, 1907, BBHC.

25. See Jack Rennert, *100 Posters of Buffalo Bill's Wild West* (New York: Darien House, 1976), pp. 60, 61.

26. Robert Wooster, *The Military and United States Indian Policy, 1865–1903* (Lincoln: University of Nebraska Press, 1988), p. 74.

27. Ibid., pp. 217–18, 48, 141–43, 74–90, 16.

28. Gaines M. Foster, *Ghosts of the Confederacy: Defeat, the Lost Cause, and the Emergence of the New South* (New York: Oxford University Press, 1987), pp. 38–39.

29. See the descriptions of Civil War monuments and commemorations in Michael Kammen, *Mystic Chords of Memory: The Transformation of Tradition in American Culture* (New York: Alfred A. Knopf, 1991), chap. 4.

30. Nate Salsbury, "An Evening with Boucicault," in typescript of "Reminiscences," c. 1901, NSP, box 2, folder 63.

31. *Brooklyn Journal*, May 31, 1894, BBHC, microfilm roll #2, Col. Cody Brooklyn Season 1894, tan book.

32. *Pictorial Weekly*, May 14, 1892, BBHC, microfilm roll #2, Col. Cody England 1892, red book.

33. *Dubuque Daily Globe Journal*, Sept. 28, 1898, BBHC, microfilm roll #2, Col. Cody Brooklyn Season 1894, tan book.

34. *New Orleans Daily Picayune*, December 16, 1884, quoted in William E. Deahl, Jr., "Buffalo Bill's Wild West Show in New Orleans," *Louisiana History* 16 (1975), p. 290.

35. *Buffalo Bill's Wild West Route Book Season of 1896*, pp. 276–80, BBHC. A silk ribbon from the Pickett dedication can be seen in BBHC, microfilm roll #2, bits from 1883–1886–1888, red-gold scrapbook.

36. Albert Johannsen, *The House of Beadle and Adams and its Dime and Nickel Novels: The Story of a Vanished Literature* (Norman: University of Oklahoma Press, 1950), vol. 2, p. 155.

37. Russell, *Lives and Legends*, p. 253.

38. Foster, *Ghosts of the Confederacy*, pp. 88–89 and 101–3.

39. Kammen, *Mystic Chords of Memory*, p. 109.

40. White, "Frederick Jackson Turner and Buffalo Bill," p. 27.

41. Foster, *Ghosts of the Confederacy*, chap. 11, and Edward L. Ayers, *The Promise of the New South: Life After Reconstruction* (New York: Oxford University Press 1992), 332–33.

42. *Brooklyn Standard-Union*, May 14, 1994, BBHC, microfilm roll #2, Col. Cody Brooklyn Season 1894, tan book.

43. Ibid.

44. A good starting point in the Custer literature is the preface to the reissue of Brian W. Dippie's *Custer's Last Stand: The Anatomy of an American Myth* (1976; reprint, Lincoln: University of Nebraska Press, 1994), in which he surveys many popular and scholarly materials.

45. Ibid., p. 52, for this story and others. For information about Busch, I am indebted to "The History of Anheuser-Busch Companies—A Fact Sheet," Anheuser-Busch Companies, Inc., 1995.

46. William F. Cody, *The Life of Hon. William F. Cody, Known as Buffalo Bill, the Famous Hunter, Scout and Guide: An Autobiography* (Hartford, Conn.: Frank E. Bliss, 1879), p. 343.

47. See White, "Frederick Jackson Turner and Buffalo Bill"; Richard Slotkin, "The 'Wild West,' " in Brooklyn Museum, ed., *Buffalo Bill and the Wild West* (Brooklyn: The Brooklyn Museum, 1981), pp. 27–44; Richard Slotkin, *Gunfighter Nation: The Myth of the Frontier in Twentieth-Century America* (New York: Atheneum, 1992); and Jonathan D. Martin, " 'The Grandest and Most Cosmopolitan Object Teacher': *Buffalo Bill's Wild West* and the Politics of American Identity, 1883–1899," *Radical History Review* 66 (Fall 1996), pp. 92–123.

48. William F. Cody, "How I Could Drive Spaniards from Cuba with 30,000 Indian Braves," *The World*, Apr. 3, 1898, BBHC, microfilm roll #1, Col. Cody 1898, red multi-colored book.

49. Ibid., *New York Herald*, Apr. 24, 1898.

50. Ibid., *Brooklyn Citizen*, Apr. 28, 1898, *Kalamazoo (Michigan) Evening News*, July 22, 1898.

51. See the discussion of the war and Cody's participation in Russell, *Lives and Legends*, pp. 416–19.

52. *The World*, March 31, 1898, unidentified clipping, June 3, 1898, BBHC, microfilm roll #1, Col. Cody 1898, red multi-colored book.

53. Advertising flier, 1898, DPL, WH 72, Cody, William, box of programs.

54. Program, Greater New York, 1899, pp. 3, 58, DPL, another box of programs.

55. Ibid., *Buffalo Bill's Wild West*, program, 1901.

56. "Electricity at the Wild West Show," *The Electrical World*, Sept. 15, 1894, BBHC, microfilm roll #2, Col. Cody Brooklyn Season 1894, tan book.

57. Charles Musser, *Edison Motion Pictures, 1890–1900* (Smithsonian Institution Press, 1997), pp. 125–45.

58. Karen C. Lund, "American Indians in Silent Film: Motion Pictures in the Library of Congress," pamphlet for Motion Picture, Broadcasting and Recorded Sound Division, Library of Congress, updated Apr. 1995.

59. "The Life of Buffalo Bill," Ernst Collection, Motion Picture, Broadcasting and Recorded Sound Division, Library of Congress, FLA 1982.

60. Edward Buscombe, ed., *The BFI Companion to the Western* (London: André Deutsch, Ltd., 1988), p. 24.

61. "Settler's Home Life," FLA 5202; "Firing the Cabin," FLA 4624; "Discovery of Bodies," FLA 4580; "Rescue of Child From Indians," FLA 5185. Paper Print Collection, Motion Picture, Broadcasting and Recorded Sound Division, Library of Congress.

62. See Lund catalogue and Bunscombe, ed., *BFI Companion*, p. 28.

63. Cited in Kevin Brownlow, *The War, the West, and the Wilderness* (New York: Alfred A. Knopf, 1979), pp. 230–32.

64. Ibid., pp. 227–33.

65. Program, *Indian War Pictures*, Tabor Grand Opera House [Denver], BBHC, MS 6, series I D, box 3, folder 1.

66. Ibid., "First Public Presentation at the Columbia Theatre, Washington, D.C."

67. *The Moving Picture World*, Nov. 21, 1914, p. 615, files of Motion Picture, Broadcasting and Recorded Sound Division, Library of Congress.

68. *Washington Herald*, Feb. 28, 1914; two unidentified clippings from Denver; *Albuquerque Morning Journal*, Mar. 19, 1914 BBHC, microfilm roll #1, Col. Cody Motion Picture Venture, Historic films, 1914, black scrapbook.

69. Don Russell, "Buffalo Bill—In Action," *Westerners Brand Book* XIX (July 1962), pp. 33–35, 40; and Brownlow, *The War, the West, and the Wilderness*, p. 235.

70. *Albuquerque Morning Journal*, March 19, 1914, BBHC, microfilm roll #1, Col. Cody Motion Picture Venture, Historic films, 1914, black scrapbook.

CONCLUSION

1. R. L. Wilson, with Greg Martin, *Buffalo Bill's Wild West, An American Legend* (New York: Random House, 1998), pp. vii, 256.

2. Stanley Kubrick, dir., *Dr. Strangelove, or, How I Learned to Stop Worrying and Love the Bomb*, 1964; J. William Fulbright, *The Arrogance of Power* (New York: Random House, 1967).

3. Sir Robert Baden-Powell, *Matabele Campaign*, quoted in Robert H. MacDonald,

Sons of the Empire: The Frontier and the Boy Scout Movement, 1890–1918 (Toronto: University of Toronto Press, 1993), p. 62 and throughout.

4. Sir Robert Baden-Powell, *Scouting for Boys* (1908; third edition, London: C. Arthur Pearson, 1910), pp. viii, 5–6.

5. Philip Deloria, *Playing Indian* (New Haven: Yale University Press, 1998), pp. 95–98.

6. Helen Cody Wetmore, *Buffalo Bill: Last of the Great Scouts: The Life Story of Col. William F. Cody ("Buffalo Bill")* (Duluth, Minn.: The Duluth Press Printing Co., 1899).

7. Edward Buscombe, ed., *The BFI Companion to the Western* (London: André Deutsch, Ltd., 1988), p. 13.

8. L. C. Moses, *Wild West Shows and the Images of American Indians 1883–1933* (Albuquerque: University of New Mexico Press, 1996), p. 179.

9. Don Russell, *The Lives and Legends of Buffalo Bill* (Norman: University of Oklahoma Press, 1960), p. 456.

10. Lee Clark Mitchell, *Westerns: Making the Man in Fiction and Film* (Chicago: University of Chicago Press, 1996), p. 3.

11. Dexter W. Fellows and Andrew A. Freeman, *This Way to the Big Show: The Life of Dexter Fellows* (New York: The Viking Press, 1936), pp. 84–85.

12. Mitchell, *Westerns*, p. 159. Jane Tompkins also suggested that violence in Western films and novels constituted a way to affirm masculinity. Jane Tompkins, *West of Everything: The Inner Life of Westerns* (New York: Oxford University Press, 1992).

13. Garry Wills, "John Wayne's Body," *The New Yorker*, Aug. 19, 1996, p. 45. See also Garry Wills, *John Wayne's America: The Politics of Celebrity* (New York: Simon & Schuster, 1997), p. 22.

14. See Miles Orvell, *The Real Thing: Imitation and Authenticity in American Culture. 1880–1940* (Chapel Hill: University of North Carolina Press, 1989); Larry Tye, *The Father of Spin: Edward L. Bernays & the Birth of Public Relations* (New York: Crown Publishers, 1998); Roland Marchand, *Advertising the American Dream* (Berkeley: University of California Press, 1985); Daniel Boorstin, *The Image, or, What Happened to the American Dream?* (New York: Atheneum, 1962); Joe McGinniss, *The Selling of the President 1968* (New York: Trident, 1969).

15. George W. S. Trow, *Within the Context of No Context* (Boston: Little, Brown and Company, 1981), p. 8 and throughout.

16. Michael Paul Rogin, *"Ronald Reagan," the Movie* (Berkeley: University of California Press, 1987), pp. 11, 6, 43, and throughout.

17. Garry Wills, "It's His Party," *New York Times Magazine*, Aug. 11, 1996, p. 30 ff.

18. Russell reports this claim, but doubts its accuracy, in *Lives and Legends*, p. 473.

19. Ibid., p. 460.

20. E. E. Cummings, Complete Poems: 1904–1962, Edited by George James Firmage (New York: Liveright, 1923, 1951, 1991), p. 90. Reprinted by permission of Liveright Publishing Corporation.

21. Rushworth M. Kidder, " 'Buffalo Bill's'—An Early Cummings Manuscript," *Harvard Library Bulletin* 24 (Oct. 1976), pp. 373–80.
22. Richard S. Kennedy, *Dreams in the Mirror: A Biography of E. E. Cummings* (New York: Liveright, 1980), pp. 23, 31, 32.
23. Kidder, " 'Buffalo Bill's,' " plate I.

LIST OF ILLUSTRATIONS

INDEX